The Best American
Travel Writing 2016

GUEST EDITORS OF
THE BEST AMERICAN TRAVEL WRITING

2000 BILL BRYSON
2001 PAUL THEROUX
2002 FRANCES MAYES
2003 IAN FRAZIER
2004 PICO IYER
2005 JAMAICA KINCAID
2006 TIM CAHILL
2007 SUSAN ORLEAN
2008 ANTHONY BOURDAIN
2009 SIMON WINCHESTER
2010 BILL BUFORD
2011 SLOANE CROSLEY
2012 WILLIAM T. VOLLMANN
2013 ELIZABETH GILBERT
2014 PAUL THEROUX
2015 ANDREW MCCARTHY
2016 BILL BRYSON

The Best American Travel Writing™ 2016

Edited and with an Introduction
by **Bill Bryson**

Jason Wilson, Series Editor

A Mariner Original

HOUGHTON MIFFLIN HARCOURT

BOSTON • NEW YORK

Contents

Foreword

WHEN I FIRST lived in Italy, and for years afterward, it seemed that many Italians could not pronounce my first name correctly. Even to this day, when I introduce myself as "Jason" to a non-English-speaking Italian, there's a strong chance he or she will reply, *"Jackson?"* Actually, for a long time what many people said was, *"Jackson? Like Michael Jackson?"* And they would often raise an eyebrow, and smirk. Some would nod their heads expectantly, as if they were waiting for me to say, *Yes, yes. You've unmasked me. I am actually not a short white guy from New Jersey, but rather I am the King of Pop. Please, allow me to moonwalk for you.* In the years since he passed away, the Michael Jackson confusion doesn't happen so much anymore. But until only the past few years, whenever I booked hotel or car rentals, or made dinner reservations, or told my phone number to someone as they typed it into a phone, it was still a 60–40 chance that I would be identified as Jackson Wilson.

One night about a decade ago, my friend Daniella and several of her cousins took me to a pizzeria in a village in the province of Cremona. We were looking at a huge chalkboard full of pizza choices. Everyone ordered, and I was taking a little too long with my decision-making, and so they began to fuss in that endearing Italian way. "What? You don't see anything you like? Do you need a translation? Should we order for you?" Finally, Daniella said, a tad impatiently, "If you don't see a pizza you like, they'll make any pizza you want." The waiter, also impatiently, reiterated this.

At that moment, for some reason, my eye lighted on the word "Gorgonzola" and then the word "pear" flittered into my brain. Gorgonzola and pears. That sounded good. It didn't seem any stranger than the "Hawaii" pizza or the "Texas BBQ" pizza on the chalkboard. And so I verbalized this: "May I have my pizza with Gorgonzola and pear?"

All conversation stopped. The waiter looked at me as if I might be mentally incompetent. He looked beseechingly at my companions as if I needed special help with my Italian. But no, I repeated my order. He rubbed his stomach as if he were ill.

Everyone at the table burst out laughing. *Who ever heard of a pizza like that? Gorgonzola! And pears! That's the craziest pizza we've ever heard of! Ah, Jason! Always the mischief-maker!*

All through dinner it went on. Every time the waiter came over, the family laughed and apologized: "Ah, he's American, you see. Don't be alarmed." I offered samples to everyone at the table, just to show them how good the pizza really was—and it was very good. But none of them would entertain one bite.

Near the end of the meal, the chef came out of the kitchen to see who was actually eating a pizza with Gorgonzola and pear. That's when everyone suggested, with a laugh, that this pizza should have a name: "Pizza Jason."

Except, here's the thing—when the chef repeated the name, he called it "Pizza Jackson" and wrote it on the chalkboard just like that. So if you happened to be passing through this small village in the province of Cremona, and for some reason you wanted a pizza that has Gorgonzola and pear, you had to ask for a Pizza Jackson.

I quite enjoy this kind of cultural misunderstanding, and usually don't correct it. Being called Jackson reminds me that despite its familiarity to Americans like me, Italy is a strange and foreign place, still full of surprises and new discoveries. In a sense, becoming Jackson remystifies Italy for me.

This process is similar to what happens every late fall when I embark on my annual reading of the year's travel writing. The best pieces I come across almost always remystify the world for me in some way, either big or small. Sadly, too much of the writing I read, and much of what we see in consumer travel magazines and newspaper travel sections, seems bent on demystifying travel. These pieces often employ a faux narrative, but their end goal is to break down some city or some experience or some mode of transportation into digestible, practical bites. These service roundups with their itineraries and lists and tips and charticles are generally competent, and probably serve their basic purpose. But they always leave me wanting more.

I've always been drawn instead to the deeper notion of travel espoused by Pico Iyer, a contributor to this year's anthology, who once wrote: "Travel is like love, mostly because it's a heightened state of awareness, in which we are mindful, receptive, undimmed by familiarity and ready to be transformed. That is why the best trips, like the best love affairs, never really end." All love affairs, all long-term relationships—travel included—demand that we keep an element of mystery alive and kicking.

These are the kinds of pieces I hope you find on the pages within this year's anthology.

The stories included here are, as always, selected from among hundreds of pieces in hundreds of diverse publications—from mainstream and specialty magazines to Sunday newspaper travel sections to literary journals to travel websites. I've done my best to be fair and representative, and in my opinion the best travel stories from 2015 were forwarded to guest editor Bill Bryson, who made our final selections.

Bill was the inaugural guest editor of this series (going way back to the 2000 edition), and it was just as much of an honor to work with him the second time around. The world has changed a great deal since Y2K, obviously. But I think you'll find that the key characteristics of great travel writing never really change. I'd also like to thank Tim Mudie, at Houghton Mifflin Harcourt, for his help in producing this year's outstanding collection, our 17th. I hope you enjoy it.

I now begin anew by reading the hundreds of stories published in 2016. As I have for years, I am asking editors and writers to submit the best of whatever it is they define as travel writing. These submissions must be nonfiction, published in the United States during the 2016 calendar year. They must not be reprints or excerpts from published books. They must include the author's name, date of publication, and publication name, and must be tear sheets, the complete publication, or a clear photocopy of the piece as it originally appeared. I must receive all submissions by January 1, 2017, in order to ensure full consideration for the next collection.

Further, publications that want to make certain their contributions will be considered for the next edition should make sure to include this anthology on their subscription list. Submissions or subscriptions should be sent to Jason Wilson, Best American Travel Writing, 230 Kings Highway East, Suite 192, Haddonfield, NJ 08033.

JASON WILSON

Introduction

MY FAVORITE PLACE in the world these days is a discreet but venerable institution on St. James's Square in London called the London Library. Founded in 1841, it's a private (though not at all exclusive) library supported by its 7,000 or so members. The *New York Times* has called it "probably the greatest lending library in the world." As you would expect of any building that smells of leather and old paper and contains a million volumes, it's just the most wonderful place. I would live there if they would let me bring a bed in.

Among its many other delights, the London Library has the most satisfyingly idiosyncratic system of organizing books, reflecting in the most arresting way the breadth and peculiarity of interests of its members over a long period. Under the broad category "Science &c.," for instance, "Horse-Shoeing" stands beside "Human Sacrifice." "Sex" comes between "Seashells" and "Sewage." "Vinegar" is twinned with "Vivisection." It can take years to learn your way around, but it is also delightfully productive because you constantly encounter subjects you would never have thought of looking into.

Thus it was recently, while browsing through books on the Western Isles of Scotland, that I chanced upon *British Lighthouses: Their History and Romance*, by J. Saxby Wryde, published in London in 1913, and therein learned the remarkable true story of the disappearing lighthouse keepers of Eilean Mòr.

Like most people, I had never heard of Eilean Mòr. It is a remote and lonely island, part of a small archipelago known as the

Flannan Isles, some 20 miles out in the cold gray waters of the North Atlantic Ocean off Scotland's rugged northwest coast. Its one forgotten moment of attention came in December 1900, when the island's three lighthouse men, its only occupants, vanished without a trace, for no apparent reason. Their names were Thomas Marshall, James Ducat, and Donald McArthur, and to this day no one knows what became of them.

All that can be said is that on the evening of December 15, the lighthouse light failed to come on, and it remained dark for several nights more until a relief crew could be dispatched from the Isle of Lewis, the nearest landmass of consequence. On arrival, the relief party found Eilean Mòr eerily quiet. No one greeted them at the jetty or answered their calls. In the lighthouse kitchen, a chair had been knocked over, but otherwise all appeared almost spookily normal. Lunch had been prepared and served but not eaten. In the men's quarters, the beds had been made. In the tower, the light had been cleaned and readied for that night's service. In an outer vestibule, two sets of oilskins were missing from their hooks, but the third set was untouched.

According to one account, the relief team found a logbook that contained this sequence of entries:

> December 12: Gale north by northwest . . . Waves very high . . . Ducat quiet. Donald McArthur crying.
> December 13: Noon, grey daylight. Me, Ducat and McArthur prayed.
> December 14: no entry.
> December 15: Storm ended, sea calm. God is over all.

That was the last entry.

In the century since the men vanished, many theories have been proposed to explain what happened—that they went to the landing stage to secure some piece of equipment and were swept away by a rogue wave, that one of them killed the other two and then himself—but all fall short of convincing plausibility. The seas off Eilean Mòr had a lot of passing ship traffic—that's why there was a lighthouse there—and none of them had reported any big waves or other unusual phenomena. The men themselves were all of equable disposition and had worked together without rancor for more than a year. Even if it was a murder-suicide, it was not easy to explain how the murderer had killed himself and then disposed of his own body. It wasn't even easy to imagine a calamity that would compel all three men to get up from their lunch and rush out—one of them without putting on rainwear.

I had never heard of Eilean Mòr or its missing lighthouse-keepers, but as soon as I came across the story I wanted to go there at once to see it for myself. If you like to travel—and I'm supposing you do or you wouldn't be reading this book—you will no doubt recognize that impulse. It seems to me an entirely natural and even admirable instinct, but it must be admitted that it sometimes has an element of irrationality about it, too—not least when it comes to wanting to visit the outermost of the Outer Hebrides.

Getting to Eilean Mòr is not an easy thing to do. From my home in southern England, it would take two plane flights (or a long train journey, car drive, and ferry crossing) just to reach Stornoway on the Isle of Lewis. Then there would be a 40-mile drive to the coastal village of Uig, and finally a crossing of perilous seas in a small boat, weather permitting.

There is very little to see when you get to Eilean Mòr other than colonies of perturbed seabirds. The lighthouse still stands, but it has been automated since 1971, so there are no keepers in residence and the building isn't open to the public. Eilean Mòr itself is just 40 acres of barren rock, and can be toured in an hour. So there really isn't anything very tangible to be gained from a visit. Even so, I would very much like to go, just to see it with my own eyes. That's the thing about travel, it seems to me. It is many attractive things—enriching, stimulating, seductive, pleasurable—but very often a touch compulsive, too.

My reason for poking about in the London Library's extensive travel section was that I was trying to answer the question that this essay naturally poses, namely: Why do I travel? Why do any of us travel? I wasn't at all sure I knew the answer. Now, after nearly two weeks buried away in the library's musty sprawl of travel narratives, histories, and sociological inquiries, I cannot say that I am a whole lot the wiser. But I do know rather more than I did about the thoughts, ambitions, and prejudices of travelers over the last 150 years or so.

In looking through books on the art and science of travel, certain recurrent themes—three in particular, all of them at least slightly off-beam, in my view—leap out. The first and most dominant is the enduring conviction that travel isn't what it used to be. Every generation makes this observation afresh. Evelyn Waugh announced the death of travel as a worthwhile pastime 70 years ago in *When the Going Was Good* (a title that is in itself telling, of course), and there is hardly a travel writer of note in our own era who hasn't at some point made a similar declaration. The idea that travel has somehow diminished in the author's own lifetime actually goes back at least as far as 1726, when Jonathan Swift has Gulliver declare wearily in *Gulliver's Travels,* "I thought we were already overstocked with books of travels."

Much as I hate to support a cliché, there is something in the argument in at least some respects. It is certainly true to say that there have never been so many tourists in the world as there are today, and their sheer numbers make many experiences a challenge. Not long ago I walked past the Anne Frank Museum in Amsterdam on a Sunday morning in March two hours before it opened, and there was already a long line forming at the door. In 2015 the Anne Frank Museum took in 1,268,095 visitors. That's about the same number as go to Bryce Canyon National Park in Utah every year, but with the obvious difference that Bryce Canyon occupies tens of thousands of acres of wilderness while the Anne Frank Museum occupies one smallish building on a quiet street in Amsterdam.

When I went to the Anne Frank Museum for the first time in 1972, I walked straight in on a summer's afternoon. I did have to wait a few minutes to gain admission to the secret annex where Anne and seven others hid from the Nazis for two years, and I clearly remember the woman at the door apologizing for the delay. Neither of us had any idea then that we were living in a kind of golden age. (I should note that in the spring of 2016 the Anne Frank Museum instituted a policy of advance-purchase tickets with timed entry, something that is bound to become more common all over as tourist numbers relentlessly grow.)

In similar manner, a year or so ago, on a bitterly cold February day—about as out of season as you could get—I fetched up at the Louvre in Paris, looking for a little cultural diversion (and ideally a little warmth, too) only to find a long and more or less stationary line of people stretching from the back of the Louvre courtyard to a distant ticket desk. I tutted and felt aggrieved, but of course I was being a hypocrite. You can't reasonably complain about what others are doing if you are trying to do it yourself.

If you do find an attraction thronged with visitors, there is always a simple solution: go somewhere else. I went across the river to the much quieter Musée d'Orsay and had an excellent time. The central feature of modern travel, it seems to me, isn't that there are too many tourists in too many places, but rather that there are too many tourists in just a few places—quite a different matter. The world is a long way away from being ruined for travel. You have only to look at many of the pieces in this anthology—and in this regard I would mention Paul Theroux in Alabama and Dave Eggers in Hollister, California, just for starters—to realize that you don't have to seek out exotic locales or go to terribly great lengths to have memorable and touristically solitary experiences.

A second enduring assumption of travel writing is that the world has become dispiritingly homogenized and isn't nearly as interesting as it used to be. I remember once being told by a *National Geographic* photographer that there is no point, in any city in the world, of going to the topmost floors of a skyscraper and taking a panoramic shot. "All cities look the same now," he explained. "It doesn't matter whether it's São Paulo, Johannesburg, Toronto, anywhere. The picture editors will never select that picture because it just looks like everywhere else."

I am old enough to recall a Europe in which each nation was a cultural oasis largely untouched by the outside world. Every country had its own cars, movies, restaurants, and stores, just as it had its own architecture, history, and language. When I arrived in Europe in the early 1970s there wasn't a single McDonald's on the continent; today there are nearly 7,500 of them. It was a world without ATMs and, except for the exceptionally rich and worldly, credit cards. The rest of us carried cash or traveler's checks. Hardly anyone outside of the Low Countries and Scandinavia reliably spoke English. Menus were almost always exclusively in the native language, so you were seldom entirely sure what you had just ordered.

If you wanted to know how things were back home, you had to have your folks write to you care of an American Express office in some exotic foreign capital, or to a post office with a poste restante service. In either case, you could expect to spend a morning standing in a long line just to learn that your cousin was pregnant and Mrs. Miller's dog had died. International phone calls were much too expensive to contemplate. The Internet of course didn't exist. To catch up with world affairs, you had to buy the *International Herald Tribune,* a costly investment but a good one because it not only gave you the baseball scores and news of American affairs, but announced you as quite a cosmopolitan fellow as you sat perusing it at a Parisian café or Venetian square.

The *International Herald Tribune* ceased publication in 2013. It lives on, in a kind of ghostly manner, as the *International New York Times,* but nobody really needs it. These days you can get all the latest news on your telephone or tablet. It is possible, indeed quite easy, to sit at a sidewalk café in Paris and forget that you are in Paris. No doubt it is a reflection of my age, but the world seems full of people with sound systems in their ears and screens in their hands who want to be anywhere but where they actually are, which seems a rather strange and depressing ambition to me. I quite like being in the world, with its noise and commotion and random distractions. One of the more resounding benefits of travel writing, I would venture, is that it reminds us just how multifariously interesting that world can be.

Which brings us to the third widespread belief of the genre, namely that travel writing is something of a doomed art. I have an old friend named John Flinn, who until his retirement was the travel editor of the *San Francisco Chronicle.* Until fairly recent times, the *Chronicle* travel section, like most Sunday travel sections, was a thing of some heft and substance. In John's day, it generally ran between 24 and 28 pages. Now it is never more than 6 and sometimes as few as 4.

"I usually ran eight feature articles a week of about fifteen hundred words each," John told me. "Now there are never more than two. Most papers just run wire copy these days. Hardly any commissioned travel articles. There are plenty of blogs you can write for, but getting paid to write travel pieces is a real challenge."

Travel magazines are often not much better. "Narrative travel writing seems to be disappearing from them. Now their bread and butter is lists of 'Ten Great Boutique Hotels' or 'Twenty Great Roller Coasters' and that sort of thing."

So it can all seem a little depressing. And yet, as the pages that follow sumptuously demonstrate, some awfully good writers are still managing to travel and get their words into print. God bless those outlets that enable them do so.

None of this, I realize, brings me a whole lot closer to answering the question I began with. To wit, what is it about travel that is so beguiling? But then I am not sure that it is a question that can be simply or satisfactorily answered. The one group of people who have addressed that question at length and in depth is academics, but alas, and to be cruelly candid, there is not a group of people on earth more densely incoherent than those who write academic texts. Here is a genuine (and genuinely typical) sentence, explaining (I think) motivation in travel writing from a book called *Travellers' Tales of Wonder* published by the University of Edinburgh Press in Scotland: "Self-reflexivity, the foregrounded consciousness of the partiality and perspectivity of the account, has its complement in the foregrounding of cultural memory. At its most fundamental poetelogical level, the narrative of a journey evokes an extraordinarily rich and varied cultural history." Or here is a wisp of thought on the nature of travel writing from *Tourists with Typewriters,* published by the University of Michigan Press: "Travel literature is a polyvalent genre that alternates between 'a semi-ethnographic, distanced, analytic mode' and 'an autobiographical, emotionally tangled mode.'"

I can't argue with any of that, mostly because I can't understand any of it. I have to say that for me it is all much simpler than that. I travel because it brings me pleasure to do so. I especially love that sense of not knowing quite what is going on, of being in a place where mundane things—an advertisement at a bus shelter, a snack from a street stall, the giant insect that lands on your shirtsleeve and preens its luminous wings—become fascinating, alarming, delightful, amusing, or otherwise notable. Henry James put it very well more than a century ago when he wrote: "I can wish the traveler no better fortune than to stroll forth in the early evening with as large a reserve of ignorance as my own." I entirely understand the feeling.

Some years ago the London *Times* sent me to Japan during the soccer World Cup to write about the spectacle of the world's greatest tournament from an outsider's perspective, as someone who doesn't follow soccer very closely. All I was expected to do was wander around and enjoy myself. I found I loved Japan, largely because I was never quite sure what was going on. I couldn't read the signs. I couldn't figure out the food. I couldn't converse with anyone. I couldn't even confidently operate the high-tech toilet in my hotel room. It was wonderful.

On my next-to-last day in the country, I flew into Tokyo from Sapporo and needed to get to Tokyo's main railroad station, called Shinjuku. I climbed into a taxi at the airport and said to the driver, "Shinjuku station, please."

He didn't seem to have any idea what I meant. I repeated my request, as articulately as I could, and he looked at me as if I had asked him to take me to Boise. I pulled a map of Tokyo out and showed him Shinjuku station. He studied this with a look of great dissatisfaction, but at length put the car in gear and we set off.

We drove for what seemed hours through the endless, numbing sprawl of Tokyo. Eventually we entered a long, deep tunnel —a kind of underground freeway, it seemed. About a mile along, the driver pulled into an emergency parking bay and stopped. He pointed to a metal door cut into the tunnel wall and indicated that I should get out and go through that door.

"You want me to go through that door?" I said in disbelief.

He nodded robustly and presented me with a bill for about a zillion yen. Everything was beginning to seem more than a touch surreal. He took my money, gave me several small bills in change, and encouraged me to depart, with a little shooing gesture. This was crazy. We were in a tunnel, for crying out loud. If I got out and he drove off, I would be hundreds of feet under Tokyo in a busy traffic tunnel with no sidewalk or other escape. You'll understand when I say this didn't feel entirely right.

"Through that door there?" I said again, dubiously.

He nodded and made another shooing gesture.

I got out with my suitcase and went up three metal steps to the door and turned the handle. The door opened. I looked back at the driver. He nodded in encouragement. Ahead of me, lit with what seemed emergency lighting, was the longest flight of stairs I had ever seen. It took a very long while to climb them all. At the top I came to another door, exactly like the one at the bottom.

I turned the handle and cautiously opened it, then stepped out onto the concourse of the world's busiest railway station.

I don't know whether this is the way lots of people get to Shinjuku or whether I am the only person in history ever to have done so. But what I do know is this: it's why I like to travel.

BILL BRYSON

The Best American
Travel Writing 2016

White Guy in a Djellaba

FROM *Bon Appétit*

WE WERE HEADING down to Fes from blue Chefchaouen and
making decent time when our driver left the autoroute for a
stretch of doubtful road. A modest sign pointed, in French and
Arabic, to some unknown town.

I considered asking Rida, our minivan driver, about the reason
for the change of route. I worked out the sentence in French in
my head. But then I let it pass. Rida was a professional, and it was
his country. In any case, I knew from long experience of travel in
foreign countries and tongues that explanations, like dreams, only
make sense while they're happening. Answers I thought I had understood perfectly when I heard them in French fell apart as read-
ily as dreams when I translated them for my wife. At that moment
I felt that I would rather not know the reason for the detour than
know that I didn't know it.

Nothing moves me more profoundly, I hasten to add, than discovering the extent of my own ignorance. That is why I travel—by
nature I'm a homebody—but sometimes it can be hard. Some days
you get tired of decoding, of interpreting, of working to understand, of constantly orienting yourself, or, to put it another way, of
being constantly lost.

"Why did you turn off the road?" my wife asked.

I looked back at Ayelet. She had a child on either side of her
—"the Bigs," Sophie and Zeke, aged 20 and 17. In the back row
were "the Littles," Rosie and Abe, 13 and 11. The boys had their
headphones on, and the landscape unspooled past them to a hip-

hop soundtrack; Action Bronson and Flatbush Zombies among the olive groves.

"Better to go this way today," Rida said. He seemed inclined to leave it at that.

"Is this the way to Volubilis?" Ayelet asked.

"No," Rida said, "the way to Zegota." Rida was handsome and soft-spoken. As with many men who have soft voices and serious eyes, it was hard to tell if he was fucking with you. I thought I saw a smile gathering momentarily on his face, but it went away. "After Zegota, Volubilis."

"Zegota," Ayelet repeated, checking with me to see if I'd heard of it. I shook my head.

"Can we get lunch there?" Rosie asked.

"Not couscous," Abe said.

We all jumped on Abe for being so rude as to disparage Rida's national dish, but we were a bunch of dirty hypocrites. Everyone was sick to death of couscous. Moroccan cuisine is delicious and comforting, but it lacks fire and, above all, breadth. The spicy harissa I had enjoyed with my couscous in Belleville and the Goutte d'Or in Paris turned out to be a Tunisian thing; in Morocco you had to ask for it, catching your hosts off-guard, at times causing mild consternation. At nearly every meal in Morocco, the tourist is presented with subtle variations on four main courses: meat and/or vegetable couscous, meat and/or vegetable tagine, meat or fish skewers, and *b'steeya*, a savory-sweet pie of pigeon or chicken. Before arriving and during the first few days, the prospect of endless couscous and *b'steeya* had seemed heavenly. But 10 days out from California, I found myself tormented by taqueria longings.

"Not couscous," Rida said. Now he smiled outright.

The country here was flat and, like so much of Morocco, under heavy cultivation with olives. In the clear late-December light, the silver leaves of the olive trees gave the day a wintry glint. Spreading plants with lush leaves grew among the endless ranks of *oliviers*. Rida said these were tobacco plants.

"Before, they grow the hashish here," he said. "Very good hashish. The best."

I saw that he expected this American whom fate had placed in the front seat of his employer's second-best minivan, dressed in a knitted wool *taqiyah*, or skullcap, and a hooded djellaba over an *Illmatic* T-shirt, to take an interest in the subject of hashish.

"Interesting," I said, trying to sound uninterested.

"Yes, but it is finished. The government says it will be better to grow the tobacco."

From a public health perspective, the underlying premise of this policy struck me as grievously flawed, but there was nothing much Rida or I could do about it. So I let it pass.

The road began to ascend, then turned abruptly horrible. At one point as we drove across a culvert, I looked down and saw that between the edge of the roadbed and the right-hand guardrail there were two feet of empty air.

The journey from Chefchaouen to Fes had seemed, on my phone, a fairly straightforward business, even with a minor detour to see what remained of Volubilis, the former capital city of the Roman province of Mauretania. So what were we even doing on this ex-road? Who was this man whom we had entrusted with our lives, knowing nothing about his temperament, intelligence, psychological history, or driving record?

"So, Zegota," I said.

"Zegota," Rida agreed. "No couscous."

I sank a little deeper into my djellaba. I'd just bought it in Chefchaouen's medina, but it was already beloved. It was a winter djellaba, woven of camel and sheep wool, patterned with vertical stripes of cream and coffee brown, and with a pointed hood that gives the wearer a wizardly air. When I wore it—though this was not my intention—I made a spectacle of myself. Seeing an American dad walking with his American family in a fine Chefchaouen djellaba seemed to put a smile on people's faces. It might be a puzzled or a mocking smile, but even these were tinged with delight. Everywhere my djellaba and I went in Morocco—and I went everywhere in my djellaba and, to this day in wintertime Berkeley, wear it every night to walk the dog—I was followed by cries of "Nice djellaba!" and "Hi, Berber Man!"

After a bumpy hour, we neared the crest of a ridge. A string of villages ran along its top for 10 or 15 miles. The road was intermittently thronged with groups of children in school uniforms headed home for lunch. In the first town, the schoolchildren shouted and waved and peered into our car eagerly, as though prepared to be astonished by the identity of its occupants. Some little joker even pounded on my door. I jumped and looked at Rida. He was grinning.

"It's like they think we're famous or something," Rosie said.

The next village was indistinguishable from the first, but here, for some reason, we barely drew a glance from the schoolchildren. It was as if all the relevant data on us had been gathered by the first group and transmitted to the second by no visible means. Word simply seemed to have spread: six Americans; Brad Pitt or Malia Obama not among them. Somehow, in the midst of our own lostness and ignorance, we found ourselves abruptly *known*.

That kind of thing happened to us all the time in Morocco. If we stiffed a kid at the far end of the medina for "helping" us find the way to a square that we already knew how to get to, a kid over in our end of town would seem to have heard about it and try to collect. When Abe felt sick on a hike in the foothills of the Atlas Mountains, a muleteer appeared, seemingly out of nowhere, and set Abe onto his ready-saddled mule so we could carry on.

Rida eased the minivan around a hairpin bend and slowed down as we came alongside a low cinder block structure with a corrugated metal roof, open on one long side. It was divided by more cinder blocks into four deep, wide bays. It looked like the loading dock for a warehouse that had never been finished and was now home to squatters. Dark smoke boiled up from the center of the building.

To our surprise, Rida pulled into a sandy patch in front. Men in djellabas, tracksuits, and sweaters and jeans passed into and out of the shadows that filled the bays. On the concrete apron, a man with a poker was jabbing at half a bisected steel drum and unraveling long gray skeins of smoke into the blue sky. Behind him, a red curtain of carcasses—lamb and cow—dangled from steel hooks.

"Meat," said Rida. "Tell him what you want and the butcher will cook it for you."

We pointed vaguely at anything that did not still have a face or testicles attached, and fled. There was also a tagine on offer, chicken with peppers, and I ordered one of those, out of confusion and panic more than any desire to eat more tagine. On the far side of the butcher shop there was a dining area with a few picnic benches, and beyond that a vague space, empty but for some carcass-red rugs and three middle-aged men with beards and expressions of dignified boredom, sitting on bentwood chairs. I went over to see what kind of fare they had on offer and they stared at me the way you might stare at a wasp as it approached your Eskimo Pie.

"That is a mosque," Rida said, pulling me gently back to the dining area.

At that moment the butcher went past, carrying a large steel basket full of ground meat on skewers, and for the first time I understood that he did not plan on feeding us an entire limb or organ, freshly hacked. You made your choice of meat and it was ground, on the spot, and mixed with the owner's proprietary blend of spices, a formula he genially refused to divulge through an interpreter. The meat and its mysterious flavorings were rolled into flattened tubes along flat skewers like steel fence pickets, then caged in the basket so that they could be turned easily on the grill without falling apart.

I have eaten good food in unprepossessing locales, but I doubt the disparity between the crude, shabby atmosphere of that nameless cement-block dispensary of protein and redemption and the quality of the lunch laid on by the butcher of Zegota will ever be matched. When it arrived, the *kefta* was easily the best we ate during our two weeks in Morocco—and we ate a lot of *kefta*. The tagine arrived sizzling in its Munchkin-hat clay oven, the long green peppers delivering a welcome and overdue burn. The ubiquitous mint tea was neither oversweetened nor bitter. The day was bright and cool, and after the meal we lingered a moment on that gritty concrete terrace, six Jews sitting in the sunshine between a mosque and a shambles, grooving on the mingled aftertastes of sugar and mint and barbecue and chiles, as happy, collectively, as we had been in Morocco or might ever be again in our lives.

"I don't get this place," Abe said, mopping the meat juices from his plastic plate with a hunk of *khoubz,* or flatbread.

I told him I knew what he meant. I thought about asking Rida if this unlikely meal was the reason he had taken such a long detour, if our growing discontent with the limited fare had somehow been guessed at and communicated—if, somehow, like the boy panhandler and the muleteer and the blasé schoolchildren, Rida had *known* that this was what we needed. But I decided to just let it pass.

SARA CORBETT

"How Can We Find More People Like You?"

FROM *The New York Times Magazine*

LET ME INTRODUCE you to Yoppy. Yoppy is young and friendly and lives in a small apartment in the Shinagawa neighborhood of Tokyo. His full name is Yuhsuke Yoshimoto, but at least with visitors who come to stay with him through his listing on Airbnb, he prefers to go by Yoppy. He wears heavy-framed black glasses, has a boyish haircut, and likes to talk to foreigners, even though his English is admittedly poor. In the one photo I've seen of him —his profile shot on Airbnb—he's wearing a navy blazer, a collared shirt, and a thin silver necklace. He smiles at the camera in a pleasant but not overbearing way. It would be hard, I imagine, not to like Yoppy if you were to meet him at a dinner party or at a gathering of pharmacists or financial planners (according to his profile, Yoppy is both a pharmacist and a financial planner), but still that says little about how you would feel when putting your toothbrush on the sink next to his late at night in a city that's far, far from home.

Amid the million or so rental listings on Airbnb, amid the castles (at last count, there were 1,200 castles) and fantasy beach spreads, amid houseboats and ski gondolas and treehouses in the jungle, amid the scores of assiduously vacuumed urban apartments showcasing vividly printed bedspreads and devotion to Ikea minimalism, Yoppy's place is eye-catching for being none of that. Its governing aesthetic is what I'd term "salaryman bachelor." In one photo, there's a dark brown couch, possibly velour, draped with a rumpled blanket. It sits in an area that is dimly lit and very narrow and has a corporate-looking whiteboard parked in one corner, maybe in the event that something needs diagramming. Another picture shows a different room, bare-walled and completely empty, where a guest can unfold a futon to sleep. The arrangement is simple: Yoppy has his own bedroom off the hallway. He will share the bathroom and kitchen and, if you need it, his hair dryer. When he is not at work, he assures you, he will be eager to hang out. "I am nice to you very much," is what he promises. All this for $42 a night.

Before flying to Japan last fall, I did a crawl through Airbnb's Tokyo listings. Maybe because I was looking only a week ahead, there wasn't a whole lot open. But still, there were options. I examined people's toilets, microwaves, and pillowcases. I assessed their cats and dogs, their workout equipment and shelves full of anime-character plushies. I felt voyeuristic and judgmental but, given that it was a business transaction, also entitled to my judgments. There is a guy named Masahiro who has an apartment he'll share with you, but be aware he already shares it with 10 snakes. Many properties have strident house rules involving not speaking to the neighbors. There were a lot of specifics about how to take out the trash and some polite but emphatic exhortations to not, in general, behave like a cretin. You could add up the various "do nots" to get a sense of all the exasperating things people actually do. This from one male host, under the heading "Keep Clean":

1. Take off your shoes when you get into my house.
2. Do not pull your luggage along the floor to prevent damage on the floor.
3. Sit on a toilet even when you take a pee (to gentlemen).

Relative to other major cities in the world, Tokyo, with its population of 13.4 million, has been slower to embrace Airbnb, with fewer hosts signing on to open their doors to strangers. There are currently about 2,500 listings in the city, less than half of what can be found in Madrid, less than one-fifteenth of what can be found in Paris, and about the same as what's available in Edinburgh, a city of half a million people. For the company, which is aggressively endeavoring to become a global superbrand and markets itself on the idea that the world is an inherently exuberant and welcoming place, this is a concern. In five years, Tokyo will host the Summer Olympics, and with that will come a wash of what the Japanese government predicts will be eight million or so eager visitors on a trip-of-a-lifetime binge, all needing places to stay. It could be an incredible boon for a growth-minded, profit-minded company like Airbnb. But so far, there are not enough Yoppys.

This is why, one morning in September, I found myself following a pair of American Airbnb employees and a Japanese translator down a leafy pedestrian street in Jiyūgaoka, an upscale residential neighborhood on the southwestern side of Tokyo. The Americans, Anne Kenny and Kathy Lee, were researchers in their mid-30s focused on user experience. They had been dispatched from headquarters in San Francisco to do a four-day anthropological deep dive, interviewing Japanese hosts, most of them designated "superhosts"—people who have excellent reviews from guests and are quick to respond to booking requests—to try to understand whether and how the San Francisco share-everything ethos works in a country like Japan.

The air was muggy and smelled faintly of cedar. Japanese commuters glided past on bikes. A flock of girls dressed in school uniforms and frilly knee socks passed us going the other way. Nobody stared, because that would be rude, but they definitely looked. We were not just foreign, but we were also accidentally louder than everyone else, if only because everyone else seemed utterly silent.

Our translator, a woman named Fujiko Suda, noticed people noticing. "It's because no tourists would really come here," she said. And true enough, inside the hushed morning routine of the neighborhood, it felt as if we had jumped a fence.

A couple of months before my trip to Japan, Airbnb overhauled its website and began an extensive effort to rebrand itself, moving away from the notion that it was merely a room-rental platform, or an "online marketplace for accommodation," as its employees often described it, but rather something warmer and fuzzier and decidedly more expansive. Brian Chesky, Airbnb's CEO and one of its three founders, announced the rebranding via a lengthy video message aimed at the site's users—"our community"—in which he unveiled the company's new credo: "We believe in a world where all seven billion of us can belong anywhere." He described Airbnb not as a business but rather as a movement, noting how people once lived in villages and understood what it was to feel a sense of belonging, but that over time—thanks to the Industrial Revolution—everything became depersonalized and dispersed and the good stuff eroded. "At a time when we've been told to look at each other with suspicion and fear," he said, "you're telling the world it's OK to trust again."

Airbnb, which makes its money by charging service fees of 9 to 15 percent on every booking, is reportedly valued at $13 billion, more than Wyndham Worldwide or Hyatt. Since its founding six years ago, the company has booked stays for 30 million people, 20 million of them last year. It now has about 1,500 employees in 20 cities worldwide. Most of the charts plotting its various growth metrics—amount of capital, number of listings—show a steep upward curve, not unlike an arm shot triumphantly at the sky. But still, there are limits, and Airbnb seems to have glimpsed them, realizing that it will continue to grow only in concert with a parallel mindset, one involving the general reliability of strangers.

Can we "belong anywhere?" Should we try? I was thinking about this as we made our way through Jiyūgaoka that September day, headed toward the home of an Airbnb host named Haruko Miki, feeling distinctly as if we didn't belong. We passed a flower shop and a placid little park and then waited at a crossing next to a quiet mother and her quiet toddler for a train to quietly whoosh past. Kenny, who is blond and blue-eyed and has a gentle matter-of-fact nature, piloted us by following 30 pages of turn-by-turn, photo-based instructions she'd received. Thirty pages seemed like a lot, but this was Kenny's second trip to Tokyo on behalf of the company, and she had already figured out that Japanese hosts tend to be heavy-handed with the directions—in part because they're trying to be helpful to people navigating the confusing streets, and in part because thoroughness and precision seem to matter for their own sake.

Earlier, over breakfast, Lee mentioned the work of a Dutch social psychologist named Geert Hofstede, who developed a matrix of cultural dimensions by which one country could be viewed against another. The original research took place in the 1960s and '70s, when Hofstede was employed by IBM International and carried out a survey of its employees in 70 countries. Using the IBM data, and later incorporating the research of other social scientists, he came up with six measures to help define and analyze the values, attitudes, and behavioral impulses of any group—from something as small as the population of a single office or factory to something as large as a nation. These include individualism versus collectivism, indulgence versus restraint, power distance (a group's acceptance or rejection of hierarchy) and, perhaps most important for Airbnb, uncertainty avoidance.

According to the Hofstede Center, an institute specializing in intercultural business practices, uncertainty avoidance has to do with "the way a society deals with the fact that the future can never be known: Should we try to control the future or just let it happen?" The 30 pages of navigational instructions seemed a vote in favor of control. The center's portrait describes Japan as a pragmatic culture that emphasizes collectivism and hierarchy and as "one of the most uncertainty-avoiding countries on earth." (Apparently Greece and Uruguay also don't enjoy uncertainty.)

Lee is tall and willowy and was dressed that day in a sleeveless knit jersey dress. She has a master's degree in behavioral psychology and another in human-computer interaction and is part of Airbnb's Insights team, which looks at user data to glean useful information about hosts and guests. Like a majority of people who work at Airbnb, she has been at the company only a couple of years. She and Kenny met when they worked together on user-experience at Microsoft; each moved to Airbnb as its growth went steroidal in 2013. While Kenny focuses on international growth, Lee specializes in doing internal studies on things like why hosts decline bookings (30 to 40 percent of booking requests on the site are rejected) and what people mean exactly when they deem a place "clean." Back at Airbnb's offices in San Francisco, Lee told me, a behavioral economist on her team has looked at user data in conjunction with cultural dimensions. "Airbnb doesn't do as well in collectivist countries," she said, citing Japan as an example. "But in a place like Australia"—which, like the United States, rates high on individualism and indulgence and low on pragmatism—"it's huge."

Chesky has characterized Airbnb's popularity as spreading "house by house, block by block, city by city," kind of like a faith-in-the-world infection, governed by good will and good behavior, transmitted from one happy traveler to the next, one continent to another. Which brought us back to the challenge at hand. It was hard not to wonder how a company that's disruptive at its core would be received ultimately in Japan, where harmonious unity —a concept known as *wa*—is something of a national virtue. How does a storm arrive in a place that's phobic about storms?

A day earlier, before meeting the Airbnb team, I had coffee with a Japanese acquaintance—an English-speaking businesswoman named Chiaki Hayashi, who often travels internationally for work. I arranged to meet her as I was on my way to check in to the place I had booked through Airbnb. It was a cute-looking apartment I would have all to myself, called "Ultimate Tokyo-Sized Experience!!" At $62 per night, it was pricier than Yoppy's spare room but still about a third of what a decent hotel would cost. Hayashi ran her finger over the map I'd printed out, pinpointing its location near the Shibuya train station, in the busiest part of the city. Ultimate Tokyo-Sized Experience!!, it turned out, sat atop something known as Love Hotel Hill, which was where, she explained, a slew of small establishments rented rooms overnight or by the hour and a lot of people in Tokyo went to have sex.

"You mean like prostitutes?" I asked. None of this had been mentioned on the Airbnb listing.

"Mainly, no," Hayashi said. "It's more young people who live with their parents. But Japanese people really don't live in that area. They wouldn't want to." When I didn't appear reassured, she smiled and told me not to worry. "It's not dangerous, not dirty," she said. "It's just . . . very . . . specific."

I asked if she thought Airbnb would eventually take off in Japan. Hayashi considered the question awhile, then gave a kind of yes-and-no answer. "Japanese people are very comfortable with the concept of sharing," she said, citing the close quarters in which many families lived and the tradition of using *sentou,* communal bathhouses. It's just that they are less accustomed to sharing with outsiders. She mentioned a restaurant nearby with a NO FOREIGNERS sign in its window and referred also to the fact that her country spent two centuries living under an isolationist government policy that pretty much forbade interaction with the outside world.

"We are not familiar living with foreign people," Hayashi said, giving a lighthearted shrug. "I mean, Japan is an island. It's like, foreign people . . . What do you even eat?"

Haruko Miki's house sits at the crest of a gentle hill, a 10-minute walk from the train station. She bowed when she opened the door. She was 75, a widow in white slacks and a hot-pink sweater. Inside the entryway, we removed our shoes. Thinking ahead to our departure, Miki leaned down and reoriented each pair so that they faced back toward the door.

She spoke virtually no English, though she did have one go-to phrase—"green towels"—which she usually deployed right off the bat when showing Airbnb guests around her place, demarcating the line between what was theirs and what was hers. Their sheets are green; their towels are green; hers are not. The system seems to work. Miki's house is small by most American standards, but by Japanese standards, it's large. There are a couple of bedrooms upstairs, where her oldest daughter lives with her husband and their three children, and some sort of open loft area, where someone had the television turned up loud. Miki is slim and grandmotherly and told us, through the translator, that for years she has made a good living selling Tupperware to friends. She signed up for Airbnb 14 months earlier, when a friend of her daughter's, who was already hosting, suggested she might like it, for both the sociability and the money. After she served tea, Miki walked us through a compact living room and a galley kitchen and then down a hallway past her own bedroom to a second tiny room.

"This is where the visitors sleep," she said, as the rest of us took turns stepping in to look. Its floor was covered by traditional strawmat tatami. There were two green futons folded up against the wall. A single window covered in rice paper filtered the light from outside. She'd had Australians, Italians, Mexicans, Chileans, Chinese, Canadians, and also, because she happens to be fluent in Korean, a good number of Koreans come through. "When I signed up, I thought it would be one or two a month, but it's all the time," she says. "Last month, I had only two days off." A family from New York—a mother, father, and baby—was staying there at the time. There was no sign of them, except some luggage piled neatly in one corner. Miki had just done their laundry, which was drying on the patio outside.

Then she donned a red apron, heated a frying pan, and started making us lunch. Kenny and Lee were recording everything Miki said. They snapped photos of the knickknacks on her shelves and the guest book in which people wrote comments about their stays. The study Kenny and Lee were making was at once methodical and impressionistic, an attempt to build a portrait of host-guest dynamics in Japan to be delivered back to San Francisco for further discussion. They would later note that Miki, despite appearing as an older woman in an apron, was both an entrepreneur and an adventurer, as evidenced by her career in Tupperware and the fact, as she told us, that she celebrated her 50th birthday in the Australian outback, skydiving over Ayers Rock. Airbnb's mission, in part, was to identify and encourage outliers like Miki. It's how the service has gained footing in every new market—adopted first by the risk-takers and then normalized over time. Kenny asked each person a set list of questions, the final and arguably most important one being, "How can we find more people like you?"

Miki, hearing the question, laughed. In an incredibly short time, she had produced a plate of scallion pancakes, a bowl of peanuts sautéed with spices, some pickled daikon radishes, and a pile of potatoes cut into perfect little pyramids, fried until crisp and then tossed in a sticky sweet sauce. She mentioned that some of her friends were interested in renting out their spare rooms, but their husbands wouldn't allow it. "They say, 'I will do it when my husband dies.'" She added that her own husband never would have approved of the menagerie of strangers now coming through their house. "You know, Japanese are really . . ." She paused, searching for the right words. "They just don't want to bring foreigners to Japan."

She herself had a high tolerance for all of it, for the people who came and the stilted conversations conducted largely through hand gestures, for the puddles they left on her bathroom floor, the laundry she did free of charge, the loads of food they consumed at her table, and the way they sometimes threw their clothes all over her tatami room. She was even tolerant of the French, whom she admitted, when pressed, could be the most challenging guests of all. It was a labor, to be sure, but it was profitable, and it also seemed to mean something to her. One of her daughters lived in Los Angeles for eight years, and Miki had gone for extended visits. She knew acutely what it felt like to be dislocated, the stun of a country that's not your own. She offered a steadying, if not particularly glamorous, refuge. She served people tea made with herbs from her garden and rice cakes wrapped in seaweed. She unfolded their green-sheeted futons before bed at night.

The more we talked with Miki, the more I wanted to go lie on her couch in front of her knickknack cabinet and wait for the next warm meal. My place, Ultimate Tokyo-Sized Experience!!, turned out to be clean and quiet (as advertised) but also strange and lonely. It was a spare, single bedroom, not more than eight feet wide, with a narrow foldout futon, a minifridge, minitelevision, and minimicrowave, and a flimsy door, behind which was a bathroom just big enough to fit a body. Like a lot of Airbnb listings, it was rented as "entire place" rather than "private room," which meant no host was in residence. But in this case, I'm not sure any host was ever in residence. The listing was run by some sort of conglomerate or management company, and checking in involved no human interaction whatsoever. To get there, I carried my luggage up a neon-lit hill—past something called Hotel Fifteen Love, past places called Pub Slow Jam, Adult Shop Joyful, and Baby Doll, and a pet store that sold fluffed-up puppies and kittens and still somehow managed to look seedy—to the concrete apartment building where it was located. The door was unlocked. A key had been left inside. I had no idea where I'd landed.

Miki, despite the language barrier, seemed to know a lot about her guests. She described a woman who came to stay with her while she was on business in Japan and developed heat exhaustion, or maybe just exhaustion in general. ("She was so busy," observed Miki.) There was a young guy who arrived from Korea, saying he just wanted to get away from his parents, who were pestering him to get married. ("He needed some quiet," she said.) An Italian man came to stay and cried the whole time, confessing to Miki that he had cheated on his Japanese wife and now she'd left him. "I took him to the Emperor's Palace to try and cheer him up," she told us, adding that it didn't work at all. Somewhere along the way, though, she delivered the kind of blunt-force, stranger-to-stranger advice that cuts handily across cultures. The man's wife eventually took him back, Miki informed us, and she was happy to claim some of the credit: "I told him," she said, shaking a finger as she described it, "he just had to stop with the affairs."

Last winter, Airbnb conducted focus groups in Tokyo, gathering people who knew nothing about the service and showing them the Japanese-language version of the Airbnb website on smartphones, complete with the castles and the treehouses, the full flight of whimsy. Anne Kenny was part of the group that watched what happened through a one-way window. "It was clear that not everyone understood the concept," she told me.

Those who did had questions—a lot of them. "It was: 'What

if this happens? What if that happens? What if I'm a guest, and my host makes me dinner, and I don't want to finish it?'" Kenny recalled one morning as we sat in a café in Shibuya, not far from Love Hotel Hill. "Here they are, they haven't booked a trip. They haven't traveled. They're just looking at a website, and already they're going through the what-ifs." One participant asked what would happen if he rented a place online and then, when he got there, it turned out to be a supermarket. Someone else studied a photo of a Western host posed casually with a coconut-water drink on her lap and, seeming flummoxed, asked, "How would I even address her?" It was, you might say, a full-on display of uncertainty avoidance, though perhaps not surprising in a country that's routinely walloped by volcanic eruptions, earthquakes, and typhoons and was, at the time, just a few years past a horrifying tsunami and the Fukushima nuclear meltdown. Still, it didn't necessarily bode well for business.

There was one woman, however, who grasped the idea immediately. "She was like: 'I can stay in a castle? You put castles on this site? That's amazing,'" Kenny said. She pulled out her laptop and showed me a photo taken at the focus group. A half-dozen young women sat around a conference-room table; five of them were dressed in gray or black. The sixth wore an electric-orange sweater. She, of course, was the castle lover, an instant icon for Kenny and her colleagues. "There was something so distinct in her mannerisms," Kenny said. "Even from behind the window, you could see she was genuinely excited about it. It was like: What is it about this woman in the bright orange sweater that makes her more interested in the idea of Airbnb, even as all her peers are focused on the worst-case scenarios?"

The woman in the orange sweater matters as an ideal, not just to Airbnb but to any company breaking into a new market, especially a market that may be inherently resistant to what's being sold. She's an early adopter in chrysalis form—curious, unconcerned with convention, seemingly willing to gamble on something unproved, ready to buy. Or sell. When I jokingly asked Kenny if they'd tried to recruit the woman as an Airbnb host in Tokyo, she laughed and said no, adding, "But we probably should have."

On the surface, the superhosts Kenny and Lee interviewed over the course of several days had little in common with one another— a husband and wife expecting their first child, a cool guy who liked to take his guests clubbing, a well-off gay couple who'd bought a second apartment as an investment—but they were all Orange Sweaters in a way. All spoke at least a little bit of English. More important, it seemed, everyone had some defining experience with outsiders. Two of the couples were multinational—Japanese natives with partners who were American and Chinese. Other hosts were Japanese by birth but had lived in other countries or traveled a lot. This appeared to give them a certain renegade perspective, a degree of global cross-pollination and comfort with strangers that seemed to put them at odds with many of the people around them, but also made them more like other Airbnb users internationally.

A number of the Tokyo hosts said they deliberately kept quiet about their involvement with Airbnb. "It's kind of like talking about your investment portfolio," one said. "You really only discuss it with the very closest of friends." Japan has a national hotel law, which requires the licensing of any business that provides accommodation, though enforcement is spotty. But there's also a tradition of individuals renting rooms to students or short-term visitors, called *minpaku,* which is considered legal. Airbnb, as it does in many countries, exists—nimbly, cannily—in a gray area. Mostly, people feared their neighbors, concerned that one poor interaction with a foreigner—one noisy night, one trampled flowerbed, one failure to interpret the boundaries of what was acceptable— might lead to a police complaint or problems with a landlord.

I was starting to see why foreigners in Japan were so worrying, so problematic. Accompanied by a translator who knew the city, Kenny, Lee, and I moved around Tokyo with relative ease, but the second she clocked out for the day, we were shucked instantly of our grace. We walked down the wrong streets, ordered things we didn't intend to at restaurants, were bumbling when counting our yen at cash registers. Kenny had taken to bowing at everyone she saw. When spoken to in Japanese, Lee and I automatically, like dummies, responded in Spanish. We swam constantly in uncertainty. We wandered the basement food court of a fancy department store in Ginza, looking at sugary pastries that were shaped like fish and raw fish that had been cut to look like candy. We stood dumbfounded in front of a cantaloupe that cost $127. I felt as alien as I'd ever felt in my life.

One morning, we visited a 27-year-old tech blogger named Ryoma Machida, who lives with his wife in a small house in a densely populated neighborhood and rents out a room on Airbnb. He also manages 11 other Airbnb properties. Machida has a mop of hair and a thoughtful demeanor. He studied international business at a university in New Zealand and first learned about Airbnb by reading Mashable. He had a picture of Steve Jobs taped to his refrigerator.

Machida was trying to start a business called Zens that would help more Japanese people host on Airbnb, taking care of bookings and guest communication and even designing custom-made furniture for compact spaces that could store bulky luggage. He was thinking ambitiously. He saw the 2020 Olympics as an opportunity not just for himself but for Japan. Sitting with his dog on his lap, he spoke about the fact that Japan's population was aging and its economy faltering. "We have 8.3 million empty homes in this country," he said. "We have smaller families, less money." He went on to describe how he'd like to start working with communities in the Japanese countryside to encourage them to open their homes to foreigners, who would then come spend money and slowly start to revitalize the economy. "Airbnb," he said, "could be a Japan-saver."

It was a difficult path to forge, however, not just because Airbnb was relatively unknown in Japan, but also because the startup mentality did not seem to play well in general there. According to the Global Entrepreneurship Monitor, which collects data on business growth, Japan has among the lowest levels of startup activity in the world, with roughly 3.7 percent of the adult population engaged in entrepreneurship—as compared with about 13 percent in the United States. Machida, though, struck me as a change-maker, an individualist who was nonetheless sensitive to his own culture's collectivist norms. He chalked up the resistance to outsiders largely to a simple lack of exposure. A number of his friends, he said, had never spoken to a foreigner in their lives. He was working to remedy this by organizing informal get-togethers between Airbnb visitors and Japanese friends a couple of times a month, spreading the word via Facebook. With neighbors who weren't sure what to make of his foreign guests, he tried to humanize them: "I say: 'Today we have guests from France. They are 35 years old, and they are teachers.'"

At the same time, he also worked to educate Airbnb guests on the Japanese way of doing things. When new guests checked in to a place he managed, he met them personally, showing them how to remove their shoes at the door and explaining that they needed to speak more quietly than maybe they did at home. Sometimes, though, the gulf between cultures felt unbridgeable, the boundaries impossible to translate. Machida described running afoul of a building co-op board, forced to close one of his listings after a visitor from Europe was spotted, to someone's apparent horror, charging her cell phone in the building's lobby.

Later, as Kenny, Lee, and Suda were debriefing at a café, I voiced my enthusiasm about Machida. Wasn't he exactly the sort of person the company was looking for? A gung-ho ambassador, an innovator, an optimist? The Airbnb researchers nodded yes, but Suda, the translator, emphatically shook her head no, declaring that Machida would never make it as a Tokyo businessman. He was too brazen, she suggested, too casual in the way he spoke about making change and making money. "You're not supposed to get rich fast," she said. "That's just Japan."

One night, on my way back up Love Hotel Hill, I decided to stop into Pub Slow Jam for a beer. It was a Monday and the eve of some sort of holiday in Japan. People were setting off firecrackers in the streets; spiky-haired teenage boys wandered around in leather jackets, girls tottered on high heels, everyone shouting into the night and snapping photos with their cell phones. Music blared from the trinket shops. The pachinko parlors had their doors open, plinking and pulsing with light. I thought that maybe Pub Slow Jam would be lively, that I might find some people to chat with in English there. But when I entered, it was a forlorn, low-ceilinged establishment with a few stools, a Formica bar, and K-pop playing in the background. A lone couple sat at the far end of the bar quietly sipping drinks, possibly gearing up for a Love Hotel experience. When I glanced at them, they looked away. The bartender greeted me in Japanese, and I said hello back—I had mastered that much—but otherwise there was nothing more either of us could say. I drank my beer in solitude, paid the bill, and went home, back to my miniature room.

Ultimate Tokyo-Sized Experience!! felt less strange than it once did. I sat on my futon, as I had every night, reading the day's news on my laptop, the world's uncertainties writ large: Ebola was raging. There were hostages in Syria. The Nigerian schoolgirls were still missing. And off the coast of Japan, a typhoon swirled ominously in the Pacific.

Around me, the building was silent—weirdly silent for its location in Shibuya, for the riotous partying going on in the streets that night. If Airbnb was going to grow in Japan, it occurred to me that it might sprout faster in places like this—in cheap impersonal residences in the city center as opposed to in the close-knit residential neighborhoods we'd been visiting. My room was next to the elevator on the third floor, which when I first arrived concerned me, until I realized it was either a very quiet elevator or else there was nobody using it. Immediately next to my door was an identical door, and right next to that door was another. The building was open in the center, so you could look up and down and see the other floors. There were maybe seven floors in the building, maybe 12 doors on every floor. I got the feeling that behind each one was a place as simple and compact as mine, like cabins on a cruise ship.

The laminated instructions left by the faceless Airbnb host/management company included strong admonishments to keep quiet and not talk to anybody else I might encounter. My checkout instructions included taking my printed map and itinerary with me when I left. "Why?" the instructions read. "Because we really don't like people we don't know finding directions to our apartment in the trash."

But the odd thing was I never saw anyone coming or going from the building, anyway—not once in four days, not another soul. Was anyone even there? I hoped so. It would be too lonely, otherwise. I could assume only that the building was populated with people who, like me, were for some reason nervous and dislocated, and therefore quiet—unsure whether they belonged. Maybe the place was full of migrant workers or runaways who'd turned to prostitution. Or could it be that behind each door was a traveler who'd rented an apartment that had looked tidy and appealing on the Airbnb website and was now just politely trying to stay hidden? I didn't know; I'd never know. In the half-conscious fog of my jet lag, the building felt to me like a giant ghost ship moving through the night, and I imagined us—whoever we were—on a dark ocean, drifting away from whatever land we understood.

DAVE EGGERS

The Actual Hollister

FROM *The New Yorker*

THE YEAR I turned 43, I woke up one morning and thought
it would be a good day to go to Hollister. I'd been seeing those
hoodies around, and the place had been on my mind. So I found
an old atlas in my garage, checked the map of California to make
sure I remembered how to get there, and left. No one was expecting me and I wasn't expecting anything. It was the kind of trip
a middle-aged man takes when his children are at a trampoline
birthday party.

The drive took two hours from the San Francisco Bay Area,
south on 280 to 85 to 101 to 25. Along 280, there are tens of
thousands of acres of heavily wooded hills surrounding the Crystal Springs Reservoir. It is incalculably valuable land, all of it protected. Eventually it flattens out a bit, and the climate gets drier as
you drop into the Central Valley. The hills go from green to gold,
but are no less beautiful. Soon, there are farms on either side of
the highway, and pumpkin sellers and stables and dust. It feels very
Old West, and you're only an hour or so from San Francisco.

Hollister emerges in no particular hurry. Tidy rows of onions,
cherry trees, and bell peppers give way to a small factory or two—a
group of women in hairnets were taking a break in front of Marich
Confectionery as I passed—and then there are diners and gas stations and, finally, a downtown that seems timeless without being
in any way quaint. There is a beautiful red brick church, Hollister
United Methodist, and, within walking distance, an array of well-
kept Victorian homes, but there are empty storefronts and vacant

offices, too. On the town's main thoroughfare, San Benito Street, I drove past an office building with a sign in the window:

THIS BUILDING IS NOT EMPTY IT IS FULL OF POTENTIAL

Nearby, a pair of women were standing on a corner holding signs that said PRAY TO END ABORTION. Behind them was a pawnshop, and down the way Hazel's Thrift Shop and a motel called Cinderella—not to be confused with the nearby quinceañera and bridal shop, which offers clothing for "both *novias* and *princesas*." The town bleeds into agriculture on all sides, and beyond the farms are the hills, largely unmarred by any construction.

It is a strangely complete town, like something out of a Richard Scarry book. There are factories, farms, schools, railroads, horses, sheep, goats, and barns. There are men wearing cowboy hats and driving pickup trucks. There is a baseball-card shop. A sign for the high-school homecoming dance advertises its theme: A DISNEY BALL.

I'd been to Hollister twice since I moved to the West Coast from Illinois, 23 years ago. Each time, I made a point of first visiting the old Hazel Hawkins Memorial Hospital. On this visit, I remembered it being close to the town center, and, sure enough, I found it easily. But something seemed different. A sign out front read PRAYER IS THE BEST WAY TO GET TO HEAVEN — BUT TRESPASSING IS FASTER. Then, on the corner of Hawkins and Monterey, I saw a large sign that said FOR LEASE. This was new to me—what was once a town centerpiece, a delicate Spanish colonial with Italianate flourishes, had apparently been carved up into small offices. I parked and looked more closely.

I figured that given the building's origin as a hospital, and its status as one of the town's oldest buildings, the occupants would be of the nonprofit sort—Junior League, Historical Society, Ladies Auxiliary. So I walked up the left-leaning white steps, noting that the sculpted cherubs on the front portico had been repainted without great care. To the right of the front door, a sign in the bay window announced, FREE FIRST MONTH RENT. GREAT DEALS. Through the window, I could see a desk, and on it an early-1990s computer in the beginning stages of decomposition. The contrast between the building's rococo exterior and its garage-sale interior was startling.

In the lobby, on a low table, there was a tidy array of brochures and business cards for taxi operators, churches, faith healers, and purveyors of bail bonds. To the left was the New Light Embassy, which billed itself as a "Whole Brain Learning & Hypnotherapy Center . . . Enriching, Developing, and Empowering, the Human Potential." Occupying much of the right wing of the building was the NewLife Worship Center.

But there was no one inside. No one in the New Light Embassy, no one in the NewLife Worship Center. "Did you know Jesus attended church?" a green leaflet asked. "This is something we do not hear about often, but it is true." Then, in the sad silence of the dormant building, there was a sound. A thumping. I followed it down the hallway to a door. A floor mat in front said ELI'S CHOP SHOP, alongside a tricolored barber pole. Voices could be heard amid the hip-hop, and for a second I was so happy to know that there was someone in this building that I thought about going inside. But instead I left.

On the front lawn, under an old willow, I stood with no clear idea of what to do. I watched a man across the street cutting his grass and I cycled through a series of conclusions and emotions. I was saddened by the state of the building. The interior was gloomy, and the tenants seemed temporary and uncommitted to the upkeep of the building. And I cared about this why?

Fifteen years ago, the word "Hollister" meant little to anyone. Now it's hard to walk around any city, from Melbourne to Montreal to Mumbai, without seeing it stitched on someone's shirt or hoodie. Abercrombie & Fitch, which launched Hollister in 2000, has done an extraordinary job with brand penetration: in 2013 there were 587 Hollister stores around the world, and the brand netted more than $2 billion in sales.

The clothes themselves rarely depart from the realm of sweatshirts and sweatpants—they're eerily similar to the comfort-wear you can buy at Target or Walmart. But a Hanes hoodie at Target is $13, while a Hollister hoodie is $44.95. This implies that "Hollister" itself means something and is worth something.

For years, employees of Hollister stores, during orientation, were given the story, and it goes something like this: John M. Hollister was born at the end of the 19th century and spent his summers in Maine as a youth. He was an adventurous boy who loved to swim in the clear and cold waters there. He graduated from Yale in 1915 and, eschewing the cushy Manhattan life suggested for him, set sail for the Dutch East Indies, where he purchased a rubber plantation in 1917. He fell in love with a woman named Meta and bought a 50-foot schooner. He and Meta sailed around the South Pacific, treasuring "the works of the artisans that lived there," and eventually settled in Los Angeles, in 1919. They had a child, John Jr., and opened a shop in Laguna Beach that sold goods from the South Pacific—furniture, jewelry, linens, and artifacts. When John Jr. came of age and took over the business, he included surf clothing and gear. (He was an exceptional surfer himself.) His surf shop, which bore his name, grew in popularity until it became a globally recognized brand. The Hollister story is one of "passion, youth and love of the sea," evoking "the harmony of romance, beauty, adventure."

None of this is true. Most of Abercrombie & Fitch's brands—including the now-defunct Gilly Hicks and Ruehl No. 925—have had fictional backstories, conceived by Mike Jeffries, the company's former CEO. Abercrombie & Fitch told the *Los Angeles Times* that the company pulled the name Hollister out of thin air, so any connection between the brand and the town is coincidental. Even so, the company's relationship with Hollister, California, population 36,000, has not exactly been one of benevolent indifference.

In 2006 a Hollister merchant put RAG CITY BLUES: HOLLISTER on vintage blue jeans and decided to file a federal trademark application for her label. She subsequently received threats from attorneys representing Abercrombie & Fitch. She was baffled; the lawyers had told her, in essence, that putting her town's name on the clothing would provoke a lawsuit—that the trademark attached to its brand superseded the rights of the town. (The company sees its legal opposition to the merchant as strictly a trademark issue, which has nothing to do with the merchant's being from Hollister.) According to the *L.A. Times,* students at a local high school worried that their sports uniforms would engender more legal letters. In an effort to smooth things over, town leaders suggested to Abercrombie that the company open an outlet in Hollister. It seemed to make sense—a Hollister store in the town of Hollister—but they were told that the company's aspirational brand would not find the right audience in Hollister. (The company does not have any recollection of this request.)

The town has no mall and few boutiques or cafés. It is not a tour-ist destination, like nearby Salinas, the home of John Steinbeck, or Gilroy, known as "the garlic capital of the world." Many of its older residents are Caucasian, but Hollister's demographics have been changing for the past 50 years, and today 67 percent of residents identify as Latino. Most of them work on the surrounding farms or in the few nearby factories. Hollister is an unglamorous town, but its name is now associated with some degree of taste and status all over the world. Which is odd, because the town benefits in almost no way from this success.

The rise of the Hollister brand has been especially strange to me, because it was my great-great-grandfather T. S. Hawkins who helped found the town of Hollister. Growing up, I was confronted daily by his white-bearded face, in an old photograph that hung in our living room in Illinois. A few feet away, his rifle, which he car-ried from Missouri to California, rested over our mantel.

The real story of Hollister begins in Marion County, Missouri, 20 miles from Mark Twain's hometown of Hannibal, in 1836. This is when T. S. Hawkins was born, the eldest of nine children, his parents farmers, their people having traveled from Ireland and England and Scotland to the early Virginia settlements.

The Hawkins family lived in two adjoining log cabins with one roof covering both. The boys of the family slept in the attic, near the clapboard roof, and listened to the tapping of the rain in the summer. "The boards made a good roof to turn off the rain," Hawkins wrote in his autobiography, *Some Recollections of a Busy Life,* self-published in 1913.

> But in the winter when the wind blew the fine snow would drift through the interstices between the boards of the roof. It was glorious up in the old-fashioned feather bed, with the blankets pulled up to one's ears, listening to the roar of the wind, the pelting of the hail and snow and the war of the elements, until one fell asleep.
>
> In the morning, we would awake to find the bedding and the floor covered an inch or more in drifted snow . . . It seems at this distance a rough life; but I do not remember that we ever considered it so, and it certainly served to make one hardy and self-reliant.

They hunted squirrels and quail and the occasional possum, and they ate their own pigs, in bacon and ham form, three times a day, for months on end. They made wool clothing for special occasions, but for everyday clothes they used bark—bark of "various trees," Hawkins notes, though it's hard to picture the clothing. You have to assume it was a fabric that breathed.

Hawkins attended the customary one-room schoolhouse, a few months a year, until he was 16. At that point, with his younger brothers able to take on his duties at the farm, Hawkins was freed to pursue his education. He made out for Kentucky, to live with his grandfather, a journey of 500 miles, which for a "diffident, awkward, backwoods boy" felt "like going out of the world."

He tried his hand at teaching, and then medicine, before returning home with $300.

> I was content to remain idle for a short time, spending my days floating down the Meramec in my canoe or resting under the shade of the trees. But this could not last long, and soon I commenced to look around for something to do. From our home the nearest village was twenty miles. Scattered here and there was a country store. There was none nearer than seven or eight miles from our place, and I conceived the idea that I could establish myself in the business . . .
>
> I immediately went to work with a carpenter, and by the end of July, I had a building twenty by forty feet, with shelving and counter complete. I had already gone to St. Louis to a firm who were engaged in the business of furnishing country stores, and as I was entirely ignorant of what I needed, they selected a stock invoicing about two thousand dollars, on which I paid my three hundred dollars, and the balance they carried for me.

It's important to note several things at this point. First, a wholesaler provided T. S. Hawkins with $2,000 worth of goods, which in today's currency would be about $50,000. Second, although Hawkins had no experience in retail sales, the wholesaler was risking the credit, with no collateral. Third, Hawkins was all of 21 years old.

The store was successful. Hawkins served as his own "clerk, janitor, bookkeeper and everything else." When it got dark, he would go home for his evening meal before returning to the store, where he would "pull a cot from under the counter, make it up, and sleep until morning with a gun by my side. As a good many rough characters visited the mountains, it was not considered safe to leave the store, a half mile from the nearest house, over night."

The next year, he married Catherine Patton, a well-bred woman

from two old southern families. Within a year, her health began to
fail, and their doctor recommended that they move to a milder,
drier climate. Hawkins sold up, and began preparing for a trip out
West. By the time he was ready, he and Catherine had a baby, a
boy named T.W., and the traveling party had grown to 20 people,
including Hawkins's father and his brother-in-law, along with 60
head of cattle, 4 wagons, 14 horses, and 17 oxen.

This was not the great emigration of the gold rush, 10 years
earlier. The Hawkinses saw other wagons only intermittently. They
expected to come across ample bison to shoot and eat, but found
none; during the journey, they were able to kill only two antelope.
Instead, they relied on trade with Indians, with other travelers,
and with settlers. There had recently been a notorious event, the
Mountain Meadows massacre, in southern Utah, in which 120
men, women, and children from Arkansas were killed by Mormon
militias masquerading as Native Americans, and so the Hawkins
party joined forces with another wagon train heading west from
Illinois. But the Mormons they encountered as they neared Salt
Lake were friendly, Hawkins wrote.

> As we had been living on bacon and salt meats, with no vegetables for
> so long, I sought out a large house which I thought gave promise of af-
> fluence. I knocked on the front door, but received no answer, so I went
> to the back of the house, where under a tree sat a large, solid-looking
> man with a babe on each knee, while a dozen other children, from two
> to eight years, were playing around. Two women were washing clothes
> in the same tub, while a third was hanging them (the clothes, not the
> women) out to dry. It was my first view of polygamy. The man, as all oth-
> ers I met later, looked fat and happy, while all the women looked tired
> and careworn.

They traveled across the Bear River, and only then did they experience the kind of hardship and tragedy that all western travelers had come to expect.

> In the Illinois company was a dare-devil of a young man, and when
> the cattle were well into the river he followed them on his horse. He
> had about reached the middle, the horse swimming gallantly, when the
> man and horse suddenly disappeared. After a time the horse came to
> the surface further across, but we never saw the young man again. We
> camped on the bank and all hands turned out to search for the body.
> The ferryman assured us that it was entirely useless, that Bear River
> never gave up its dead.

They traversed the Sierra Nevadas. They found Angels Camp and French Camp and crossed the Livermore Valley southwest to San Francisco Bay, near Milpitas. Hawkins finally arrived in Mountain View in 1860.

"So ended our journey across the plains," he wrote. "I have read somewhere the saying that the 'Good Lord takes care of children and fools.' Looking backward, I cannot but feel that we must have belonged to one or both of those divisions of humanity."

The health of Catherine Hawkins initially improved, but she died less than two years after the journey. To some, this would have seemed like a cruel trick played by a malevolent god. But Hawkins decided to stay in California.

> Only those who have lost the companion of their young manhood can know the utter darkness that can come and the feeling that the bottom has dropped out of one's hopes and aspirations, that the world has come to an end, so far as one's own life is concerned. I realized, however, that hard work and unceasing work was the only panacea for me.

Hawkins bought 200 acres just north of Gilroy and married Emma Day, the daughter of a farmer. In 1864 they had their first child, Charles, and by 1867 Hawkins was a father of four and a prosperous farmer. Though he was largely self-taught, that year he shipped, he wrote, 10,000 centals of wheat to San Francisco.

Hawkins soon heard about a Colonel W. W. Hollister, who owned 21,000 acres of agricultural land nearby. For many years, that land had been in the hands of Spanish clergy, after most of its Native American inhabitants had been expelled or drawn into the mission system. When Mexico gained independence from Spain, much of it was given to Mexican soldiers and settlers. After the Mexican-American War, Hollister bought his tract of land from Francisco Pérez Pacheco. Hollister had followed a southern path to California, from Ohio down through New Mexico and Arizona to Santa Barbara and then north. He'd started out with 8,000 or 9,000 head of sheep, intending to move the largest herd of its kind across the continent. By the end, he had only a few thousand left, but when the Civil War began, Hollister made a fortune selling wool that outfitted the Union Army.

By 1868 Hollister was ready to sell his property, part of a ranch known as San Justo. Hawkins organized a group of local farmers to buy the parcel for $370,000. They split the land into 50 tracts, leaving 100 acres in the center for a town site. They were about to name the town San Justo when one of the men objected. Does every town in California have to be named after a saint? he asked. And so, after much debate, the farmers settled on Hollister, honoring the character Hawkins called "one of the noblest men I ever knew."

Hawkins had one more child, and gave up farming to establish the Bank of Hollister. Eventually, his 5 children had 11 children among them, and all but one thrived. Hazel Hawkins, born in 1892, died at the age of nine, of appendicitis, although the illness isn't mentioned in *Some Recollections*. In the 161 pages of his memoir, Hawkins seems stoic, even cavalier, about any adversity or loss, but the death of Hazel Hawkins left him devastated.

"She had lived with us all her little life. She was my constant companion, and we loved each other with a devotion I had never known before. All of her days she had striven unselfishly to make all around her happy," Hawkins wrote. "On the fifth of March, as I stood by her bedside, she opened her eyes and looking at me said in her sweet voice, 'Good-night, Grandpa,' and then fell asleep, to waken in the Paradise of God."

To some extent, Hawkins blamed his granddaughter's death on the lack of proper health care in rural Hollister, so he threw himself into the construction of a solution and a monument. He named it the Hazel Hawkins Memorial Hospital.

I stood on its white stone steps, wondering what had happened. Looking for some insight into the state of the building, I went to Hollister's chamber of commerce. But first I had to wait. The chamber's president and CEO, Debbie Taylor, was occupied with a woman who wanted to know about the local Boy Scout troop. She was a new arrival, and a talkative one, having high expectations for the Scouts of Hollister. While I waited, I flipped through the brochures on a table in the office. WANTED! a flier said. Apparently the Hollister Hills Junior Off-Highway Rangers, a group of young ATV riders, were looking for members to rampage through the surrounding golden hills.

When I got a chance to talk to Taylor, I asked about the golden hills, commending the city for preserving them. Taylor was not so sure she agreed. It might not have been the official chamber-of-commerce line, but Taylor implied that the town would not mind anyone building on the hills. They wouldn't mind economic development of any kind. The recession had been tough, Taylor said, and they were looking for any bright spots. There were too many tattoo parlors, she told me, and she lamented the karate studio that had recently closed under suspicious circumstances.

Without much prompting, we arrived at the subject of Abercrombie & Fitch, and Taylor talked about the litigation the company threatened and about the interesting fact that it refused to open a Hollister store in Hollister. But, she said, the town would soon have a Walgreens, and everyone was excited about that—no one more so than Debbie Taylor.

She asked me what brought me to Hollister, and I told her about T. S. Hawkins and my connection to him. She flipped through my copy of *Some Recollections,* and I showed her the photo of young Hazel Hawkins and explained the connection between her and the hospital in her name.

"Oh!" Taylor said. "You know there's a ribbon-cutting tonight at five-thirty?" I didn't know. I had no idea what she was talking about. She explained that a new wing of the relocated Hazel Hawkins Hospital, a women's center, had just been built, and a few hours hence there would be an opening. She gave me the address —it was far from the site of the original building—and I left, the two of us marveling at the lucky timing of my visit.

It seemed as good a reason as any to get a haircut.

I went back to the old Hazel Hawkins Memorial Hospital building and opened the door of Eli's Chop Shop to find a large tattooed man behind a barber's chair cutting the hair of another large tattooed man. In a second barber's chair, there was a third large tattooed man, apparently just hanging out. They seemed baffled to see me.

Then I saw a mother and her middle-school-aged son sitting on a couch, waiting their turn. I didn't look like the rest of the clientele, and I was far older—even the mom seemed a decade younger than I am—but I still had my hand on the doorknob, so I had to do something. I could have turned and left them in peace, but instead I asked, "Is it first come, first served?"

"Yup," the barber said.

I sat on the couch, a wide and low-slung black leather model, and began watching *SportsCenter* on the flat-screen TV mounted near the ceiling. Loud hip-hop overwhelmed the room.

I could tell that the three men were wondering why I was there, but they got back to talking among themselves, and, in an effort to disappear and to put them at ease, I watched *SportsCenter* so intensely I must have looked as though I were listening for coded messages from space.

There were some hugs and backslaps when the occupant of the barber's chair stood up, and then the boy took his turn. The barber, in the meantime, had changed the TV channel to a reality show called *World's Dumbest Criminals*.

The mom and I laughed at the show, which was periodically very funny, and then she lifted her chin at me and said, "You're up." The barber had carved an elaborate geometric design into the hair on the lower part of the boy's head. It had been done with a confident hand, and the boy was thrilled. He and his mother left, and I sat down. The man who'd got a haircut was leaning against the counter where all the gels and combs and washes were kept. The man in the other chair crossed his arms, revealing a pair of tattoos: FAMILY on one arm, FIRST on the other.

"So what's it gonna be?" the barber asked.

He was looking at the back of my head, and his two friends were looking at me. I told them it had been 22 years since I'd had a professional haircut.

"Looks like it," the barber said, and we all chuckled. "How come?"

I explained the budgetary benefits of cutting one's own hair, and the guys all nodded.

"I gotta come in here once a week," Family First said. He turned his head side to side, revealing an intricate design that would require regular upkeep. It was the work of an artist.

I told the barber to just take an inch off anywhere he saw the need, and he got started. Another man entered, athletic and tanned, with an array of tattoos on his arms. He sat under *World's Dumbest Criminals* and talked with the barber about an upcoming UFC fight in Sacramento.

Then the barber turned to me. "So how'd you hear about this

place?" He said this with a mixture of nonchalance and wariness. It was the question his two friends had been waiting for. Even the guy on the couch turned around.

I told them the story about T. S. Hawkins coming to this land, about how he built the former hospital where we were sitting, that the structure was dedicated to his granddaughter who had died young. All four men nodded respectfully.

Then something happened. The TV was on loud, and there was the stereo, too, so I heard nothing new, but the two friends were suddenly wondering what a certain sound was.

"Hear that?" the one with the new haircut said.

"Hear it?" Family First said. "Is that you?" he asked me.

I didn't know what they were talking about. The men said something about some ring or some electronic sound they'd just heard.

"Is someone here wearing a wire?" Family First asked. His friend laughed and patted himself down briefly, running his hands over his chest and ample stomach. Now they were looking at me again, and it finally dawned on me that they thought I was a narc.

"Aw, man," the barber said, about the possibility that I was wearing a wire. "I'd be out the window, I don't care."

The three of them discussed what they'd do if cops showed up, or were already in the room. I suddenly remembered the sign in front of the building, indicating that trespassers would be shot, sent to heaven, etc. The atmosphere was still lighthearted, but the three friends around me were uncomfortable. It was odd: they continued to be polite to me, and my hair was being cut with great care, all while they were talking about the possible narc in the room as if he were some other person—not me.

Trying to change the subject, I asked Family First and his friend where they were from. Only then did I realize it was the kind of awkward question that a normal person would not ask but that a narc would find brilliant. One of the guys said he was from Visalia. The other didn't answer. The barber tilted my head down to work on the back of my neck. When I tilted my head up again, the two friends had gone.

The silence stretched out, and I decided to fill it.

I asked the barber how long he'd been in Hollister.

"I don't know. Not long," he said.

"You like it here?" I asked.

"Nah," he said. "It sucks."

He said he was from Gilroy, and he liked it much better there. Gilroy is not a booming metropolis—except maybe during the garlic festival—and is only 15 miles away, but it's bigger than Hollister, and that's what mattered to him.

I asked him how he'd chosen the former Hazel Hawkins Memorial Hospital as the location for his barbershop, and he shrugged. The rent was cheap enough, he said. I asked how he stayed in business when there was no sign facing the street. Except for the doormat, there was no sign at all, come to think of it. He said that he had enough customers through word of mouth. I said something about the building having charm and history, but he didn't like the building, either.

"You know there was a coroner's office in the basement?" he asked.

For him, this was another reason to leave. He believed the building was haunted.

With the utmost professionalism, he trimmed around my ears and brushed the hair from my neck. He removed the bib. The haircut was $15, and I paid him and thanked him—the haircut was flawless—but we were both very confused about all that had just transpired.

"See you in another ten years," he said. I was halfway through the door when he added, cheerfully, "I probably won't be here then, though."

Hollister, like many towns of its size and socioeconomics, has been affected by gang activity and by the related spike in meth and heroin use. The town had been discussing the possibility of adding police officers to address the drug trade and the gang presence. Maybe the barber thought I was one of these new cops—and he'd assumed that I'd made assumptions about him and his friends. I thought about going back to apologize, but wouldn't that be exactly what a narc would do?

Gang activity, real and imagined, has a historical echo in Hollister. In the early part of the 20th century, the American Motorcyclist Association started the Gypsy Tours, for which bikers were encouraged to hold races, rallies, shows, and picnics. During the Second World War, the rallies were suspended, but afterward they were revived. The atmosphere, though, was different. Many of the young men returning from Europe and the Pacific were shattered, disillusioned. Men who otherwise would have expected to stay in their rural homes or work in urban factories had now seen the world, had seen unnameable horrors, and were no longer beholden to pedestrian life paths. Motorcycling became more popular than ever, and the rallies became bigger and wilder.

And so, on July 4, 1947, the Gypsy Tour descended on Hollister, and, by some estimates, the town's population of 4,500 doubled overnight, with all kinds of clubs—the Boozefighters, the Market Street Commandos, the Galloping Goose, the Pissed Off Bastards of Bloomington. The members rode through town, making noise, drinking beer, breaking bottles, and generally causing low-level mayhem. Police struggled to control the crowds.

Rumors of the unruly bikers morphed into rumors of rioting, and six years later Marlon Brando was playing a confused and misunderstood leather-clad young man, caught up in a riot in Hollister. *The Wild One* terrified law-abiding citizens, but to rebellious bike-riding men it seemed like a blueprint for life. Soon enough, the Hells Angels took note, and they began to attend yearly gatherings, although the locals were divided on the advantages of their patronage. In any case, the town saw fit, in 1997, to commemorate the "riot" of 1947 with a 50th-anniversary party.

The celebrations have continued over the years, only occasionally called off owing to lack of interest or the fluctuating tolerance of the town. Debbie Taylor was quick to point out that though the rally hadn't happened the year before, they were planning to reinstate it. "Definitely next year," she said. (There was indeed a rally the following year. It would be Debbie Taylor's last. She's moved on from the chamber of commerce and away from Hollister. Eli's Chop Shop has closed, too.)

After I left the chamber of commerce, I meandered through the town, passing Hazel Street and Hawkins Street and Steinbeck Street, and the middle school and the high school, the students, most of them Latino, finishing the day and heading home. The afternoon was aging, and I figured it was time to make my way to the modern incarnation of the hospital. Only then did I realize that I hadn't come across one person, all day, wearing the Hollister name. It seemed like a remarkable inversion: anywhere else in the world, seeing thousands of kids leaving school, you'd see the word "Hollister" on someone's chest or hat or shorts. But here, where the word might mean the most, you don't see it at all.

When I got to the hospital, the sun was setting and the shock was real. The complex was large and modern. Signs everywhere featured the name Hazel Hawkins prominently. And the new women's center was a gleaming addition, with its own roundabout and a two-story atrium.

Already there were a few dozen people gathered, all of them well dressed. I was wearing shorts and a torn brown brandless hoodie. I walked in, carrying my copy of *Some Recollections,* with pages of Hazel and T. S. flagged. And then, moving among the attendees in their suits and dresses, I realized with great clarity that I was that peculiar relative: the poorly dressed and unshaven man who shows up carrying a hundred-year-old book with certain pages marked. My new haircut, given to me by a man who thought I was a cop, was the only thing that made me look presentable or sane.

I saw Debbie Taylor. She introduced me to a number of doctors and dignitaries, always as the descendant of Hazel Hawkins. Most of them didn't know the story behind the name and were even more surprised to hear that Hazel Hawkins was a child when she left this world. I told truncated versions of the tale, always pointing to the book, trying not to appear as unhinged as I looked.

Otherwise, the ceremony was practical and funny and joyous. Gloria Torres, the hospital's director of Maternal and Child Health, said that this new facility was what the community needed and deserved—she called the complex's previous birthing center "embarrassing." Gordon Machado, the president of the San Benito Health Care District Board, noted that the construction was done by local labor, and this news received some sturdy applause. The project manager, Liam McCool, was introduced, after Machado joked that though he was Irish, McCool showed up every morning, even the day after St. Patrick's. McCool waved and smiled at the audience, whose diversity reflected the particular blend of people in today's Central Valley: there were the older, whiter representatives, there were the second- and third-generation Latino families whose parents were laborers and whose children might be college graduates, there were nurses and doctors who had immigrated from India and China and beyond.

There are those who think that California is a state where Spanish speakers should have natural sway. And there are those who think that this is a state where English speakers have preeminence, and there are those who insist that if we have any sense of history, of decency, the native peoples of California should be given the first seat at the table. And then there are those who have no idea at all about the history of the state and do not care.

But California has always been a state of visitors, of late arrivals, of seekers innocent and not so innocent. Though it might not be good enough for a Hollister clothing outlet, this is the real Hollister, a place where people work hard and sometimes struggle with their past and their present but look with great practicality toward the future. They build new hospitals that will bring new Californians into the world, new hospitals named after a young white pioneer child few ever knew existed.

GRETEL EHRLICH

Rotten Ice

FROM *Harper's Magazine*

I FIRST WENT TO Greenland in 1993 to get above tree line. I'd
been hit by lightning and was back on my feet after a long two-year
recovery. Feeling claustrophobic, I needed to see horizon lines,
and off I went with no real idea of where I was going. A chance
meeting with a couple from west Greenland drew me north for a
summer and part of the next dark winter. When I returned the
following spring, the ice had failed to come in. I had planned to
travel up the west coast by dogsled on the route that Knud Rasmussen took during his 1916–18 expedition. I didn't know then that
such a trip was no longer possible, that the ice on which Arctic
people and animals had relied for thousands of years would soon
be nearly gone.

In the following years I went much farther up the coast, to the
two oldest northernmost villages in the world: Qaanaaq and Siorapaluk. From there I traveled with an extended family of Inuit
subsistence hunters who represent an ice-evolved culture that
stretches across the Polar North. Here, snowmobiles are banned
for hunting purposes; against all odds, traditional practices are
still carried on: hunting seals and walrus from dogsleds in winter,
spring, and fall; catching narwhals from kayaks in summer; making
and wearing polar-bear pants, fox anoraks, sealskin mittens and
boots. In Qaanaaq's large communal workshop, 21st-century tools
are used to make Ice Age equipment: harpoons, dogsleds, kayaks.
The ways in which these Greenlanders get their food are not much
different than they were a thousand years ago, but in recent years
Arctic scientists have labeled Greenland's seasonal sea ice "a rotten

ice regime." Instead of nine months of good ice, there are only two or three. Where the ice in spring was once routinely 6 to 10 feet thick, in 2004 the thickness was only 7 inches even when the temperature was –30 degrees Fahrenheit. "It is breaking up from beneath," one hunter explained, "because of the wind and stormy waters. We never had that before. It was always clear skies, cold weather, calm seas. We see the ice not wanting to come back. If the ice goes it will be a disaster. Without ice we are nothing."

Icebergs originate from glaciers; ice sheets are distinct from sea ice, but they, too, are affected by the global furnace: 2014 was the hottest year on earth since record keeping began, in 1880. Greenland's ice sheet is now shedding ice five times faster than it did in the 1990s, causing ice to flow down canyons and cliffs at alarming speeds. In 2010 the Petermann Glacier, in Greenland's far north, calved a 100-square-mile "ice island," and in 2012 the glacier lost a chunk twice the size of Manhattan. Straits and bays between northwest Greenland and Ellesmere Island, part of Canada's Nunavut territory, are often clogged with rotting, or unstable, ice. In the summer of 2012 almost the whole surface of Greenland's ice sheet turned to slush.

What happens at the top of the world affects all of us. The Arctic is the earth's natural air conditioner. Ice and snow radiate 80 percent of the sun's heat back into space, keeping the middle latitudes temperate. Dark, open oceans and bare land are heat sinks; open water eats ice. Deep regions of the Pacific Ocean have heated 15 times faster over the past 60 years than during warming periods in the preceding 10,000, and the effect on both glaciers and sea ice is obvious: as warm seawater pushes far north, seasonal sea ice disintegrates, causing the floating tongues of outlet glaciers to wear thin and snap off.

By 2004 the sea ice in north Greenland was too precarious for us to travel any distance north, south, or west from Qaanaaq. Sea ice is a Greenlander's highway and the platform on which marine mammals—including walrus, ring seals, bearded seals, and polar bears—Arctic foxes, and seabirds travel, rest, breed, and hunt. "Those times we went out to Kiatak and Herbert Islands, up Politiken's Glacier, or way north to Etah and Humboldt Glacier," the Inuit hunters said, "we cannot go there anymore." In 2012 the Arctic Ocean's sea ice shrank to a record minimum. Last year the rate of ice loss in July averaged 40,000 square miles per day.

The Greenland ice sheet is 1,500 miles long, 680 miles wide, and covers most of the island. The sheet contains roughly 8 percent of the world's freshwater. GRACE (Gravity Recovery and Climate Experiment), a satellite launched in 2002, is one of the tools used by scientists to understand the accelerated melting of the ice sheet. GRACE monitors monthly changes in the ice sheet's total mass, and has revealed a drastic decrease. Scientists who study the Arctic's sensitivity to weather and climate now question its stability. "Global warming has fundamentally altered the background conditions that give rise to all weather," Kevin Trenberth, a scientist at the National Center for Atmospheric Research, in Boulder, Colorado, says. Alun Hubbard, a Welsh glaciologist, reports: "The melt is going off the scale! The rate of retreat is unprecedented." To move "glacially" no longer implies slowness, and the "severe, widespread, and irreversible impacts" on people and nature that the most recent report of the Intergovernmental Panel on Climate Change (IPCC) warned us about have already come to fruition in Greenland.

It was in Qaanaaq in 1997 that I first experienced climate change from the feet up. I was traveling with Jens Danielsen, headed for Kiatak Island. It was spring, and six inches of snow covered the sea ice. Our 15 dogs trotted slowly; the only sound was their percussive panting. We had already encountered a series of pressure ridges —steep slabs of ice piled up between two floes—that took us five hours to cross. When we reached a smooth plain of ice again, we thought the worst was over, but the sound of something breaking shocked us: dogs began disappearing into the water. Jens hooked his feet over the front edge of the sled, lay on the trace lines, and pulled the dogs out. Afterward, he stepped down onto a piece of rotten ice, lifted the front of the sled, and laid it on a spot that was more stable, then jumped aboard and yelled at the dogs to run fast. When I asked if we were going to die, he smiled and said, "Imaqa." Maybe.

Ice-adapted people have amazing agility, which allows them to jump from one piece of drift ice to another and to handle half-wild dogs. They understand that life is transience, chance, and change. Because ice is so dynamic, melting in summer and reforming in September, Greenlanders in the far north understand that nothing is solid, that boundaries are actually passages, that the world is a permeable place. On the ice they act quickly and precisely, flexing mind as well as muscle, always "modest in front of the weather," as Jens explained. Their material culture represents more than 10,000 years of use: dogsleds, kayaks, skin boats, polar bear and sealskin pants, bone scrapers, harpoons, bearded-seal-skin whips—all designed for beauty, efficiency, and survival in a harsh world where most people would be dead in a day.

From 1997 to 2012 I traveled by dogsled, usually with Jens and his three brothers-in-law: Mamarut Kristiansen, Mikile Kristiansen, and Gedeon Kristiansen. The dogtrot often lulled me to sleep, but rough ice shook me to attention. "You must look carefully," Jens said. From him I began to understand about being *silanigtalersarput:* a person who is wise about things and knows the ice, who comes to teach us how to see. The first word I learned in Greenlandic was *sila,* which means, simultaneously, weather, animal and human consciousness, and the power of nature. The Greenlanders I traveled with do not make the usual distinctions between a human mind and an animal mind. Polar bears are thought to understand human language. In the spring, mirages appear, lifting islands into the air and causing the ice to look like open water. Silver threads at the horizon mark the end of the known world and the beginning of the one inhabited by the imagination. Before television, the Internet, and cell phones arrived in Greenland, the coming of the dark time represented a shift: anxiety about the loss of light gave way to a deep, rich period of storytelling.

In Qaanaaq the sun goes down on October 24 and doesn't rise again until February 17. Once the hood of completely dark days arrives, with only the moon and snow to light the paths between houses, the old legends are told: "The Orphan Who Became a Giant," "The Orphan Who Drifted Out to Sea." Now Jens complains that the advent of television in Qaanaaq has reduced storytelling time, though only three channels are available. But out on the ice the old ways thrive. During the spring of 1998, when I traveled with Jens and his wife, Ilaitsuk, along with their five-year-old grandchild, installments of the legends were told to the child each night for two weeks.

That child, now a young man, did not become a subsistence hunter, despite his early training. He had seen too many springs when there was little ice. But no one suspected the ice would disappear completely.

The cycle of thinning and melting is now impossible to stop. The enormous ice sheet that covers 80 percent of the island is increasingly threaded with meltwater rivers in summer, though when I first arrived in Greenland, in 1993, it shone like a jewel. According to Konrad "Koni" Steffen, a climate scientist who has established many camps on top of the Greenland ice sheet, "in 2012 we lost 450 gigatons of ice—that's five times the amount of ice in the Alps. All the ice on top has pulled apart. It used to be smooth; now it looks like a huge hammer has hit it. The whole surface is fractured."

In 2004, with a generous grant from the National Geographic Expeditions Council, I returned to Qaanaaq for two month-long journeys—in March and in July. The hunters had said to come in early March, one of the two coldest months in Greenland, because they were sure the ice would be strong then. They needed food for their families and their dogs. We would head south to Savissivik, a hard four-day trip. The last part would take us over the edge of the ice sheet and down a precipitous canyon to the frozen sea in an area they called Walrus El Dorado. It was −20 degrees when we started out with 58 dogs, four hunters—including Jens, Gedeon, Mamarut, and a relative of Jens's named Tobias—and my crew of three. We traveled on *hikuliaq*—ice that has just formed. How could it be only seven inches thick at this temperature? I asked Jens. He told me: "There is no old ice, it's all new ice and very salty: hard on the dogs' feet, and, you'll see, it melts fast. Dangerous to be going out on it." But there we were.

After making camp we walked single file to the ice edge. The ice was so thin that it rolled under our feet like rubber. One walrus was harpooned. It was cut up and laid on our sleds. I asked about the pile of intestines left behind. "That's for the foxes, ravens, and polar bears," Mamarut said. "We always leave food for others." Little did we know then that we would get only one walrus all month, and that soon we would be hungry and in need of meat for ourselves and the dogs.

The cold intensified and at the same time more ice broke up. We traveled all day in frigid temperatures that dropped to what Jens said was −40, and found refuge in a tiny hut. We spent the day rubbing ointment onto our frostbitten faces and fingers, and eating boiled walrus for hours at a time to keep warm. A day later we traveled south to Moriusaq, a village of 15, where the walrus hunting had always been good. But the ice there was unstable, too. We were told that farther south, around Savissivik, there was no ice at all. Mamarut's wife, Tekummeq, the great-granddaughter of the explorer Robert Peary, taught school in the village. She fed us and heated enough water for a bath. Finally we turned around and headed north toward Qaanaaq, four days away. Halfway there, a strong blizzard hit and we were forced to hole up in a hut for three days. We kept our visits outside brief, but after even a few minutes any exposed skin burned: fingers, hands, cheeks, noses, foreheads, and asses. The jokes flowed. The men kept busy fixing dog harnesses and sled runners. Evenings, they told hunting stories—not about who got the biggest animal but who made the most ridiculous mistake—to great laughter.

Days were white, nights were white. On the ice, dogs and humans eat the same food. The dogs lined up politely for the chunks of frozen walrus that their owners flung into their mouths. Inside the hut, a haunch of walrus hung from a hook, dripping blood. Our heat was a single Primus burner. Breakfast was walrus-heart soup; lunch was what Aleqa, our translator (who later became the first female prime minister of Greenland), called "swim fin"—a gelatinous walrus flipper. Jens, the natural leader of his family and the whole community, told of the polar bear with the human face, the one who could not be killed, who had asked him to follow, to become a shaman. "I said no. I couldn't desert my family and the community of hunters. This is the modern world, and there is no place in it for shamans."

When the temperature moderated, we spent three weeks trying to find ice that was strong enough to hold us. We were running out of food. The walrus meat was gone. Because Greenlandic freight sleds have no brakes, Jens used his legs and knees to slow us as we skidded down a rocky creekbed. At the bottom, we traveled down a narrow fjord. There was a hut and a drying rack: the last hunter to use the shed had left meat behind. The dogs would eat, but we would not—the meat was too old—and we were still a long way from home. The weather improved but it still averaged 30 degrees below zero. "Let's go out to Kiatak Island," Jens said. "Maybe we can get a walrus there." After crossing the strait, we traveled on an ice foot—a belt of ice that clung to the edge of the island. Where it broke off we had to unhook the dogs, push the sleds over a 14-foot cliff, and jump down onto rotting disks of ice. Sleds tipped and slid as dogs leaped over moats of open water from one spinning pane to the next. We traveled down the island's coast to another small hut, happy to have made it safely. From a steep mountain the men searched the frozen ocean for walrus with binoculars, but the few animals they saw were too far out and the path of ice to get to them was completely broken.

A boy from Siorapaluk showed up the next morning with a fine team, beautifully made clothing, a rifle, and a harpoon. At 15 he had taken a year off from school to see whether he had the prowess to be a great hunter, and he did. But the ice will not be there for him in the future; subsistence hunting will not be possible. "We weren't born to buy and sell things," Jens said sadly, "but to live with our families on the ice and hunt for our food."

Spring weather had come. The temperature had warmed considerably, and the air felt balmy. As we traveled to Siorapaluk, a mirage made Kiatak Island appear to float like an iceberg. Several times, while we stopped the dogs to rest, we stretched out on the sled in our polar-bear pants to bask in the warmth of the sun.

North of Siorapaluk there are no more habitations, but the men of the village go up the coast to hunt polar bears. When Gedeon and his older brother Mamarut ventured north for a few hours to see whether the route was an option for us, all they saw was a great latticed area of pressure ice, polynyas (perennially open water), and no polar bears. They decided against going farther. We had heavy loads, and the dogs had not eaten properly for a week, so after a rest at Siorapaluk we turned for home, traveling close to the coast on shore-fast ice.

On our arrival in Qaanaaq, the wives, children, and friends of the hunters greeted us and helped unload the sleds. The hunters explained that we had no meat. With up to 15 dogs per hunter, plus children, the sick, and the elderly, there were lots of mouths to feed. Northern Greenland is a food-sharing society with no private ownership of land. In these towns families own only the houses they build and live in, along with their dogs and their equipment. No one hunts alone; survival is a group effort. When things go wrong or the food supply dwindles, no one complains. They still have in their memories tales of hunger and famine. Greenland has its own government but gets subsidies from Denmark. In the old days, before the mid-1900s, an entire village could starve quickly, but now Qaanaaq has a grocery store, and with Danish welfare and help from extended families, no one goes without food.

Back in town after a month on the ice, we experienced "village shock." Instead of being disappointed about our failed walrus hunt, we celebrated with a bottle of wine and a wild dance at the local community hall, then talked until dawn. Finally my crew and I made our rounds of thanks and farewells and boarded the once-a-week plane south. It was the end of March, and just beginning to get warm. When I returned to Qaanaaq four months later, in July, the dogsleds had been put away, new kayaks were being built, and the edges of paddles were being sharpened to cut through roiling fjord water. I camped with the hunters' wives and children on steep hillsides and watched for pods of narwhals to swim up the fjord. "Qilaluaq," we'd yell when we saw a pod, enough time for Gedeon to paddle out and wait. As the narwhals swam by, he'd glide into the middle of them to throw a harpoon. By the end of the month enough meat had been procured for everyone. In August a hint of darkness began to creep in, an hour a day. Going back to Qaanaaq in Jens's skiff, I was astonished to see the moon for the first time in four months. Jens was eager to retrieve his dogs from the island where they ran loose all summer and to get out on the ice again, but because of the changing climate, the long months of darkness and twilight no longer marked the beginnings and endings of the traditional hunting season.

The year 2007 saw the warmest winter worldwide on record. I'd called the hunters in Qaanaaq that December to ask when I should come. It had been two years since I'd been there, and Jens was excited about going hunting together as we had when we first met. He said, "Come early in February when it's very cold, and maybe the ice will be strong." The day I arrived in Greenland I was shocked to find that it was warmer at the airport in Kangerlussuaq than in Boston. The ground crew was in shirtsleeves. I thought it was a joke. No such luck. Global air and sea temperatures were on the rise. The AO, the Arctic Oscillation, an index of high- and low-pressure zones, had recently switched out of its positive phase —when frigid air is confined to the Arctic in winter—and into its negative phase—when the Arctic stays warm and the cold air filters down into lower latitudes.

Flying north the next day to Qaanaaq, I looked down in disbelief: from Uummannaq, a village where I had spent my first years
in Greenland, up to Savissivik, where we had tried to go walrus
hunting, there was only open water threaded with long strings of
rotting ice. As global temperatures increase, multiyear ice—ice
that does not melt even in summer, once abundant in the High
Arctic—is now disappearing. Finally, north of Thule Air Base
and Cape York, ice had begun to form. To see white, and not the
black ink of open water, was a relief. But that relief was short-lived.
Greenland had entered what American glaciologist Jason Box calls
"New Climate Land."

Jens, Mamarut, Mikile, and Gedeon came to the guesthouse
when I arrived, but there was none of the usual merriment that
precedes a long trip on the ice. Jens explained that only the shore-
fast ice was strong enough for a dogsled, that hunting had been
impossible all winter. Despondent, he left. I heard rifle shots. What
was that? I asked. "Some of the hunters are shooting their dogs
because they have nothing to feed them," I was told. A 50-pound
bag of dog food from Denmark cost more than the equivalent of
50 U.S. dollars; one bag lasts two days for 10 dogs.

Gedeon and Mikile offered to take me north to Siorapaluk. What
was normally an easy 6-hour trip took 12 hours, with complicated
pushes up and over an edge of the ice sheet. On the way, Gedeon
recounted a narrow escape. He had gone out hunting against the
better judgment of his older brother. His dogsled drifted out onto
an ice floe that was rapidly disintegrating. He called for help. The
message was sent to Thule Air Base, and a helicopter came quickly.
Gedeon and the dogs (unhooked from the sled) were hauled up
into the hovering aircraft. When he looked down, his dogsled and
the ice on which he had been standing had disappeared.

We arrived at Siorapaluk late in the day, and the village was
strangely quiet. It had once been a busy hub, with dogsleds coming and going, and polar-bear skins stretched out to dry in front of
every house. There was a school, a chapel, a small store with a pay
phone (from which you could call other Greenland towns), and
a post office. Mail was picked up and delivered by helicopter; in
earlier times, delivery of a letter sent by dogsled could take a year.
Siorapaluk once was famous for its strong hunters who went north
along the coast for walrus and polar bears. By 2007 everything had
changed. There were almost no dog teams staked out on the ice,

and quotas were being imposed on the harvest of polar bears and narwhals.

At the end of the first week I called a meeting of hunters so that I could ask them how climate change was affecting their lives. Otto Simigaq, one of the best Siorapaluk hunters, was eager to talk: "Seven years ago we could travel on safe ice all winter and hunt animals. We didn't worry about food then. Now it's different. There has been no ice for seven months. We always went to the ice edge in spring west of Kiatak Island, but the ice doesn't go out that far now. The walrus are still there, but we can't get to them." Pauline Simigaq, Otto's wife, said, "We are not so good in our outlook now. The ice is dangerous. I never used to worry, but now if Otto goes out I wonder if I will ever see him again. Around here it is depression and changing moods. We are becoming like the ice."

After the meeting I stood and looked out at the ruined ice. Beyond the village was Kiatak, and to the north was Neqe, where I had watched hunters climb straight up rock cliffs to scoop little auks, or dovekies, out of the air with long-handled nets. Farther north was the historic (now abandoned) site of Etah, the village where, in 1917, a half-starved Knud Rasmussen, returning from his difficult attempt to map the uninhabited parts of northern Greenland, came upon the American Crocker Land Expedition and the welcoming sound of a gramophone playing Wagner and Argentine tangos. Explorers and visitors came and went. Siorapaluk, Pitoravik, and Etah were regular stops for those going to the North Pole or to Ellesmere Island. Some, most notably Robert Peary, fathered children during their expeditions. The Greenlanders—and those children—stayed, traveling only as far as the ice took them. "We had everything here," Jens said. "Our entire culture was intact: our language and our way of living. We kept the old ways and took what we wanted of the new."

It wasn't until 2012 that I returned to Qaanaaq. I hadn't really wanted to go: I was afraid of what I would find. I'd heard that suicides and drinking had increased, that despair had become contagious. But a friend, the artist Mariele Neudecker, had asked me to accompany her to Qaanaaq so that she could photograph the ice. On a small plane carrying us north from Ilulissat she asked a question about glaciers, so I yelled out: "Any glaciologists aboard?" Three passengers, Poul Christoffersen, Steven Palmer, and Julian

Dowdeswell, turned around and nodded. They hailed from Cambridge University's Scott Polar Research Institute and were on their way to examine the Greenland ice sheet north of Qaanaaq. As we looked down, Steve said, "With airborne radar we can identify the bed beneath several kilometers of ice." Poul added: "We're trying to determine the consequences of global warming for the ice." They talked about the linkages between ocean currents, atmosphere, and climate. Poul continued: "The feedbacks are complicated. Cold ice-sheet meltwater percolates down through the crevasses and flows into the fjords, where it mixes with warm ocean water. This mixing has a strong influence on the glaciers' flow."

Later in the year, they would present their new discovery: two subglacial lakes just north of Qaanaaq, half a mile beneath the ice surface. Although common in Antarctica, these deep hidden lakes had eluded glaciologists working in Greenland. Steve reported, "The lakes form an important part of the ice sheet's plumbing system connecting surface lakes to the ones beneath. Because the way water flows beneath ice sheets strongly affects ice-flow speeds, improved understanding of these lakes will allow us to predict more accurately how the ice sheet will respond to anticipated future warming."

Steve and Poul talked about four channels of warm seawater at the base of Petermann Glacier that allowed more ice islands to calve, and the 68-mile-wide calving front of the Humboldt Glacier, where Jens and I, plus seven other hunters, had tried to go one spring but were stopped when the dogs fell ill with distemper and died. Even with healthy dogs we wouldn't be able to go there now. Poul said that the sea ice was broken and dark jets of water were pulsing out from in front of the glacier—a sign that surface and subglacial meltwater was coming from the base of the glacier, exacerbating the melting of the ice fronts and the erosion of the glacier's face.

The flight from Ilulissat to Qaanaaq takes three hours. Below us, a cracked elbow of ice bent and dropped, and long stretches of open water made sparkling slits cuffed by rising mist. Even from the plane we could see how the climate feedback loop works, how patches of open water gather heat and produce a warm cloud that hangs in place so that no ice can form under it. "Is it too late to rewrite our destiny, to reverse our devolution?" I asked the glaciologists. No one answered. We stared at the rotting ice. It was

down there that a modern shaman named Panippaq, who was said
to be capable of heaping up mounds of fish at will, had committed suicide as he watched the sea ice decline. Steve reminded me
that the global concentration of carbon dioxide in the atmosphere
had almost reached 400 parts per million, and that the Arctic had
warmed at least five degrees. Julian Dowdeswell, the head of the
institute at Cambridge, had let the younger glaciologists do the
talking. He said only this: "It's too late to change anything. All we
can do now is deal with the consequences. Global sea level is rising."

But when Mariele and I arrived in Qaanaaq, we were pleasantly
surprised to find that the sea ice was three feet thick. Narwhals,
beluga, and walrus swam in the leads of open water at the ice edge.
Pairs of eider ducks flew overhead, and little auks arrived by the
thousands to nest and fledge in the rock cliffs at Neqe. Spirits rose.
I asked Jens whether they'd ever thought of starting a new community farther north. He said they had tried, but as the ice retreated
hungry polar bears had come onto the land, as they were doing in
Vankarem, Russia, and Kaktovik, Alaska. The bears were very ag-
gressive. "We must live as we always have with what the day brings
to us. And today, there is ice," he said.

Jens had recently been elected mayor of Qaanaaq and had
to leave for a conference in Belgium, but Mamarut, Mikile, and
Gedeon wanted to hunt. When we went down to the ice where
the dogs were staked, I was surprised to see Mikile drunk. Usually mild-mannered and quiet, he lost control of his dogs before
he could get them hitched up, and they ran off. With help from
another hunter, it took several hours to retrieve them. Perched on
Mikile's extra-long sled was a skiff; Mamarut tipped his kayak side-
ways and lashed it to his sled. Gedeon carried his kayak, paddles,
guns, tents, and food on his sled, plus his new girlfriend, Bertha.
The spring snow was wet and the going was slow, but it was wonderful to be on a dogsled again.

I had dozed off when Mamarut whispered, "Hiku hina," in my
ear. The ice edge. Camp was set up. Gedeon sharpened his harpoon, and Bertha melted chunks of ice over a Primus stove for tea.
The men carried their kayaks to the water's edge. Glaucous gulls
flew by. The sound of narwhal breathing grew louder. "Qilaluaq!"
Gedeon whispered. The pod swam by but no one went after them.
It was May, and the sun was circling in a halo above our heads, so

we learned to sleep in bright light. It was time to rest. We laid our sleeping bags under a canvas tent, on beds made from two sleds pushed together. The midnight sun tinted the sea green, pink, gray, and pale blue.

Hours later, I saw Gedeon and Mikile kneeling in snow at the edge of the ice, facing the water. They were careful not to make eye contact with passing narwhals: two more pods had come by, but the men didn't go after them. "They have too many young ones," Gedeon whispered, before continuing his vigil. Another pod approached and Gedeon climbed into his boat, lithe as a cat. He waited, head down, with a hand steadying the kayak on the ice edge. There was a sound of splashing and breathing, and Gedeon exploded into action, paddling hard into the middle of the pod, his kayak thrown around by turbulent water. He grabbed his harpoon from the deck of the kayak and hurled it. Missed. He turned, smiling, and paddled back to camp. There was ice and there was time—at least for now—and he would try again later.

In the night, a group of Qaanaaq hunters arrived and made camp behind us on the ice. It's thought to be bad practice to usurp another family's hunting area. They should have moved on but didn't. No one said anything. The old courtesies were disintegrating along with the ice. The next morning, a dogfight broke out, and an old man viciously beat one of his dogs with a snow shovel. In 20 years of traveling in Greenland, I'd never seen anyone beat a dog.

Hunting was good the next day, and the brothers were happy to have food to bring home for their families. Though the ice was strong, they knew better than to count on anything. We were all deeply upset about the beating we had witnessed, but there was nothing we could do. In Greenland there are unwritten codes of honor that, together with the old taboos, have kept the society humming. A hunter who goes out only for himself and not for the group will be shunned: if he has trouble on the ice no one will stop to help him. Hunters don't abuse their dogs, which they rely on for their lives.

To become a subsistence hunter, the most honorable occupation in this society, is no longer an option for young people. "We may be coming to a time when it is summer all year," Mamarut said as he mended a dog harness. Once the strongest hunter of the family and also the jokester, he was now too banged up to hunt and rarely smiled. He'd broken his ankle going solo across the ice sheet in a desperate attempt to find food—hunting muskoxen instead of walrus—and it took him two weeks to get home to see a doctor. Another week went by before he could fly to Nuuk, the capital of Greenland, for surgery. Now the ankle gives him trouble and his shoulder hurts: one of his rotator cuffs is torn. The previous winter his mother died—she was still making polar-bear pants for her sons, now middle-aged—and a fourth brother committed suicide. "They want us to become fishermen," Mamarut said. "How can we be something we are not?"

On the last day we camped at the ice edge, the hunters got 2 walrus, 4 narwhals, and 10 halibut. As the men paddled back to camp, their dogs broke into spontaneous howls of excitement. Mamarut had opted to stay in camp and begin packing. In matters of hunting, his brash younger brother, Gedeon, had taken his place. Eight years earlier I had watched Gedeon teach his son, Rasmus, how to handle dogs, paddle a kayak, and throw a harpoon. Rasmus was seven at the time. Now he goes to school in south Greenland, below the Arctic Circle, and is learning to be an electrician. Mamarut and his wife, Tekummeq, have adopted Jens and Ilaitsuk's grandchild, but rather than being raised in a community of traditional hunters, the child will grow up on an island nation whose perennially open waters will prove attractive to foreign oil companies.

At camp, Mamarut helped his two brothers haul the dead animals onto the ice. One walrus had waged an urgent fight after being harpooned and had attacked the boat. Unhappy that the animal did not die instantly, Gedeon had pulled out his rifle and fired, ending the struggle that was painful to watch. The meat was butchered in silence and laid under blue tarps on the dogsleds. Breakfast was fresh narwhal-heart soup, rolls with imported Danish honey, and *mattak*—whale skin, which is rich in vitamin C, essential food in an environment that can grow no fruits or vegetables.

We packed up camp, eager to leave the dog beater behind. It was the third week of May and the temperature was rising: the ice was beginning to get soft. We departed early so that the three-foot gap in the ice that we had to cross would still be frozen, but as soon as the sun appeared from behind the clouds, it turned so warm that we shed our anoraks and sealskin mittens. "Tonight that

whole ice edge where we were camped will break off," Mamarut
said quietly. The tracks of *ukaleq* (Arctic hare) zigzagged ahead of
us, and Mamarut signaled to the dogs to stay close to the coast lest
the ice on which we were traveling break away. We camped high
on a hill in a small hut near the calving face of Politiken's Glacier,
which in 1997 had provided an easy route to the ice sheet but was
now a chaos of rubble. Mamarut laid out the topographic map
I had brought to Greenland on my first visit, in 1993, and scru-
tinized the marks we had made over the years showing the ice's
retreat. Once the ice edge in the spring extended far out into the
strait; now it barely reached beyond the shore-fast ice of Qaanaaq.
Despite seasonal fluxes, the ice kept thinning. Looking at the map,
Mamarut shook his head in dismay. "Ice no good!" he blurted out
in English, as if it were the best language for expressing anger. On
our way home to Qaanaaq the next day, he got tangled in the trace
lines while hooking up the dogs and was dragged for a long way
before I could stop them. These were the final days of subsistence
hunting on the ice, and I wondered if I would travel with these
men ever again.

The news from the Ice Desk is this: the prognosis for the future of
Arctic ice, and thus for human life on the planet, is grim. In the
summer of 2013 I returned to Greenland, not to Qaanaaq but to
the town of Ilulissat in what's known as west Greenland, the site
of the Jakobshavn Glacier, the fastest-calving glacier in the world.
I was traveling with my husband, Neal, who was on assignment to
produce a radio segment on the accelerated melting of the Greenland ice sheet. In Copenhagen, on our way to Ilulissat, we met with
Jason Box, who had moved to Denmark from the prestigious Byrd
Polar and Climate Research Center to work in Greenland. It was
a sunny Friday afternoon, and we agreed to meet at a canal where
young Danes, just getting off work, piled onto their small boats,
to relax with a bottle of wine or a few beers. Jason strolled toward
us wearing shorts and clogs, carrying a bottle of hard apple cider
and three glasses. His casual demeanor belies a gravity and intelligence that becomes evident when he talks. A self-proclaimed climate refugee, and the father of a young child, he said he couldn't
live with himself if he didn't do everything possible to transmit his
understanding of abrupt climate change in the Arctic and its dire
consequences.

Jason has spent 24 summers atop Greenland's great dome of ice. "The ice sheet is melting at an accelerated pace," he told us. "It's not just surface melt but the deformation of the inner ice. The fabric of the ice sheet is coming apart because of increasing meltwater infiltration. Two to three hundred billion tons of ice are being lost each year. The last time atmospheric CO_2 was this high, the sea level was seventy feet higher."

We flew to Ilulissat the next day. Below the plane, milky-green water squeezed from between the toes of glaciers that had oozed down from the ice sheet. Just before landing, we glided over a crumpled ribbon of ice that was studded with icebergs the size of warehouses: the fjord leading seaward from the calving front of the Jakobshavn Glacier. Ice there is moving away from the central ice sheet so fast—up to 150 feet a day—and calves so often that the adjacent fjord has been designated a World Heritage Site, an ironic celebration of its continuing demise. Ilulissat was booming with tourists who had flocked to town to observe the parade of icebergs drift by as they sipped cocktails and feasted on barbecued muskoxen at the four-star Hotel Arctic; it was also brimming with petroleum engineers who had come in a gold-rush-like flurry to find oil. But the weather had changed: many of the well sites were nonproducers, and just below the fancy hotel were the remains of several tumbled houses and a ravine that had been dredged by a flash flood, a rare weather event in a polar desert.

Neal and I hiked up the moraine above town to look down on the ice-choked fjord. We sat on a promontory to watch and listen to the ice pushing into Disko Bay. Nothing seemed to be moving, but at the front of stranded icebergs fast-flowing streams of meltwater spewed out, crisscrossing one another in the channel. Recently several subglacial lakes were discovered to have "blown out," draining as much as 57,000 gallons per minute and then refilling with surface meltwater, softening the ice around it, so that the entire ice sheet is in a process of decay. From atop another granite cliff we saw an enormous berg, its base smooth but its top all jagged with pointed slabs. Suddenly, two thumping roars, another sharp thud, and an entire white wall slid straight down into the water. Neal turned to me, wide-eyed, and said: "This is the sound of the ice sheet melting."

Later, we gathered at the Hotel Icefiord with Koni Steffen and a group of Dartmouth glaciology students. Under a warm sun

we sat on a large deck and discussed the changes that have occurred in the Arctic in the past five years. Vast methane plumes
were discovered boiling up from the Laptev Sea, north of Russia,
and methane is punching through thawing seabeds and terrestrial
permafrost all across the Arctic. Currents and air temperatures are
changing; the jet stream is becoming wavier, allowing weather conditions to persist for long periods of time; and the movements of
high- and low-pressure systems have become unpredictable. The
new chemical interplay between ocean and atmosphere is now so
complex that even Steffen, the elder statesman of glaciology, says
that no one fully understands it. We talked about future scenarios
of what we began to call, simply, bad weather. Parts of the world
will get much hotter, with no rain or snow at all. In western North
America, trees will keep dying from insect and fungal invasions,
uncovering more land that in turn will soak up more heat. It's
predicted that worldwide demand for water will exceed the supply
by 40 percent. Cary Fowler, who helped found the Svalbard Global
Seed Vault, predicts that there will be such dire changes in season-
ality that food growing will no longer align with rainfall, and that
we are not prepared for worsening droughts. Steffen says, "Water
vapor is now the most plentiful and prolific greenhouse gas. It is
altering the jet stream. That's the truth, and it shocks all the environmentalists!"

In a conversation with the biologist E. O. Wilson on a morning in Aspen so beautiful that it was difficult to imagine that anything on the planet could go wrong, he advised me to stop being
gloomy. "It's our chance to practice altruism," he said. I looked
at him skeptically. He continued: "We have to wear suits of armor
like World War II soldiers and just keep going. We have to get used
to the changes in the landscape, to step over the dead bodies, so
to speak, and discipline our behavior instead of getting stuck in
tribal and religious restrictions. We have to work altruistically and
cooperatively, and make a new world."

Is it possible we haven't fully comprehended that we are in
danger? We may die off as a species from mere carelessness. That
night in Ilulissat, on the patio of the Hotel Icefiord, I asked one
of the graduate students about her future. She said: "I won't have
children; I will move north." We were still sitting outside when the
night air turned so cold that we had to bundle up in parkas and
mittens to continue talking. "A small change can have a great ef-

fect," Steffen said. He was referring to how carelessly we underestimate the profound sensitivity of the planet's membrane, its skin of ice. The Arctic has been warming more than twice as fast as anywhere else in the world, and that evening, the reality of what was happening to his beloved Greenland seemed to make Steffen go quiet. On July 30, 2013, the highest temperature ever recorded in Greenland—almost 80 degrees Fahrenheit—occurred in Maniitsoq, on the west coast, and an astonishing heat wave in the Russian Arctic registered 90 degrees. And that was 2013, when there was said to be a "pause" in global heating.

Recently, methane plumes were discovered at 570 places along the East Coast of the United States, from Cape Hatteras, North Carolina, to Massachusetts. Siberian tundra holes were spotted by nomadic reindeer herders on the Yamal Peninsula, and ash from wildfires in the American and Canadian West fluttered down, turning the southern end of the Greenland ice sheet almost black.

The summer after Neal and I met with Koni Steffen in Ilulissat, Jason Box moved his camp farther north, where he continued his attempts to unveil the subtle interactions between atmosphere and earth, water, and ice, and the ways algae and industrial and wildfire soot affect the reflectivity of the Greenland ice sheet: the darker the ice, the more heat it absorbs. As part of his recent Dark Snow Project, he used small drones to fly over the darkening snow and ice. By the end of August 2014, Jason's reports had grown increasingly urgent. "We are on a trajectory to awaken a runaway climate heating that will ravage global agricultural systems, leading to mass famine and conflict," he wrote. "Sea-level rise will be a small problem by comparison. We simply must lower atmospheric carbon emissions." A later message was frantic: "If even a small fraction of Arctic seafloor methane is released to the atmosphere, we're fucked." From an IPCC meeting in Copenhagen last year, he wrote: "We have very limited time to avert climate impacts that will ravage us irreversibly."

The Arctic is shouldering the wounds of the world, wounds that aren't healing. Long ago we exceeded the carrying capacity of the planet, with its seven billion humans all longing for some semblance of First World comforts. The burgeoning population is incompatible with the natural economy of biological and ecological systems. We have found that our climate models have been too conservative, that the published results of science-by-committee are unable to keep up with the startling responsiveness of Earth to our every footstep. We have to stop pretending that there is a way back to the lush, comfortable, interglacial paradise we left behind so hurriedly in the 20th century. There are no rules for living on this planet, only consequences. What is needed is an open exchange in which sentience shapes the eye and mind and results in ever-deepening empathy. Beauty and blood and what Ralph Waldo Emerson called "strange sympathies" with otherness would circulate freely in us, and the songs of the bearded seal's ululating mating call, the crack and groan of ancient ice, the Arctic tern's cry, and the robin's evensong would inhabit our vocal cords.

Off Diamond Head

FROM *The New Yorker*

THE BUDGET FOR moving our family to Honolulu was tight, judging from the tiny cottage we rented and the rusted-out Ford Fairlane we bought to get around. My brother Kevin and I took turns sleeping on the couch. I was 13; he was 9. But the cottage was near the beach—just up a driveway lined with other cottages, on a street called Kulamanu—and the weather, which was warm even in January, when we arrived, felt like wanton luxury.

I ran to the beach for a first, frantic survey of the local waters. The setup was confusing. Waves broke here and there along the outer edge of a mossy, exposed reef. All that coral worried me. It was infamously sharp. Then I spotted, well off to the west, and rather far out at sea, a familiar minuet of stick figures, rising and falling, backlit by the afternoon sun. Surfers! I ran back up the lane. Everyone at the house was busy unpacking and fighting over beds. I threw on a pair of trunks, grabbed my surfboard, and left without a word.

I had been surfing for nearly three years when my father got the job that took us to Hawaii. He had been working, mostly as an assistant director, in series television—*Dr. Kildare, The Man from U.N.C.L.E.* Now he was the production manager on a new series, a half-hour musical variety show based on a local radio program, *Hawaii Calls*. The idea was to shoot Don Ho singing in a glass-bottomed boat or a calypso band by a waterfall or hula girls dancing while a volcano spewed and call it a show. "It won't be the Hawaiian Amateur Hour," my father said. "But close."

"If it's really bad, we'll pretend we don't know you," my mother said.

I was beside myself with excitement just to be in Hawaii. All surfers, all readers of surf magazines—and I had memorized nearly every line, every photo caption, in every surf magazine I owned—spent the bulk of their fantasy lives, like it or not, in Hawaii. Now I was there, walking on actual Hawaiian sand (coarse, strange-smelling), tasting Hawaiian seawater (warm, strange-smelling), and paddling toward Hawaiian waves (small, dark-faced, windblown).

Nothing was what I'd expected. In the mags, Hawaiian waves were always big and, in the color shots, ranged from a deep, mid-ocean blue to a pale, impossible turquoise. The wind was always offshore (blowing from land to sea, ideal for surfing), and the breaks themselves were the Olympian playgrounds of the gods: Sunset Beach, the Banzai Pipeline, Makaha, Ala Moana, Waimea Bay.

All that seemed worlds away from the sea in front of our new house. Even Waikiki, known for its beginner breaks and tourist crowds, was over on the far side of Diamond Head—the glamorous western side—along with every other part of Honolulu anybody had heard of. We were on the mountain's southeast side, down in a little saddle of sloping, shady beachfront west of Black Point. The beach was just a patch of damp sand, narrow and empty.

I paddled west along a shallow lagoon, staying close to the shore, for half a mile. The beach houses ended, and the steep, brushy base of Diamond Head itself took their place across the sand. Then the reef on my left fell away, revealing a wide channel—deeper water, where no waves broke—and, beyond the channel, 10 or 12 surfers riding a scatter of dark, chest-high peaks in a moderate onshore wind. I paddled slowly toward the lineup—the wave-catching zone—taking a roundabout route, studying every ride.

The surfers were good. They had smooth, ungimmicky styles. Nobody fell off. And nobody, blessedly, seemed to notice me. I circled around, then edged into an unpopulated stretch of the lineup. There were plenty of waves. The takeoffs were crumbling but easy. Letting muscle memory take over, I caught and rode a couple of small, mushy rights. The waves were different—but not too different—from the ones I'd known in California. They were shifty but not intimidating. I could see coral on the bottom but nothing too shallow.

There was a lot of talk and laughter among the other surfers. Eavesdropping, I couldn't understand a word. They were probably speaking pidgin. I had read about pidgin in James Michener's *Hawaii*, but I hadn't actually heard any yet. Or maybe it was some foreign language. I was the only haole (white person—another word from Michener) in the water. At one point, an older guy paddling past me gestured seaward and said, "Outside." It was the only word spoken to me that day. And he was right: an outside set was approaching, the biggest of the afternoon, and I was grateful to have been warned.

As the sun dropped, the crowd thinned. I tried to see where people went. Most seemed to take a steep path up the mountainside to Diamond Head Road, their pale boards, carried on their heads, moving steadily, skeg first, through the switchbacks. I caught a final wave, rode it into the shallows, and began the long paddle home through the lagoon. Lights were on in the houses now. The air was cooler, the shadows blue-black under the coconut palms. I was aglow with my good fortune. I just wished I had someone to tell: "I'm in Hawaii! Surfing in Hawaii!" Then it occurred to me that I didn't even know the name of the place I'd surfed.

It was called Cliffs. It was a patchwork arc of reefs that ran south and west for half a mile from the channel where I first paddled out. To learn any new spot in surfing, you first bring to bear your knowledge of other breaks—all the other waves you've learned to read closely. But at that stage my archives consisted of 10 or 15 California spots, and only one that I really knew well: a cobblestone point in Ventura. And none of this experience especially prepared me for Cliffs, which, after that initial session, I tried to surf twice a day.

It was an unusually consistent spot, in the sense that there were nearly always waves to ride, even in what I came to understand was the off-season for Oahu's South Shore. The reefs off Diamond Head are at the southern extremity of the island, and thus pick up every scrap of passing swell. But they also catch a lot of wind, including local williwaws off the slopes of the crater, and the wind, along with the vast jigsaw expanse of the reef and the swells arriving from many different points of the compass, combined to produce constantly changing conditions that, in a paradox I didn't appreciate at the time, amounted to a rowdy, hourly refutation of the notion of consistency. Cliffs possessed a moody complexity beyond anything I had known.

Mornings were especially confounding. To squeeze in a surf before school, I had to be out there by daybreak. In my narrow experience, the sea was supposed to be glassy at dawn. In coastal California, early mornings are usually windless. Not so, apparently, in the tropics. Certainly not at Cliffs. At sunrise, the trade winds often blew hard. Palm fronds thrashed overhead as I tripped down the lane, board on my head, and from the seafront I could see whitecaps outside, beyond the reef, spilling east to west on a royal-blue ocean. The trades were said to be northeasterlies, which in theory was not a bad direction, for a south-facing coast, but somehow they were always sideshore at Cliffs, and strong enough to ruin most spots from that angle.

And yet the place had a growling durability that left it ridable even in those battered conditions. Almost no one else surfed it in the early morning, which made it a good time to explore the main takeoff area. I began to learn the tricky, fast, shallow sections, and the soft spots where a quick cutback was needed to keep a ride going. Even on a waist-high, blown-out day, it was possible to milk certain waves for long, improvised, thoroughly satisfying rides. The reef had a thousand quirks, which changed quickly with the tide. And when the inshore channel began to turn a milky turquoise—a color not unlike some of the Hawaiian fantasy waves in the mags—it meant, I came to know, that the sun had risen to the point where I should head in for breakfast. If the tide was extra low, leaving the lagoon too shallow to paddle, I learned to allow more time for trudging home on the soft, coarse sand, struggling to keep my board's nose pointed into the wind.

Afternoons were a different story. The wind was lighter, the sea less seasick, and there were other people surfing. Cliffs had a crew of regulars. After a few sessions, I could recognize some of them. At the mainland spots I knew, there was usually a limited supply of waves, a lot of jockeying for position, and a strictly observed pecking order. A youngster, certainly one lacking allies, such as an older brother, needed to be careful not to cross, even inadvertently, any local big dogs. But at Cliffs there was so much room to spread out, so many empty peaks breaking off to the west of the main takeoff—or, if you kept an eye out, perhaps on an inside shelf that had quietly started to work—that I felt free to pursue my explorations of the margins. Nobody bothered me. Nobody vibed me. It was the opposite of my life at school.

I had never thought of myself as a sheltered child. Still, Kaimuki Intermediate School was a shock. I was in the eighth grade, and most of my new schoolmates were "drug addicts, glue sniffers, and hoods"—or so I wrote to a friend back in Los Angeles. That wasn't true. What was true was that haoles were a tiny and unpopular minority at Kaimuki. The "natives," as I called them, seemed to dislike us particularly. This was unnerving, because many of the Hawaiians were, for junior high kids, quite large, and the word was that they liked to fight. Asians were the school's most sizable ethnic group, though in those first weeks I didn't know enough to distinguish among Japanese and Chinese and Korean kids, let alone the stereotypes through which each group viewed the others. Nor did I note the existence of other important tribes, such as the Filipinos, the Samoans, or the Portuguese (not considered haole), nor all the kids of mixed ethnic background. I probably even thought the big guy in wood shop who immediately took a sadistic interest in me was Hawaiian.

He wore shiny black shoes with long, sharp toes, tight pants, and bright flowered shirts. His kinky hair was cut in a pompadour, and he looked as if he had been shaving since birth. He rarely spoke, and then only in a pidgin that was unintelligible to me. He was some kind of junior mobster, clearly years behind his original class, just biding his time until he could drop out. His name was Freitas—I never heard a first name—but he didn't seem to be related to the Freitas clan, a vast family with several rambunctious boys at Kaimuki Intermediate. The stiletto-toed Freitas studied me frankly for a few days, making me increasingly nervous, and then began to conduct little assaults on my self-possession, softly bumping my elbow, for example, while I concentrated over a saw cut on my half-built shoeshine box.

I was too scared to say anything, and he never said a word to me. That seemed to be part of the fun. Then he settled on a crude but ingenious amusement for passing those periods when we had to sit in chairs in the classroom section of the shop. He would sit behind me and, whenever the teacher had his back turned, hit me on the head with a two-by-four. *Bonk . . . bonk . . . bonk*, a nice steady rhythm, always with enough of a pause between blows to allow me brief hope that there might not be another. I couldn't understand why the teacher didn't hear all these unauthorized, resonating *clonks*. They were loud enough to attract the attention of our classmates, who seemed to find Freitas's little ritual fascinating. Inside my head the blows were, of course, bone-rattling explosions. Freitas used a fairly long board—five or six feet—and he never hit too hard, which permitted him to pound away without leaving marks, and to do it from a certain rarefied, even meditative distance, which added, I imagine, to the fascination of the performance.

I wonder if, had some other kid been targeted, I would have been as passive as my classmates were. Probably. The teacher was off in his own world, worried only about his table saws. I did nothing in my own defense. While I eventually understood that Freitas wasn't Hawaiian, I must have figured that I just had to take the abuse. I was, after all, skinny and haole and had no friends.

Discreetly, I studied the surfing of some of the regulars at Cliffs— the ones who seemed to read the wave best, who found the speed pockets and wheeled their boards so neatly through their turns. My first impression was confirmed: I had never seen such smoothness. Hand movements were strikingly in sync with feet. Knees were more deeply bent than in the surfing I was used to, hips looser. There wasn't much nose-riding, which was the subspecialty rage at the time on the mainland and required scurrying, when the opportunity arose, to the front of one's board—hanging five, hanging ten, defying the obvious physics of flotation and glide. I didn't know it then, but what I was looking at was classic Island style. I just took my mental notes from the channel, and began, without thinking about it, to walk the nose less.

There were a few young guys, including one wiry, straight-backed kid who looked to be about my age. He stayed away from the main peak, riding peripheral waves. But I craned to see what he did. Even on the funky little waves he chose, I could see that he was uncommonly quick and poised. In fact, he was the best surfer my age I had ever seen. He rode an unusually short, light, sharp-nosed board—a bone-white clear-finish Wardy. He caught me watching him, and he seemed as embarrassed as I was. He paddled furiously past me, looking affronted. I tried to stay out of his way after that. But the next day he cocked his chin in greeting. I hoped my happiness didn't show. Then, a few days later, he spoke.

"Mo' bettah that side," he said, throwing his eyes to the west as we pushed through a small set. It was an invitation to join him at one of his obscure, uncrowded peaks. I didn't need to be asked twice. His name was Roddy Kaulukukui. He was 13, same as me. Roddy and I traded waves warily, and then less warily. I could catch waves as well as he could, which was important, and I was learning the spot, which became something of a shared enterprise. As the two youngest guys at Cliffs, we were both, at least half-consciously, in the market for an age mate. But Roddy didn't come out there alone. He had two brothers and a sort of honorary third brother —a Japanese guy named Ford Takara. Roddy's older brother, Glenn, was a lineup mainstay. Glenn and Ford were out every day. They were only a year older than we were, but both of them could compete with anybody in the main peak. Glenn, in particular, was a superb surfer, with a style that was already flowing and beautiful. Their father, Glenn Sr., also surfed, as did their little brother, John, though he was too young for Cliffs.

Roddy began to fill me in on some of the other guys. The fat one who appeared on bigger days, taking off far outside and ripping so hard that the rest of us stopped surfing to watch, was Ben Aipa. (Years later, Aipa photos and stories began to fill the mags.) The Chinese guy who showed up on the biggest day I had seen yet at Cliffs—a solid, out-of-season south swell on a windless, overcast afternoon—was Leslie Wong. He had a silky style, and deigned to surf Cliffs only when conditions were exceptionally good. Leslie Wong caught and pulled into the wave of the day, his back slightly arched, his arms relaxed, making the extremely difficult—no, come on, the ecstatic—look easy. If I ever grew up, I wanted to be Leslie Wong. Among the Cliffs regulars, I got to know who was likely to waste a wave—fail to catch it, or fall off—and then how to snag the wave myself without showing disrespect. Even in a mild-mannered crowd, it was important not to show anyone up. Male egos (I never saw a girl out at Cliffs) were always, subtly or otherwise, on the line in the water.

Here's how ridable waves form. A storm out at sea churns the surface, creating chop—smaller and then larger wavelets, which amalgamate, with enough wind, into heavy seas. What we are waiting for on distant coasts is the energy that escapes from the storm, radiating outward into calmer waters in the form of wave trains—groups of waves, increasingly organized, that travel together. Each wave sets off a column of orbiting water, most of it below the surface. The wave trains produced by a storm constitute what surfers call a swell. A swell can travel thousands of miles. The more powerful the storm, the farther the swell may travel. As it travels, the swell becomes more organized—the distance between each wave in a train, known as the interval, becomes uniform. In a long-interval train, the orbiting water may extend more than a thousand feet beneath the ocean surface. Such a train can pass easily through surface resistance like chop or other smaller, shallower swells that it crosses or overtakes.

As waves from a swell approach the shoreline, they begin to feel the sea bottom. Wave trains become sets—groups of waves that are larger and longer-interval than their locally generated cousins. The approaching waves refract (bend) in response to the shape of the sea bottom. The visible part of the wave grows. The resistance offered by the sea bottom increases as the water gets shallower, slowing the progress of the wave. Finally, it becomes unstable and prepares to topple forward—to break. The rule of thumb is that it will break when its height reaches 80 percent of the water's depth—an 8-foot wave will break in 10 feet of water. But many factors, some of them endlessly subtle—wind, bottom contour, swell angle, currents—determine exactly where and how each wave breaks. As surfers, we're just hoping that it has a catchable moment (a take-off point), and a ridable face, and that it doesn't break all at once (close out) but, instead, breaks gradually, successively (peels), in one direction or the other (left or right), allowing us to travel roughly parallel to the shore, riding the face, for a while, in that spot, in that moment, just before it breaks.

My parents had sent me to Kaimuki Intermediate, I later decided, under a misconception. This was 1966, before the Proposition 13 tax revolt, and the California public school system, particularly in the middle-class suburbs where we had lived, was among the nation's best. The families we knew never considered private schools for their kids. Hawaii's public schools were another matter—impoverished, mired in colonial, plantation, and mission traditions, miles below the American average academically.

Ignorant of all this, my parents sent two of my younger siblings (I have three) to the nearest elementary school, which happened to be in a middle-class area, and me to the nearest junior high, up in working-class Kaimuki, on the inland side of Diamond Head crater, where they assumed I was getting on with the business of the eighth grade but where I was occupied almost entirely by the rigors of bullies, loneliness, fights, and finding my way, after a lifetime of unconscious privileged whiteness in the segregated suburbs of California, in a racialized world. Even my classes felt racially constructed. For academic subjects, at least, students were assigned, on the basis of test scores, to a group that moved together from teacher to teacher. I was put in a high-end group, where nearly all my classmates were Japanese girls. The classes, which were prim and undemanding, bored me in a way that school never had before. To my classmates, I seemed not to exist socially. And so I passed the class hours slouched in back rows, keeping an eye on the trees outside for signs of wind direction and strength, drawing page after page of surfboards and waves.

My orientation program at school included a series of fistfights, some of them formally scheduled. There was a cemetery next to the school grounds, with a well-hidden patch of grass down in one corner where kids went to settle their differences. I found myself facing off there with a number of boys named Freitas—none of them, again, apparently related to my hairy tormentor from wood shop. My first opponent was so small and young that I doubted that he even attended our school. The Freitas clan's method for training its members in battle, it seemed, was to find some fool without allies or the brains to avoid a challenge, then send their youngest fighter with any chance at all into the ring. If he lost, the next biggest Freitas would be sent in. This went on until the nonkinsman was defeated. It was all quite dispassionate, the bouts arranged and refereed by older Freitases, and more or less fairly conducted.

My first match was sparsely attended—really of no interest to anyone—but I was still scared sick, having no seconds in my corner and no idea what the rules were. My opponent turned out to be shockingly strong for his size, and ferocious, but his arms were too short to land punches, and I eventually subdued him without much damage to either of us. His cousin, who stepped up immediately, was more my size, and our sparring was more consequential. I held my own, but we both had shiners before a senior Freitas stepped in, declaring a draw. There would be a rematch, he said, and, if I won that, somebody named Tino would come and kick my ass, no questions asked. Team Freitas departed. I remember watching them jog, laughing and loose, a happy family militia, up the long slope of the graveyard. They were evidently late for another appointment. My face hurt, my knuckles hurt, but I was giddy with relief. Then I noticed a couple of haole guys my age standing in the bushes at the edge of the clearing, looking squirrelly. I half recognized them from school, but they left without saying a word.

I won the rematch, I think. Then Tino kicked my ass, no questions asked.

There were more fights, including a multiday brawl with a Chinese kid in my agriculture class who refused to give up even when I had his face shoved deep in the red mud of a lettuce patch. This bitter tussle went on for a week. It resumed each afternoon, and never produced a winner. The other boys in the class, enjoying the show, made sure that the teacher, if he ever came round, didn't catch us at it.

I don't know what my parents thought. Cuts and bruises, even a black eye, could be explained. Football, surfing, something. My hunch, which seems right in retrospect, was that they couldn't help, so I told them nothing.

A racist gang came to my rescue. They called themselves the In Crowd. They were haoles and, their laughable gang name notwithstanding, they were impressively bad. Their leader was a jolly, dissolute, hoarse-voiced, broken-toothed kid named Mike. He was not physically imposing, but he shambled around school with a rowdy fearlessness that seemed to give everyone but the largest Samoans pause. Mike's true home, one came to understand, was a juvenile detention center somewhere—this school-going was just a furlough, which he intended to make the most of. He had a younger sister, Edie, who was blond and skinny and wild, and their house in Kaimuki was the In Crowd's clubhouse. At school, they gathered under a tall monkeypod tree on a red-dirt hill behind the unpainted bungalow where I took typing. My induction was informal. Mike and his buddies simply let me know that I was welcome to join them under the monkeypod. And it was from the In Crowd kids, who actually seemed to include more girls than boys, that I began to learn first the broad outlines and then the minutiae of the local racial setup. Our main enemies were the "mokes"— which seemed to mean anyone dark and tough. "You been beefin' with mokes already," Mike said to me.

That was true, I realized.

But my fighting career soon tailed off. People seemed to know that I was now part of the haole gang, and elected to pick on other kids. Even Freitas in wood shop started easing up on me. But had he really put away his two-by-four? It was hard to imagine that he would be worried by the In Crowd.

Day in, day out, Glenn Kaulukukui, Roddy's brother, was my favorite surfer. From the moment he caught a wave, gliding catlike to his feet, I couldn't take my eyes off the lines he drew, the speed he somehow found, the improvisations he came up with. He had a huge head, which appeared always to be slightly thrown back, and long hair, sun-bleached red, also thrown lushly back. He had thick lips, and black shoulders, and he moved with unusual elegance. But there was something else—call it wit, or irony—that accompanied his physical confidence and beauty, something bittersweet that allowed him, in all but the most demanding situations, to seem as if he were both performing intently and, at the same time, laughing quietly at himself.

He also laughed at me, though not unkindly. When I overpowered a kick-out, trying to put a flourish on the end of a ride, slicing awkwardly over the shoulder and into parallel with his board in the channel, Glenn said, "Geev 'um, Bill. Geev 'um da lights." Even I knew that this was a pidgin cliché—an overused exhortation. It was also a dense little piece of satire. He was mocking me and encouraging me both. We paddled out together. When we were nearly outside, we watched Ford catch a set wave from a deep position and pick a clever line to thread through a pair of difficult sections. "Yeah, Fawd," Glenn murmured appreciatively. "Spahk dat." ("Look at that.") Then he began to outsprint me toward the lineup.

One afternoon, Roddy asked where I lived. I pointed east, toward the shady cove inside Black Point. He told Glenn and Ford, then came back, looking abashed, with a request. Could they leave their boards at my house? I was happy for the company on the long paddle home. Our cottage had a tiny yard, with a stand of bamboo, thick and tall, hiding it from the street. We stashed our boards in the bamboo and washed off in the dark with a garden hose. Then the three of them left, wearing nothing but trunks, dripping wet, but clearly stoked to be unburdened of their boards, for distant Kaimuki.

The In Crowd's racism was situationist, not doctrinaire. It had no historical pretensions—unlike, say, the skinheads who came along later, claiming descent from Nazism and the Klan. Hawaii had seen plenty of white supremacism, particularly among its elites, but the In Crowd knew nothing of elites. Most of the kids were hardscrabble, living in straitened circumstances, though some had been kicked out of private schools and were simply in disgrace. Among Kaimuki Intermediate's smattering of haole students, most were actually shunned by the In Crowd as insufficiently cool. These unaffiliated haoles seemed to be mainly military kids. They all looked disoriented, scared. The structural privilege that came with being white was all but invisible to me at school.

I thought the In Crowd's main activity would be gang fighting, and there was certainly continual talk of impending warfare with various rival "moke" groups. But then Mike always seemed to be leading a peace delegation to some powwow, and bloodshed would be avoided through painstaking, face-saving diplomacy. Truces would be formalized by solemn underage drinking. Most of the group's energy actually went into gossip, parties, petty theft and vandalism, and being obnoxious on the city bus after school. There were a number of pretty girls in the In Crowd, and I was serially smitten with each of them. Nobody in the gang surfed.

Roddy and Glenn Kaulukukui and Ford Takara all went to Kaimuki Intermediate, it turned out. But I didn't hang with them there. That was a feat, since the four of us spent nearly every afternoon and weekend together in the water, and Roddy was soon established as my new best friend. The Kaulukukuis lived at Fort Ruger, on the north slope of Diamond Head crater, near the cemetery that abutted our school. Glenn Sr. was in the army, and their apartment was in an old military barracks tucked into a kiawe grove below Diamond Head Road. Roddy and Glenn had lived on the island of Hawaii, which everybody called the Big Island. They had family there. Now they had a very young stepmother, and she and Roddy didn't get along.

Confined to quarters after a fight with his stepmother, he poured out his misery in bitter whispers in the stifling room he shared with Glenn and John.

I thought I knew something about misery: I was missing waves that afternoon in a show of solidarity. There wasn't even a surf mag to leaf through while grimacing sympathetically. "Why he have to marry *her*?" Roddy keened.

Glenn Sr. occasionally came surfing with us. He was a formidable character, heavily muscled, severe. He ordered his sons around, not bothering with niceties. He seemed to loosen up in the water, though. Sometimes he even laughed. He rode a huge board in a simple, old-fashioned style, drawing long lines, perfectly balanced, across the long walls at Cliffs. In his day, his sons told me proudly, he had surfed Waimea Bay.

Waimea was on the North Shore of Oahu. It was considered the heaviest big-wave spot in the world. I knew it only as a mythical place—a stage set, really, for the heroics of a few surf celebrities, hyped endlessly in the mags. Roddy and Glenn didn't talk much about it, but to them Waimea was obviously a real place, and extremely serious business. You surfed it when you were ready. Most surfers, of course, would never be ready. But, for Hawaiian kids like them, Waimea, and the other great North Shore breaks, lay ahead, each a question, a type of final exam.

I had assumed that only famous surfers rode Waimea. Now I saw that local fathers rode it, too, and in time, perhaps, their sons would as well. These people never appeared in mainland magazines. And there were many families like the Kaulukukuis in Hawaii—multigenerational surfing families, *ohanas* rich in talent and tradition, known only to one another.

Glenn Sr. reminded me, from the first time I saw him, of Liloa, the old monarch in a book I loved, *Umi: The Hawaiian Boy Who Became a King*. It was a children's book, first given to my father, according to a faded flyleaf inscription, by two aunts who had bought it in Honolulu in 1939. The author, Robert Lee Eskridge, had also done the illustrations, which I thought magnificent. They were simple but fierce, like lushly colored woodcuts. They showed Umi and his younger brothers and their adventures in old Hawaii: sailing down mountainsides on morning-glory vines ("From vine to vine the boys slid with lightning speed"), diving into pools formed by lava tubes, crossing the sea in war canoes ("Slaves shall accompany Umi to his father's palace in Waipio"). Some of the illustrations showed grown men, guards and warriors and courtiers, whose faces scared me—their stylized cruelty, in a pitiless world of all-powerful chiefs and quaking commoners. At least the features of Liloa, the king (and Umi's secret father), were softened at times by wisdom and paternal pride.

Roddy believed in Pele. She was the Hawaiian goddess of fire. She lived, people said, on the Big Island, where she caused the volcanoes to erupt when she was displeased. She was famously jealous and violent, and Hawaiians tried to propitiate her with offerings of pork, fish, liquor. She was so famous that even tourists knew about her, but Roddy made it clear, when he professed his belief to me, that he wasn't talking about the kitsch character. He meant a whole religious world, something from the time before the haoles came—a Hawaiian world with elaborate rules and taboos and secret, hard-won understandings about the land, the ocean, birds, fish, animals, and the gods. I took him seriously. I already knew, in rough outline, what had happened to the Hawaiians—how American missionaries and other haoles had subjugated them, stolen their lands, killed them en masse with diseases, and converted the survivors to Christianity. At the time, I felt no responsibility for this cruel dispossession, no liberal guilt, but I knew enough to keep my junior atheist's mouth shut.

We started surfing new spots together. Roddy wasn't afraid of coral the way I was, and he showed me spots that broke among the reefs between my house and Cliffs. Most were ridable only at high tide, but some were little keyholes, slots between dry reef—sweet waves hiding in plain sight, essentially windproof. These breaks, Roddy said, were customarily named after the families who lived, or had once lived, in front of them—Patterson's, Mahoney's. There was also a big-wave spot, known as the Bomb, that broke outside Patterson's. Glenn and Ford had ridden it once or twice. Roddy had not. I had seen waves feathering (their crests throwing spray as the swells steepened) out there on big days at low tide, but had never seen it big enough to break. Roddy talked about the Bomb in a hushed, strained voice. He was obviously working up to it.

"This summer," he said. "First big day." In the meantime, we had Kaikoos. It was a deepwater break off Black Point, visible from the bottom of our lane. It was hard to line up, and always bigger than it looked, and I found it frightening. Roddy led me out there the first time, paddling through a deep, cross-chopped channel that had originally been cut, he told me, by Doris Duke, the tobacco heiress, to serve a private yacht harbor that was still tucked into the cliff under her mansion. He pointed toward the shore, but I was too worried about the waves ahead to check out Doris Duke's place.

Thick, dark-blue peaks seemed to jump up out of deep ocean, some of them unnervingly big. The lefts were short and easy, really just big drops, but Roddy said the rights were better, and he paddled farther east, deeper into the break. His temerity seemed to me insane. The rights looked closed-out (unmakable), and terribly powerful, and, even if you made one, the ride would carry you straight into the big, hungry-looking rocks of outer Black Point. If you lost your board in there, you would never see it again. And where could you even swim in to shore? I darted around, dodging peaks, way out at sea, half-hysterical, trying to keep an eye on Roddy. He seemed to be catching waves, though it was hard to tell. Finally, he paddled back to me, looking exhilarated, smirking at my agitation. He took pity on me, though, and said nothing.

Roddy was transferred, for some reason, to my typing class. Listening to him report to the teacher, I was stunned. He abandoned, briefly, his normal pidgin and spoke standard English. Glenn, I learned later, could do the same thing. The Kaulukukui boys were bilingual; they could "code switch," as we would say now. There just weren't many occasions in our daily rounds—indeed, almost none—when they had to drop their first language.

But keeping my two worlds separate got suddenly trickier. Roddy and I started hanging out at school, far from the In Crowd's monkeypod. In the cafeteria, we ate our saimin and chow fun together in a dim corner. But the school was a small pond. There was nowhere to hide. So there should have been a scene, a confrontation, perhaps with Mike himself—*Hey, who's this moke?*

There wasn't, though. Glenn and Ford were around then, too. Maybe Glenn and Mike hit it off over some shared laugh, nothing to do with me. All I knew was that, seemingly overnight, Glenn and Roddy and Ford were showing up not only at the In Crowd's schoolyard spot under the monkeypod but also at Mike and Edie's house in Kaimuki on Friday nights—when Mike's uncle supplied the Primo (local beer) and mod Steve, one of the gang's cooler kids, supplied the Kinks. The In Crowd had been integrated, with no visible fuss.

This was at a time when the Pacific Club, the leading local private club, where much of Hawaii's big business was conducted over cocktails and paddle tennis, was whites-only. The Pacific Club, apparently unmoved by the fact that Hawaii's first U.S. representative and one of its first two senators were Asian American (both were also distinguished veterans of the Second World War; one of them, Daniel Inouye, had lost an arm), still formally excluded Asian Americans from membership. This sort of bald discrimination wasn't exactly un-American—legal segregation was still in force in much of the country—but it was badly out of date in Hawaii. Even the low-rent haole kids in the In Crowd were more enlightened. They saw that my friends were cool guys—particularly, I think, Glenn—and, at least for gang purposes, just let the race thing go. It wasn't worth the trouble. It was radioactive crap. Let's party.

Not that kicking it with the In Crowd was the fondest ambition of Glenn, Ford, or Roddy. From what I knew, which was a lot, it was no big deal to them. It was only a big deal to me. In fact, after Roddy got to know a couple of the girls I had been telling him about—In Crowd girls I had agonized over—I could see that he was unimpressed. Roddy had been suffering his own romantic torments, which I had also heard much about, but the object of his affections was a modest, notably old-fashioned, quietly beautiful girl whom I would never have noticed if he hadn't pointed her out. She was too young to go steady, she told him. He would wait years, if necessary, he said wretchedly. Looking at my erstwhile girlfriends through his eyes, I didn't like them any less, but I began to see how lost they were, in their delinquent, neglected-child glamour, their sexual precocity. In truth, they were more sexually advanced than I was, which made me timid.

And so I developed a disastrous crush on Glenn's girlfriend, Lisa. She was an older woman—14, in ninth grade—poised, amused, kind, Chinese. Lisa was at Kaimuki Intermediate but not of it. That was how I saw her. She and Glenn made sense as a couple only because he was a natural-born hero and she was a natural-born heroine. But he was a wild man, an outlaw, a laughing truant, and she was a good girl, a good student. What could they possibly talk about? I would just wait, impatiently, for her to come to her senses and turn to the haole boy who struggled to amuse her, and worshiped her. I couldn't tell if Glenn noticed my hapless condition. He had the good grace, anyway, to say nothing off-color about Lisa within my hearing. (No "Spahk *dat*"—which boys were always saying to one another, popping their eyes at girlish rumps and breasts.)

Lisa helped me understand Ford. She knew his family, including his hardworking parents, who owned a gas station. I knew that Ford was considered unusual for a Japanese kid. Glenn sometimes teased him, saying things about "da nip-o-nese" and what a disappointment Ford, who cared for nothing except surfing, must be to his family. But he rarely got a rise out of him. Ford had a powerful inwardness about him. He could not have been more different, I thought, from the kids in my academic classes. They looked to teachers, and to one another, blatantly, fervently, for approval. I had become friendly with some of the funnier girls, who could be very funny indeed, but the social wall between us stayed solid, and their brownnosing in class still offended my sense of student-teacher protocol. Ford, on the other hand, was from my planet.

My father's Hawaii was a big, truly interesting place. He was regularly in the outer islands, herding film crews and talent into rainforests, remote villages, tricky shoots on unsteady canoes. He even shot a Pele number on a Big Island lava field. His job involved constant battling with local labor unions, especially the teamsters and the longshoremen, who controlled freight transportation. There was abundant private irony in these battles, since my father was a strong union man, from a union family (railroaders) in Michigan.

My dad gained enough sense of local working-class culture to know that the streets of Honolulu (and perhaps the schools) might be a challenge for a haole kid. If nothing else, there was a notorious unofficial holiday called Kill a Haole Day. This holiday got plenty of discussion, including editorials (against) in the local papers, though I never managed to find out precisely where on the calendar it fell. "Any day the mokes want," Mike, our In Crowd chief, had said. I also never heard whether the holiday had occasioned any actual homicides. The main targets, people said, were off-duty servicemen, who generally wandered in packs around Waikiki and the red-light district downtown. I think my father took comfort in seeing that my best friends were the local kids who kept their surfboards in our yard. They looked like they could handle themselves.

He had always worried about bullies. When confronted by bigger boys, or outnumbered, I should, he told me, "pick up a stick, a rock, whatever you can find." He grew alarmingly emotional giving me this advice. My dad seemed scared of no one. Indeed, he had a cantankerous streak that could be mortifying. He wasn't afraid to raise his voice in public. I found his combativeness intensely embarrassing. He sometimes asked the proprietors of shops and restaurants that posted signs asserting their right to refuse service to anyone what, exactly, that meant, and if he didn't like their answers he angrily took his business elsewhere. This didn't happen in Hawaii, but it happened plenty of times on the mainland. I didn't know that such notices were often code for "whites only." I just quailed and stared desperately at the ground as his voice began to rise.

Now, in Hawaii, I felt myself drifting away from my family. My parents knew me only as Mr. Responsible. That had been my role at home since shortly after the other kids began arriving. There was a substantial age gap between me and my siblings, and I could usually be counted on to keep the little ones undrowned, unelectrocuted, fed, watered, rediapered. But I resented my babysitting duties, and the snug fracas of the family dinner felt vestigial. Mom and Dad knew less and less about me. I had been leading a clandestine life, not only at school but in the water. Nobody asked where I went with my board, and I never talked about good days at Cliffs or my triumphs over fear at Kaikoos.

The surf changed as spring progressed. There were more swells from the south, which meant more good days at Cliffs. Patterson's, the gentle wave between wide panels of exposed reef out in front of our house, started breaking consistently and a new group of surfers materialized to ride it—old guys, girls, beginners. Roddy's younger brother, John, came out. He was 9 or 10, and fantastically nimble. My brother Kevin began to show some interest in surfing, perhaps influenced by John, who was about his age and kept his board in our yard. I was surprised. Kevin was a terrific swimmer. He had been diving into the deep end of the swimming pool since he was 18 months old. Pigeon-toed, he had a piscine ease in water, and was an expert bodysurfer already at 9. He had always professed indifference to my obsession, though. It was my thing; it would not be his. But now he paddled out at Patterson's on a borrowed board and within days was catching waves, standing, turning. He was a natural. We found him a used board, an old Surfboards Hawaii tanker, for $10. I was proud and thrilled. The future suddenly had a different tinge.

But one day at Patterson's I heard people calling me from the shore. "It's your brother!" I paddled in, frantic, and found Kevin lying on the beach, people standing around him. He looked bad —pale, in shock. He'd been hit in the back by a board. Apparently he had got the wind completely knocked out of him. Little John Kaulukukui had saved him from drowning. Kevin was still breathing heavily, coughing, crying. We carried him up to the house. Everything hurt, he said. Mom cleaned him up, calmed him down, and put him to bed. I went out to surf some more. I figured he would be back in the water in a few days. But Kevin never surfed again. He did resume bodysurfing, and as a teenager became one of the hotshots at Makapu'u and Sandy Beach, two serious bodysurfing spots on the eastern tip of Oahu. As an adult, he has had back trouble. Recently, an orthopedist, looking at a spinal x-ray, asked him what had happened when he was a child. It looked as if he had suffered a serious fracture.

I eventually learned to like the rights at Kaikoos. The spot was often empty, but there were a few guys who knew how to ride it, and, watching them on good days from the Black Point rocks, I began to see the shape of the reef and how to avoid, with a little luck, catastrophe. Still, it was a gnarly spot by my standards, and when I bragged in letters to my friend in Los Angeles about riding this scary, deep-water peak, I was not above spinning tall tales about being carried, with Roddy, by huge currents halfway to Koko Head, which was miles away to the east. My detailed description of scooting through a big tube—the cavern formed by a hard-breaking wave—on a Kaikoos right contained, on the other hand, a whiff of authenticity. I still half remember that wave.

But surfing always had this horizon, this fear line, that made it different from other things, certainly from other sports I knew.

You could do it with friends, but when the waves got big, or you got into trouble, there never seemed to be anyone around.

Everything out there was disturbingly interlaced with everything else. Waves were the playing field. They were the goal. They were the object of your deepest desire and adoration. At the same time, they were your adversary, your nemesis, even your mortal enemy. The surf was your refuge, your happy hiding place, but it was also a hostile wilderness—a dynamic, indifferent world. At 13, I had mostly stopped believing in God, but that was a new development, and it had left a hole in my world, a feeling that I'd been abandoned. The ocean was like an uncaring God, endlessly dangerous, power beyond measure.

And yet you were expected, even as a kid, to take its measure every day. You were required—this was essential, a matter of survival—to know your limits, both physical and emotional. But how could you know your limits unless you tested them? And if you failed a test? You were also required to stay calm if things went wrong. Panic was the first step, everybody said, to drowning. As a kid, too, your abilities were assumed to be growing. What was unthinkable one year became thinkable, possibly, the next. My letters from Honolulu in 1966 were distinguished less by swaggering bullshit than by frank discussions of fear: "Don't think I've suddenly gotten brave. I haven't." But the frontiers of the thinkable were quietly, fitfully edging back for me.

That was clear on the first big day I saw at Cliffs. A long-interval swell had arrived overnight. The sets were well overhead, glassy and gray, with long walls and powerful sections. I was so excited to see the excellence that my backyard spot could produce that I forgot my usual shyness and began to ride with the crowd at the main peak. I was overmatched there, and scared, and got mauled by the biggest sets. I wasn't strong enough to hold on to my board when caught inside by six-foot waves, even though I "turned turtle" —rolled the board over, pulled the nose down from underwater, wrapped my legs around it, and got a death grip on the rails. The whitewater tore the board from my hands, then thrashed me, holding me down for sustained, thorough beatings. I spent much of the afternoon swimming. Still, I stayed out till dusk. I even caught and made a few meaty waves. And I saw surfing that day—by Leslie Wong, among others—that made my chest hurt. Long moments of grace that felt etched deep in my being: what I wanted, somehow, more than anything else. That night, while my family slept, I lay awake on the bamboo-framed couch, heart pounding with residual adrenaline, listening restlessly to the rain.

My parents were dutiful, if not particularly enthusiastic, Catholics. Mass every Sunday, Saturday catechism for me, fish sticks on Friday. Then, around my 13th birthday, while we were still in California, I received the sacrament of confirmation, becoming an adult in the eyes of the church, and was thunderstruck to hear my parents say that I was no longer required to go to mass; that decision was now mine. Were they not worried about the state of my soul? Their evasive, ambiguous answers shocked me again. They had been fans of Pope John XXIII. But they did not, I realized, actually believe in all the doctrine and the prayers—all those oblatios, oratios, frightening confiteors, and mealy-mouthed acts of contrition that I had been memorizing and struggling to understand since I was small. It was possible that they didn't even believe in God. I immediately stopped going to mass. God was not visibly upset. My parents continued to drag the little ones to church. Such hypocrisy! This joyful ditching of my religious obligations happened shortly before we moved to Hawaii.

And so, on a spring Sunday morning, I found myself slowly paddling back from Cliffs through the lagoon while my family was sweating it out at Star of the Sea, a Catholic church in Waialae. The tide was low. My skeg gently bumped on the bigger rocks. Out on the exposed reef, wearing conical straw hats, Chinese ladies bent, collecting eels and octopuses in buckets. Waves broke here and there along the reef's outer edge, too small to surf.

I felt myself floating between two worlds. There was the ocean, effectively infinite, falling away forever to the horizon. This morning, it was placid, its grip on me loose and languorous. But I was lashed to its moods now. The attachment felt limitless, irresistible. I no longer thought of waves being carved in celestial workshops, as I once did. I was getting more hardheaded. Now I knew that they originated in distant storms, which moved, as it were, upon the face of the deep. But my absorption in surfing had no rational content. It simply compelled me; there was a profound mine of beauty and wonder in it. Beyond that, I could not have explained why I did it. I knew vaguely that it filled a psychic cavity of some kind—connected, perhaps, with leaving the church, or with, more likely, the slow drift away from my family—and that it had replaced many things that came before it.

The other world was land: everything that was not surfing. Books, girls, school, my family, friends who did not surf. "Society," as I was learning to call it, and the exactions of Mr. Responsible. Hands folded under my chin, I drifted. A bruise-colored cloud hung over Koko Head. A transistor radio twanged on a seawall where a Hawaiian family picnicked on the sand. The sun-warmed shallow water had a strange boiled-vegetable taste. The moment was immense, still, glittering, mundane. I tried to fix each of its parts in memory. I did not consider, even in passing, that I had a choice when it came to surfing. My enchantment would take me where it chose.

ALICE GREGORY

Climb Every Mountain

FROM *T Magazine*

THE ONLY HIKING I've ever known or half-enjoyed has involved
flat terrain, a swimmable body of water as a destination, and at
least one parent to whine to along the way. But in September I
found myself 5,000 feet up a mountain, lost, alone, without a
working cell phone, not even close to where I was supposed to be
going, and completely happy. As I gnawed my way up the Dolomite
peak of Kronplatz mountain, I had to stop every 100 yards and
catch my breath. It hadn't even occurred to me that the trek would
be difficult or that I should bring water. But whatever panic and
thirst and lung-burn I experienced was mitigated by the frosted
clover and edelweiss and enzian, which I could see the sun thawing in real time as I walked. The air smelled sweetly of manure and
cut grass; the tinkle of cowbells and the call of actual cuckoo birds
echoed through the valleys.

I was promised, via translated emails, that waiting for me at the
top of the mountain would be Reinhold Messner, who is, at least
in the glaciated, barely oxygenated part of the world where he was
born and still lives, extremely famous. South Tyrol, the autono-
mous, Austria-bordering province of Northern Italy where Messner scaled his first mountain in the mid-1940s at the age of five,
is plastered with blown-up pictures of his leathered face. In the
decades that followed his first kindergarten ascent, Messner went
on to climb another 3,500 peaks and in the process became one
of the most celebrated and sport-advancing, and correspondingly
wealthiest, mountaineers of the 20th century.

In 1978 he and his partner Peter Habeler became the first

people to climb Mount Everest without using bottled oxygen; two years later he became the first to do it alone. Messner was also the first to ascend all 14 "eight-thousanders" (mountains with peaks over 8,000 meters), and has scaled the highest mountains on all seven continents. Unlike most of his contemporaries, Messner packed with extreme asceticism and maintains that he has always gone without supplemental oxygen. He has traversed both Antarctica and the Gobi Desert on foot, and spent a not insignificant amount of time searching for yetis.

Messner, who has only three remaining toes (frostbite) and does not know how to swim ("It is not necessary"), has written more than 50 books, lent his name to a line of toiletries, and represented the Italian Green Party in the European Parliament. With his full beard and mass of rock-colored hair, he has the appearance of a man who might be featured on a limited-edition postage stamp. It's Messner, and perhaps only Messner, who defies author-adventurer Jonathan Waterman's claim that "climbing is one of the few sports in which the arena—the cliffs, the mountains and their specific routes—acquires a notoriety that outpopulates, outshines and outlives the actual athletes."

Now 71, Messner no longer climbs, at least not professionally. Instead, he has spent the past decade focusing on the Messner Mountain Museum, his constellation of six thematically curated, high-altitude institutions devoted to the history and culture of mountain climbing.

The first museum was opened in 1995 in Sigmundskron Castle; the entire project is estimated to have cost over $30 million. The latest museum, Corones, is a 1,000-square-meter concrete crashed-spaceship of a building designed by the Iraqi-British architect Zaha Hadid. Construction, which began in 2013, involved the excavation of 140,000 cubic feet of Kronplatz mountain, the nearly 7,500-foot Dolomite peak that I exuberantly and somewhat stupidly volunteered to climb.

Though more contemporary than the five museums built before it (three of which are in castles), this one, like the others, recreates, in a pleasurably primitive way, the experience of scaling a mountain. The multilevel space is cool and smells faintly of snow. A hip-high grotto houses a collection of amethyst geodes, and making your way through the galleries' tunnels, you often find yourself disoriented, returned almost to where you began, as if having miscalculated a switchback. Staircases are mirrored with diagonal glass vitrines filled with ice picks, boots, scrapbooks, and carabiners; there are semi-relevant quotes printed on the walls from the Buddha, Nietzsche, John Ruskin, and, of course, Messner himself. Chamois congregate in a pen outside, as do copper-haired couples in Hogan hiking boots and Brunello Cucinelli quarter-zip sweaters.

"In mountaineering, there is not only the activity, but the philosophy behind it," Messner told me outside the museum at 10:00 a.m. When I arrived, slicked with sweat and dragging an irresponsibly empty, hotel-supplied backpack, he was already there, staring silently out a biomorphic window. And then he added, unbidden, "Some say a moral, but I am against that because all morality is dangerous. All nationalism is dangerous; all religions are dangerous."

As he spoke, Messner's face became enveloped in a thin cloud of condensation.

"What is this strange religion they have in America now?" he asked.

"Scientology."

"Oh, yes, it is very dangerous."

For someone who has spent his entire life climbing mountains, the appeal of which rivals only theistic rituals, Messner's conception of religion, and even of morality, struck me as surprisingly literal.

At this point a group of full-grown adults approached us tentatively to ask if Messner would agree to be in a few photographs and, by implication, if I would make myself scarce. He obliged, and for the next five minutes various permutations of people, all dutifully wearing the website-prescribed "stout footwear," rearranged themselves in semi-symmetrical formations, always with him at the center.

After his fans retreated, Messner urged me to look north. "See?" he said. "Look out."

Below us were verdant pastures and distant outcroppings that mirrored the view behind us. We both inhaled. "You don't see one bad situation." Then, in a humble concession to reality, Messner pointed to a distant smokestack, and squinted with vague contempt. "Only there, I guess, a little bit."

*

Driving north from Venice, it's obvious the moment you cross from
Italy proper into the affluent, Everglades-size region of South Tyrol. The radio, seconds ago playing telenovela-style pop, goes static
and then suddenly comes in again, this time with Mahler. There
are clusters of timber farmhouses with blooming window boxes;
tiny white churches with spires that, like the surrounding pine
trees, cast long and elegant shadows upon vast expanses of emerald-green grass. The brooks actually babble; the sky seems always
to be cloudless. It looks like a Walt Disney creation—impossibly
synthetic-seeming, almost edible—what a four-year-old girl might
draw up were she encouraged to design her dream landscape.
There are miniature ponies. And rainbows. And lakes so blue that
the most accurate comparisons (to blue raspberry Gushers, to
Smurfs, to aquarium gravel) feel sacrilegious. The only piece of
litter I saw in an entire week was—honest to God—a Ritter Sport
wrapper, and it was from the "whole almonds" flavor, meaning the
plastic was forest-green and all but invisible in the shrubbery.

In the centuries before the High Alps were first explored in
the mid-1700s, mountains were not generally considered beautiful. Samuel Johnson called them "considerable protuberances"
and they were often referred to as boils and warts. Well into the
18th century, cross-continental voyagers who were forced to travel
through the range elected to do so blindfolded. "Natural scenery
was appreciated largely for the extent to which it spoke of agricultural fecundity," writes Robert Macfarlane in his elegant and often
quite funny 2003 book *Mountains of the Mind*. "Tamed landscapes,
in other words, were attractive: landscapes which had had a human order imposed upon them by the plough, the hedgerow and
the ditch . . . Mountains, nature's roughest productions, were not
only agriculturally intractable, they were also aesthetically repel-
lent."

But to a modern onlooker, it's the white peaks of the Dolomites,
which rise up, evil-looking, all around, that make the apparent
mirth and merry of the meadow-rich valleys at all palatable. The
sinister, toothy mountains both exaggerate the loveliness below
and cut it with the necessary bit of harshness that is otherwise lacking from the saccharine, sentimental landscape. It's all too easy to
imagine, in a fairy tale–like way, a local child growing up with these
threatening peaks forever in his peripheral vision and feeling as

though his character was contingent upon a successful confrontation with them. Which is, of course, exactly Messner's story.

"I am a man who is realizing ideas," he told me, looking out from the museum's prowlike balcony. "For me, when I was a child —a boy, let's say—I went beside this beautiful mountain there"— at this, he pointed west toward a pleasingly round summit—"and I looked up for a few days with binoculars, and I invented a line where I could climb up. Then, one Sunday I went up with my brother and we did it. It's like a piece of art. The same thing with the museum. I have an idea, I do it."

Messner spent the entirety of our conversation orienting my gaze in different directions as he told me about his life and the history of South Tyrol. "I was born behind this first chain," he said, gesturing out toward the same general area as before. "My mother came from that left-hand valley; my grandfather came from a place a bit south of the Dolomites, so my roots are here. I am a South Tyrolean. I identify with this land."

His mother was unusually well educated and his father a strict, proudly Teutonic schoolteacher. Messner grew up a German-speaking Italian citizen (the signage in South Tyrol is still in both languages) charged with chopping wood, slaughtering chickens, and exploring the nearby mountains with his eight siblings, each of whom was unofficially responsible for the one just younger than themselves. For Reinhold, this was Günther, his shy brother two years his junior. By the time they were 13 and 11, Reinhold and Günther were devoted amateur climbers known for their agility and speed. Forced by their father to pursue traditional professions, Reinhold trained as an architect and Günther worked in finance, but the brothers took every possible opportunity to climb together and toughen up, often staying out for days at a time without food. By 1969 they had gained a reputation as local semi-celebrities and were invited on a Himalayan expedition.

In 1970 the two brothers traveled to Pakistan as part of a group trek up Nanga Parbat. As they reached the summit, Günther grew ill from the altitude. They made their way to lower ground but, as night fell, were forced to pitch and sleep in an emergency bivouac shelter. In the morning, they continued their descent, Reinhold in the long lead. At one point he waited for Günther to catch up and when he didn't, Reinhold turned back to find him; instead he

found the remnants of an avalanche. He searched for a day and a
night to no avail. He even returned the following year. Günther's
remains were not recovered for another 34 years.

A week after we met, not far from where the two grew up, Messner left for Africa to direct his first movie: a re-creation of a near-
fatal climb (also taken in 1970) by two Austrian mountain climbers up Mount Kenya.

No sport encourages the ostensibly paradoxical impulses of meditative, in-the-moment focus and past-tense memorializing quite
like mountain climbing. It seems that everyone who has even dabbled in the endeavor has gone on to document it. A mountain
presents not just an invitation to climb it but also a provocation to
represent that climb. How to do it in a way that begins to approxi-
mate the scale of even a small hill?

For Messner, the answer has been interdisciplinary. He told me
that he learned how to open and organize a museum by doing
it himself, "not by going to museums." His autodidacticism is apparent in the Mountain Museums, which are at once charming
and confounding and weirdly ambitious. Ripa, the northernmost
museum, in the quaint and mostly cobblestoned town of Brunico,
holds the most interesting collection. Housed in a crenelated castle carpeted with lichen and strung with Tibetan prayer flags is
an extensive collection of fascinating, bewildering cultural artifacts
often presented without context. There is a room filled with doll-
houses made to look like the kind of traditional mountain homes
found in places like Patagonia, Peru, and Kandahar. (They are re-
markably similar.) There is a gallery devoted to international water vessels, another stocked with Tibetan musical instruments, and
another for Incan weapons. There are beautiful, cowry-shell-laced
articles of clothing from the Hindu Kush and a few human skulls
(unlabeled) thrown in for good measure.

Seventy-five miles southwest is Juval, the 13th-century castle
where Messner lives with his family for a part of the year, and
which he opens to visitors. It sits atop a modest mountain covered
in both apple orchards and terraced Riesling vineyards. There is
a small zoo on the premises, along with a sprawling collection of
Asian masks and effigies. (The theme is holy mountains.) Messner's personal library, consisting mostly of books about Alpinism,
is kept here in an ornately carved room, complete with catwalk,

flokati rugs, Lucite chairs, and a custom porcelain stove painted with some of the more impressive mountains he has climbed.

If the concept of a museum about mountain climbing seems odd in a dancing-about-architecture type of way, consider this: just two months ago, Ralph Nader opened the American Museum of Tort Law in his hometown of Winsted, Connecticut. There are also museums devoted to, among other topics: dialysis (Seattle), ventriloquism (Kentucky), ramen (Osaka), tap water (Beijing), and dog collars (England). In the grand scheme of things, the premise of the Messner Mountain Museums isn't so far-fetched.

Positioned at what was the highest place of the former Austro-Hungarian Empire, the Ortles museum is "devoted to the world of ice." What this mostly means for the visitor is that it is bone-chillingly cold inside. There are some walking sticks, some ice picks, some skis, reportedly 200 years' worth of mountaineering boots, a rescue sled from 1940, and Shackleton's binoculars. But these items are the outliers. The ratio of artifacts to art seems particularly miscalculated at this location: most of the museum's contents are paintings, dozens from the late 19th and early 20th centuries and a not insignificant number of contemporary works, all of which depict ice, a creative goal that Messner considers to be supremely difficult. "I don't want to draw a line between kitsch and art," he explains in the wall text.

Sadly, my trip did not coincide with Almabtrieb, an annual South Tyrolean festival held each fall in which, per Messner's description, local farmers "bring the young cows down to valleys with coronas of flowers and big bells and *boom, boom, boom,* it is beautiful." Though he finds the tradition lovely, Messner does not participate. "I personally have yaks," he said solemnly. "My yaks are going home alone. In fall with the first cold days they go. They go alone."

I saw no sign of yaks outside the museum, though in front of a roaring fire in the on-site restaurant I ate some. The dish was cooked in red wine and served with mushroom dumplings. Like everything else I ate on the trip—homemade yolk noodles with raspberry-laced ragu, elk medallions garnished with violets and pansies—it looked and tasted like something a besotted hunter might prepare for a lost princess.

Bolzano, the largest city in South Tyrol, is also the site of the largest museum, Firmian. The castle it is housed in, dating back to

A.D. 945, was far more treacherous to navigate than any hike I'd been on. Focused, however vaguely, on "man's encounter with the mountain," the place was packed with people on a weekday morning.

In part organized by mountain range, the curatorial plan seemed to have been often abandoned; in the gallery supposedly about the Matterhorn, for instance, there was a bronze statue of Krishna and also looped audio of Bob Dylan's "Blowin' in the Wind." Artifacts collected here include, but are not limited to: ancient and wildly inaccurate maps; a first edition of Edward Whymper's famous 1871 book, *Scrambles Amongst the Alps;* old hiking "boots" that were really just wooden paddles with hand-forged iron cleats hammered into footbeds made of straw; Nepalese crystals; an intricately constructed proto–French press intended to be used over an open flame; vintage postcards; a model heart in a case playing an audio track of its beating and a German voiceover explaining, presumably, the altitude's effect on the pulmonary system; a contemporary, Joseph Beuys–inspired sculpture consisting of 12 cots made up in gray felt; leather-strapped goggles; and a plexiglass chamber filled with "Everest refuses," i.e., garbage (rusty cans, discarded clothing, tarps, candy wrappers, a teapot).

"In the museum, I'm telling stories about mountains. This is not a classical museum; it's not an art museum or a museum of natural science. It's a museum where I tell stories about the mountains," Messner said. "We are a touristic destination for mountain aficionados who come to climb or hike or be in the mountains in a nice hotel with a nice bottle of wine in the evenings and sit on the balconies enjoying the sun. I give to this country, which is based on mountain tourism, the cultural aspect."

This seemed like the proud, self-assured mission statement of someone convinced that his time is being well spent. But Messner has sworn that the Hadid-designed Corones will be the last of the museums and tells me that the plan is for his 27-year-old daughter Magdalena, who has studied both art history and economics and whom he charmingly referred to as a "young head," to take over the project.

Standing atop Kronplatz, I asked Messner why this should be, why this museum will be the last, and his answer was comically unsatisfying. "There is no other issue," he said in a throaty German accent.

Issue?

"One museum is for the ice, one is for the rocks, one is on mountain people, one is on holy mountains, and this one is on the traditional Alpinism," he says impatiently. "There is no other issue."

"Mountains are not fair or unfair—they are dangerous," Messner has written. Maybe that's the real appeal of climbing one, something that books and films and museums—all so safe—can't ever quite re-create. In a world that can so often feel rigged, there is an undeniable relief to experiencing so impersonal a struggle, a challenge so absolutely free of conspiracy.

It was embarrassing how quickly I came to feel as though it were an absolute necessity I climb to the rest of Messner's museums, all of which are accessible by car. Messner's feats were to my "climbing" what a professional swimmer's are to taking a bath, but I still found myself grinning with unseemly pride every time I made it to the top. If there's one thing missing from the lives of people I know—and from my own—it's the self-generated feeling of achievement that comes from choosing to start, and then being able to finish, an arbitrarily chosen task. Ideally, this task is difficult, though incrementally surmountable, and unrelated to everything else that comprises a coherent sense of self-worth. A graduate student doing a jigsaw puzzle. A hedge fund manager reading *Clarissa*. A writer climbing a mountain.

The Foreign Spell

FROM *Lapham's Quarterly*

THE FOREIGN HAS long been my stomping ground, my sanctuary, as one who grew up a foreigner wherever I happened to be. Born to Indian parents in Oxford, England, I was seven when my parents moved to California; by the third grade, I was a foreigner on all three of the continents that might have claimed me—a little Indian boy with an English accent and an American green card. Foreignness became not just my second home, but my theme, my fascination, a way of looking at every place as many locals could not. As some are born with the blessing of beauty or a musical gift, as some can run very fast without seeming to try, so I was given from birth, I felt, the benefit of being on intimate terms with outsiderdom.

It's fashionable in some circles to talk of Otherness as a burden to be borne, and there will always be some who feel threatened by —and correspondingly hostile to—anyone who looks and sounds different from themselves. But in my experience, foreignness can as often be an asset. The outsider enjoys a kind of diplomatic immunity in many places, and if he seems witless or alien to some, he will seem glamorous and exotic to as many others. In open societies like California, someone with Indian features such as mine is a target of positive discrimination, as strangers ascribe to me yogic powers or Vedic wisdom that couldn't be further from my background (or my interest).

Besides, the very notion of the foreign has been shifting in our age of constant movement, with more than 50 million refugees;

every other Torontonian you meet today is what used to be called a foreigner, and the number of people living in lands they were not born to will surpass 300 million in the next generation. Soon there'll be more "foreigners" on earth than there are Americans. Foreignness is a planetary condition, and even when you walk through your hometown—whether that's New York or London or Sydney—half the people around you are speaking in languages and dealing in traditions different from your own.

Yet for all the global culture and busy crossroads we might share, it's treacherous to assume these imply common values or assumptions. It's one thing to note with amusement how there are "two-and-three" counts at the ballparks in Japan, or to be unable to distinguish the characters for left and right on the signs in China. It's quite another to be somewhere where you're not even sure who's living and who's dead. "O brave new world, / That has such people in't!" exclaims innocent Miranda in Shakespeare's *The Tempest,* as she sees the first foreigners she's ever glimpsed (though in truth they come from Milan, as she originally did). "'Tis new to thee" is her wise father Prospero's dry response.

The first time I set foot on Indonesia's Hindu island of Bali, I was enchanted by everything I didn't recognize, as if it were out of a fairy tale: the nymphs performing eye-rolling dances in the temple courtyards before bare-chested men plunged mock-daggers into their hearts to simulate mass exorcisms; the fact that children weren't allowed to touch the ground their first many months on earth, so they'd remain closer to the realm of angels; the stories people told me of how, if I wore green, I'd be swept away by the ocean; the jangled, hypnotic near-melodies of the gamelan, clangorous notes between the trees, playing well into the night. Foreignness took many forms, but most of them, as I came to find, proved indecipherable. I had been keen to see foreignness as part souvenir and part snapshot, like any postcard-seeking tourist, and yet just as often it was rising up all around me, devouring, and reminding me of how far from useful my judgments could be.

"When you in America want to communicate with each other," I once heard a Balinese matter-of-factly declare, "you communicate by telephone. When I need to say something to my brother, we communicate by telepathy. I send a thought and he catches it." He wasn't playing only to foreign credulity, and I didn't know quite what to make of his claim. I only sensed that he believed this to be true. And when I was stepping onto his island, I was stepping into his belief system, whether I wanted to or not.

From the moment Westerners began living in Bali, soon after World War I, they sent back two messages, more or less contradictory: first, they were no longer foreign—they had gone native, and felt wonderfully at home in Eden; second, the rest of us would always remain outsiders, the gates to the garden having closed behind them. By 1930 Hickman Powell, a reporter from Duluth, was entitling his book on Bali *The Last Paradise;* soon thereafter, the Mexican artist Miguel Covarrubias, author of *Island of Bali,* was wondering if Paradise was lost when its denizens began wearing shorts. Here was a truly unfallen place, every newcomer seemed to report, which would fall as soon as the next newcomer disembarked.

This is the point of the foreign. We don't travel halfway across the world to find the same things we could have seen at home. Those who undertake long and dangerous journeys have every incentive in stressing their discovery of a world far better than the one they left behind. Paul Gauguin became a "true savage, a real Maori," he wrote, after he traveled deep into the jungles of Polynesia (having found his first port of call, Papeete, a place polluted by "the absurdities of civilization"). His outsider's appeal in the South Seas put to shame his Everyman status as an artist of uncertain prospects back in Paris. Somerset Maugham later adapted Gauguin's story into a novel, *The Moon and Sixpence,* reminding readers that any distant port might be more liberating and richer in romance than a stockbroker's life.

Around the same time, D. H. Lawrence was thrashing through his own "savage pilgrimage" in which, famously, he alighted on Australia, Ceylon, and New Mexico in quick succession, pronouncing each one heaven until, within a few days, he decided it was hell. The violence of his responses reflected the tumult of his relations with everyone around him—he had the gift, perhaps, of conflating the foreign and the familiar—but in each place, he saw a tabula rasa onto which he could project his fear or hope. Gertrude Bell had noted that "the East is full of secrets—no one understands their value better than the Oriental; and because she is full of secrets she is full of entrancing surprises." One thing Bell chose not to acknowledge was that for the "Orientals" around her she was the real surprise—and keeper of secrets—as an unmarried Englishwoman who appeared only to want to live far from home, scaling mountains and studying ruins.

Nowadays, we're eager to note how much travel reveals our shared humanity: idealistic kids returning from a semester abroad in Cape Town or Jerusalem are likely to stress the similarities between places—the kinship they found, the friendships they formed. In earlier times, perhaps, the length and severity of a journey intensified a traveler's sense of shock when docking in Africa or India; now that a Dreamliner can whisk us to Tibet with only a two-hour layover in Hong Kong, it's much easier to underestimate —and dangerously elide—our differences.

My first night ever on the island of Bali, in 1984, I fell under what I later came to see was a spell cast on me by a young local woman, who led me into the unlit back alleyways and wound me around her almost as if I were helpless. I had done what I could to domesticate the island on arrival: I bought a pirated Dire Straits cassette and an owl mask as a good-luck souvenir; I mapped out a routine, locating where I could get good cake, where to post my letters home. In any case, a part of me was still in Manhattan, where I'd been closing a long article on Iran in the 25th-floor offices of *Time* only a day before. And so when this youngish woman came up to me at sunset on Kuta Beach, I was pleasantly surprised —I'd entered *A Midsummer Night's Dream,* I thought—even as she coaxed me through the alleyways into the thick forests only minutes away.

It wasn't long before I realized how out of my depth I was in this charged, supersaturated, animist landscape. Romance in most circumstances can have the aspect of a foreign country, but in an alien setting the unsettledness can overwhelm you. When I revisited the island a year later, I took pains not to alert my former friend. Yet there she was, next to the check-in desk my first night back, as if she'd been expecting me. I tried to assert some distance —a foreigner shouldn't travel too deeply into what he doesn't understand, I told her—and she cast another spell on me, as my skeptical mind was obliged to acknowledge, and I lay poleaxed in my room for seven days and nights.

The light switches on my wall I took to be geckos. The purrs and sighs of a Balinese girl in the next room, making a fuss over her

Aussie boyfriend, were a moment-by-moment torment. I couldn't sleep and I couldn't not sleep; I thought of how the owl mask I'd bought a year before had proved so potent when I put it up on my wall on 20th Street in New York that I had to tear it down minutes later. A doctor might have told me that I'd caught the flu —though I showed no external symptoms—or dismissed my ailment as something in my head. But really the truth of it was that the girl—or her culture—had gotten inside my head, and now I could no longer tell what she had wrought and what was mere circumstance.

I still often meet travelers who rhapsodize about the seductions of this fantasy island, as if to deny that Paradise is a place with a serpent and a Tree of the Knowledge of Good and Evil that it's fatal to eat from. An anthropologist's nirvana with its complex customs—foreigners cannot hang their laundry higher than a temple, and signs strictly remind you not to enter certain sites while menstruating—Bali also has long been a tourist's delight: you can fly bird-headed kites, learn that everyone, male or female, has one of the same four names, or hear about room 327 in the Grand Bali Beach Hotel reserved for a goddess (when a fire destroyed the place in 1993, it was one of the only rooms to survive). In case the swaying love songs of *South Pacific* and the ready epiphanies of the New Age needed any refueling, Julia Roberts sat before a wise-eyed, twinkling Balinese sage in the 2010 movie *Eat Pray Love,* and, lo and behold, by the end of the film she was sharing a cabana with Javier Bardem.

But Elizabeth Gilbert, in the book that inspired the movie, was too shrewd and seasoned an observer to think that the foreign could be tamed so easily. One of the island's earliest visitors wrote that "the Balinese are a fierce, savage, perfidious and bellicose people," and although that was the language—perhaps the prejudice —of the day, the place was most famous by the 17th century for its slaves and human sacrifices. Over the centuries that followed, other Indonesians came to view Bali—whose gamelan music is all dissonance and cacophony next to the elegant restraint of, say, Java—with much more watchfulness and distance than most foreigners would. And when, in 1965, anticommunist riots erupted across Indonesia, the rivers of Bali ran red with blood as temple-goers cut down their neighbors with machetes and sticks. Eighty thousand people were slaughtered all but overnight. Violence was terrible throughout the land, but nowhere was it as hideous as in Bali, where killers were said to have drunk their victims' blood.

The foreign is never going to be a pure and simple thing on an island with a temple guarded by poisonous sea snakes and a cave filled with thousands of bats. The dances that transfix tourists in Bali play out an ancient, implacable battle between good and evil, even if one we can grab with our iPhones. It is from the languages around this archipelago that our word "amok" comes, to refer to those possessed; and if, as most guidebooks tell us, there are more temples than homes on the island, it only follows, surely, that you are walking, as a foreigner, through an atmosphere thick with totems, taboos, and demons.

Growing up, I soon saw that I was ill-equipped for many things by my multicontinental upbringing—I would never enjoy settling down in any one place, and I wouldn't vote anywhere for my first half-century on earth—but I saw, too, that I had been granted a kind of magic broomstick that few humans before me had ever enjoyed. By the age of nine, flying alone over the North Pole six times a year—between my parents' home in California and my schools in England—I realized that only one generation before, when my parents had gone to college in Britain, they had had to travel for weeks by boat, sometimes around the stormy Cape of Good Hope. When they bid goodbye to their loved ones—think of V. S. Naipaul hearing of his father's death while in England, but unable to return to Trinidad—they could not be sure they'd ever see them again.

At 17, I was lucky enough to spend the summer in India, the autumn in England, the winter in California, and the spring bumping by bus from Tijuana down to Bolivia—and then up the west coast of South America. I wasn't rich, but the door to the world was swinging open for those of us ready to live rough and call ourselves foreigners for life. If my native India, the England of my childhood, and the America of my official residence were foreign, why not spend time in Yemen and on Easter Island?

In retrospect, it seems inevitable that I would move, in early adulthood, to what still, after 27 years of residence, remains the most foreign country I know, Japan. However long I live here, even if I speak the language fluently, I will always be a *gaikoku-jin,* an "outsider person," whom customs officials strip-search and children stare at as they might a yeti. I'm reminded of this on a daily basis. Even the dogs I pass on my morning walks around the neighborhood bark and growl every time they catch wind of this butter-reeking alien.

Japan remains itself by maintaining an unbreachable divide between those who belong to the group and those who don't. This has, of course, left the country behind in an ever more porous world of multiple homes, and is a source of understandable frustration among, say, those Koreans who have lived in the country for generations but were—until relatively recently—obliged to be fingerprinted every year and denied Japanese passports. Yet for a lifelong visitor, the clarity of its divisions is welcome; in free-and-easy California, I always feel as accepted as everyone else, but that doesn't make me feel any more Californian. Besides, I know that Japan can work as smoothly as it does only by having everyone sing their specific parts from the same score, creating a single choral body. The system that keeps me out produces the efficiency and harmony that draws me in.

I cherish foreignness, personally and internationally, and feel short-shrifted when United Airlines, like so many multinationals today, assures me in a slogan, "The word 'foreign' is losing its meaning"; CNN, for decades, didn't even use the word, in deference to what it hoped would be a global audience. Big companies have an investment in telling themselves—and us—that all the world's a single market. Yet all the taco shacks and Ayurvedic doctors and tai chi teachers in the world don't make the depths of other cultures any more accessible to us. "Read *The Sheltering Sky*," I want to tell my neighbors in California as they talk about that adorable urchin they met in the souk in Marrakesh. Next time you're in Jamaica—or Sri Lanka or Cambodia—think of Forster's Marabar Caves as much as of the postcard sights that leave you pleasantly consoled. Part of the power of travel is that you stand a good chance of being hollowed out by it. The lucky come back home complaining about crooked rug merchants and dishonest taxi drivers; the unlucky never come home at all.

On my most recent visit to Bali—my fifth trip since 1984—a part of me was almost relieved, on arrival, to see that the roads leading away from the airport housed an almost unbroken sequence of massage parlors—smile, bliss, relaxation—tending to the less ex-

alted needs of foreigners. (A massage in Bali, given only by old ladies, often blind, when first I visited, is now the province of young
girls and boys who all but guarantee a "happy ending.") Gaudy
karaoke parlors poked above the trees, assault rifles were on sale
near signs advertising extreme combat weekends. The first word
that greeted me in the airport was "death"—for those who bring
drugs into Bali; the signs spelling out such rules in Chinese and
Arabic might have been reminding us that this was now a place
consecrated to foreign pleasure.

Up in the hills, honoring the island's longtime segregation of
its foreign markets, was a labyrinth of exquisite, candlelit spas
and restaurants, mostly in identical minimalist style; lanterns led
through a temple entrance to what might be the more spiritual
forms of massage or daily bread. Emerald pools gleamed in the
dark, and visitors sipped at apple mojitos while wondering when to
sample some Hindu meditation. Brahma Kumaris World Spiritual
University was, I noticed, not far from the Foreign Development
Investment Council.

But the beauty of Bali, as I see it, is that the world of and for
foreigners, the tantra courses and salsa workshops and Mexican
restaurants, don't begin to intersect with the currents surging below and above us; we are as far from the people around us as the
"rude mechanicals" in *A Midsummer Night's Dream* are from the
courtiers and gods who toy with them. The Balinese man I met my
first night on the island on this trip said, "We are afraid of going
out at night. There are people who can turn into animals, who can
do anything if they want." As he drove me back to the luxury villa
I'd been given free of charge—private swimming pool attached
—he spoke of *leyak* witches who fly through the air here and "left-
handed tantra masters" who travel these days by Beemer or Suzuki
Shogun. I didn't know what he was going on about, and it didn't
matter. Even if I had understood, it wouldn't have protected me
against what would always remain foreign.

Among the Beverly Hills–worthy sanctuaries that encircle the
village of Ubud—full of signs for paradise regained, bikini parties,
and furniture stores called Reincarnation—people will tell you
that Bali is "spoiled," as if choosing to forget that this is what the
island has been tempting every visitor to say since the beginning.
And as if the so-called spoiling makes the place any less eerie or
unsettling or unfathomable. Pundits assure us the world is homog-

enized now—there are KFCs everywhere on Bali, and DHL will now send your owl masks back to Santa Monica almost overnight —but 40 years of travel, from Bolivia to Ladakh to Ethiopia, Beirut, and North Korea, have only convinced me of the opposite.

Not long ago, I was walking along a narrow lane beside a quiet stream north of Kyoto, a picturesque scene worthy of a Hiroshige woodcut. I saw a small shrine up a flight of stairs, and was about to climb up to inspect it—lots of other visitors were looking around —when my wife, born in Kyoto, stiffened; this, she said, was where black rites were conducted at midnight, and human sacrifices. This sounded implausible to me in her Westernized, highly secular homeland, but she was determined not to go closer, and I thought to myself that Japan is one foreignness I've chosen to live with. After more than a quarter of a century here, I feel I know which boundaries not to overstep.

But in a place I'm just visiting—in the local paintings you see all over Bali, it's impossible to see where the trees end and the humans begin—I can't make out where the boundaries are demarcated. I was walking through my ancestral homeland, India, one warm evening in 2009, and recalling, with amusement, the signs I'd seen earlier in the day, advertising McVeggies with cheese at the local Golden Arches, the little shacks calling themselves Glorious Ladies Tailors, the billboards that announced BRITISH SCHOOL FOR LANGUAGES IS NOW TROUNCE EDUCATION. It's a blessing to be a foreigner everywhere, detached and able to see the fun in things.

Then I noticed an orange glow in the air and looked along the holy Ganges to where bodies were being burned. Excited crowds of men raced through the narrow lanes of the old town to commit their loved ones to the flickering flames; bonfires burned along the riverbanks to the south and to the north. As so often in India, it was hard to tell whether I was in a riot or a festival. I'm of Hindu origin myself, and this sacred city might be one of the places that I could call home. But all I thought then was that nearly everywhere I knew was foreign, which meant that nearly everywhere had the power to unsettle and surprise me, forever.

ANDREW W. JONES

The Marlboro Men of Chernivtsi

FROM *The Morning News*

THE 7:10 A.M. bus to Suceava was almost entirely empty and quiet. Well, except for the bus driver. With foamy spittle amassing on his lips as he spoke in a language I couldn't understand, he kept thrusting a carton of cigarettes in my face, waving it wildly. And with each new response from me—all versions of "No, thank you" in any language I could butcher—both the cigarettes and the spittle came closer. My girlfriend, Erin, sitting next to me, was just as perplexed.

We'd arrived in Chernivtsi, the largest city in southwestern Ukraine, the afternoon before, and now were on our way to Romania. In the summer of 2008, well before Ukrainian borders were crossed by invading Russian troops, we didn't think much of what lay ahead of us. We'd been bouncing around Eastern Europe for three weeks and figured our jaunt into Romania would be a forgettable affair.

"He doesn't want to sell you the cigarettes," a brown-haired man declared in British-accented English. "He wants you to take them across the border for him."

With this, the driver sensed an opening and stopped waving the carton at us.

"Take them?"

"Well, he wants you to put the carton of cigarettes in your bag for him. He wants you to help him smuggle the cigarettes across the border."

"*Smuggle?*"

"I guess that's the technical term," the British man laughed.

"But I wouldn't worry about it. It's quite normal. This is the way things work here."

Feeling peer-pressured in ways I hadn't since I was 13 years old, I saw I had little choice. I couldn't claim I didn't understand what was happening, and now this episode had received the green light from a fellow English-speaker. Even if I wanted to say no, it didn't seem like the bus driver was going to take no for an answer, and this was the only bus of the day. With a shrug from Erin—this was normal, right?—I accepted the cigarettes from the gleeful bus driver, opened up my backpack, and stuffed the carton of Marlboros inside.

What's the big deal? I thought. I was just doing this bus driver a favor—all part of the international experience. How serious could taking a carton of cigarettes across the Ukraine-Romania border be?

In 2015 the dominant news stories about crossing the Ukrainian border involve armies and weapons. From the east, the Russian army has already marched into and annexed Crimea. The furious fighting right now in Donetsk and Luhansk, both near the border with Russia, has Western leaders perplexed over how to stop the bloodshed and secure Ukraine's sovereignty. But before the Ukrainian border became a dangerous war zone, it was a profitable smuggling arena. And while weapons are now being smuggled across the border, the smugglers' main product before this conflict broke out was cigarettes.

In 2008 in Ukraine, the international cigarette companies that control 99 percent of the cigarette market there manufactured and imported 130 billion cigarettes. And for a country that adores smoking like few others—according to *The Tobacco Atlas,* the *average* Ukrainian in 2008 smoked 2,526 cigarettes—you'd have to assume that all 130 billion would be gobbled up by the populace. You wouldn't expect, however, that nearly 25 percent of them were not.

Officially, according to the four leading international cigarette companies in Ukraine—Philip Morris International, Japan Tobacco International, Imperial Tobacco, and British American Tobacco—30 billion cigarettes were "lost." The reality was that these cigarettes were sold wholesale to international cigarette traffickers. According to Tobacco Underground, a group of journalists determined to uncover the rampant cigarette smuggling throughout the world, cigarettes are the most smuggled legal substance on earth. After the fall of communism, major players in the tobacco industry chose Eastern Europe for the expansion of the capitalist cigarette industry. During the 1990s, antismoking campaigns in the West were well underway, but this wasn't the case in Eastern Europe. Smoking was ingrained in the communist culture and represented one of the few freedoms Eastern Europeans had. They weren't about to give it up with the fall of the Berlin Wall. So Western cigarette companies moved in.

They weren't the only ones who saw an opening in Eastern Europe, though. More daring than making a profit from these "lost" cigarettes, one manufacturer in particular, the Baltic Tobacco Company, was established solely for the purpose of smuggling.

Ukraine's tangled relationship with Russia makes it an interesting case study for how international cigarette smuggling works. The Orange Revolution of 2004–2005 represented the first time in modern history that Ukraine broke away from Russia since the collapse of the Soviet Union. But as an impoverished state where the GDP per capita was $1,800 U.S. in 2005, the break from Russia didn't immediately lead to a better life for most Ukrainians. Between 2005 and 2015 Ukrainians have seen wild swings in their economic fortunes and the notion of a stable economy has seemed like an illusion. It comes as no surprise that a country with a flailing economy would have so many people turn to smuggling.

And cigarette companies, it seems, have been eager to play along. Seizing an opportunity in a country with some of the lowest cigarette taxes in the world, international companies are thriving in Ukraine. But Ukraine wasn't always the culmination of their cigarette market. There were smokers all over Europe, but in recent years, many countries had seen a decline in smoking because of the added cost of massive taxes on cigarettes, levied to give smokers a financial incentive to quit and young people no incentive to start. In Ukraine in 2008, a pack of Philip Morris Marlboros cost $1.05 U.S. In Romania, that pack of cigarettes would cost at least double. That pack could cost at least five times as much in Germany, and even farther west, in Great Britain, it could cost over $10.

The international cigarette companies in Ukraine had a different, unofficial plan: make money by selling cheap cigarettes with low taxes to a smoking-hungry population, and then add to it with extra sales of "lost" cigarettes to smugglers who would be eager to flood European markets with cheap, tax-free cigarettes.

This plan was humming along when I unknowingly joined it. The production of Marlboros—the most popular brand in Ukraine—rocketed skyward 85 percent from 2003 to 2008. A portion of these cigarettes were illegally smuggled on the European black market, which in 2008 was a $2.1 billion industry. By 2015 the numbers have become even more staggering. According to the European Commission, the European Union loses €10 billion annually in tax and customs revenue due to cigarette smuggling. And in a study conducted from 2006 to 2012, illegal cigarette consumption in the EU has spiked by 30 percent. Worldwide, cigarette smuggling now costs governments $50 billion in lost revenue.

The cigarette companies sell the cigarettes wholesale to buyers, and in some cases they might be aware they're selling to smugglers. In other cases, they might not. It's always possible that any wholesale purchase could be for legal purposes, so for them, it's not in their best interest to ask too many questions. And once the smugglers have the cigarettes, the only issue is how to get them safely across the border.

We settled in for the 75-kilometer ride to the Romanian border. Factoring in the bad roads and the crawl our 1970s bus would be chugging along at, we knew this ride would take several hours. But I still found myself surprised that every one or two kilometers, the bus would sputter its way over to the side of the road and out of the trees would emerge a small colony of overweight, elderly Ukrainian women.

At our first stop, five of them trudged onto the bus. Less than five minutes later, we stopped again, allowing a new group of grandmothers to board. This was followed by another stop to pick up more of these women.

When the bus had departed from the station in Chernivtsi, including us, there were only six or seven people on it. Now, after a mere 10 kilometers, we were crammed to capacity.

The women were dressed in the typical fashion: headscarves; long, dark skirts; and baggy blouses dulled by years of wear. Their most notable aspect was their luggage: each was carrying at least two—sometimes three or four—identical large black plastic bags

with the same striking white typeface: BOSS etched on top with
HUGO BOSS in smaller print neatly below.

The bags all seemed to contain the same rectangular objects,
rounded out as the women stuffed items of clothing on top.

Money began changing hands on the bus. This would be a normal occurrence as people typically passed their fare forward to the
bus driver, but here, the women weren't exchanging Ukrainian
hryivna but U.S. dollars, mostly $20 bills.

"Do you understand any of this?" I asked Erin, whose nose was
in a book.

"Wait a minute," she nodded in the direction of two women
standing in the aisle adjacent to us, "what exactly is she doing?
She's not, she's not—is she?"

One of the women was reaching down into her shirt and stuffing
her bra full of packs of cigarettes. Once she'd sufficiently loaded
up her bra, she moved to her skirt. More packs of Marlboros were
headed for her underwear.

"Oh my God," Erin whispered urgently. "They're all doing it!"

This was a cigarette-smuggling bus. Each woman now had two
Hugo Boss bags, and each bag appeared to hold about eight cartons—1,600 cigarettes. Our quick math led us to believe there
were around 500 cartons—100,000 cigarettes—on this bus.

The Romanian border had to be getting close, and these women
were all gearing up for the crossing. This seemed to be the least
devious act of smuggling I could imagine. Even if cigarette smuggling were normal, wouldn't it also be normal to try harder to hide
it? But maybe they knew something I didn't.

And maybe I shouldn't have been worried about how the
women were concealing their stash of Marlboros when I was a part
of it, too. With that thought, sweat started to trickle down my neck.
I leaned down and stuffed my carton of cigarettes deeper into my
backpack.

Though we didn't know it then, using a medium-sized bus
to transport approximately 100,000 cigarettes was a small-time
scheme. From Ukraine, it wasn't uncommon for hang gliders to
take off near the border and float their way into Hungary or Romania. Once they hovered in the general vicinity of the drop spot,
they'd release their cargo—hundreds, even thousands of cartons
of cigarettes—make a hasty turn, and head back.

Sometimes vans would be equipped with secret compartments

underneath the floor and roof panels. Trucks legally transporting materials would save room for illegal cigarettes. Bigger smuggling operations employed secret panels inside liquid gas tankers, providing space for thousands, sometimes even millions of cartons. (The largest seizure of cigarettes of all time occurred in 2009 when 4.4 million cigarettes were found inside a tanker.) Boats would include space for secret cigarette cargo among their other legally transported goods. Shipments of fruits and vegetables could be littered with illegal cigarettes.

In 2012 Slovakian authorities unearthed a 700-meter-long underground tunnel crossing the Ukraine-Slovakian border used for cigarette smuggling. The tunnel even included a railcar system. And even worse was their speculation that this tunnel was used for human trafficking as well.

The rampancy of cigarette smuggling isn't just limited to faraway Ukraine. A 2014 study in New York State revealed that 57 percent of cigarettes smoked in New York had been smuggled into the state in order to dodge taxes. This led to a massive bust of 500,000 illegal cigarettes on Staten Island in November 2014.

Organized crime flourished with the introduction of the Eastern European illegal cigarette trade in the 1990s. These syndicates weren't entirely responsible for the global trade of smuggled cigarettes, but the market was too good to pass up. Not only were there huge profits, the penalties for getting caught were light. The Ukrainian government's punishment for cigarette smuggling amounted to a slap on the wrist. In 2008 66 million cigarettes were seized by Ukrainian police and border officials: less than 1 percent of what was believed to be smuggled that year.

And the international cigarette companies in Ukraine didn't actually mind when their product was seized. They had already claimed these cigarettes as "lost" and would receive no penalty. In fact, they'd typically receive a sales boost, as the smugglers would just buy more cigarettes from the manufacturer for another run. Cigarette companies actually profited from the authorities busting the smugglers; smuggling was part of their business model.

But this was only an issue when the Ukrainian government seized the cigarettes and arrested the traffickers, which in 2008 rarely happened. For the smuggling operation to work fluidly, border guards needed to be bribed to look the other way. The entire process had the potential to be so profitable to so many players that it's easy to see why authorities were reticent to stop it. It starts with the cigarette companies who are eager to make a profit, selling 30 billion cigarettes wholesale to smugglers in Ukraine. (These "lost" cigarettes must be accounted for on the books somehow, but how this transpires is something that I was unable to account for in many hours of research.) The smugglers support themselves and their families. The border guards receive a nice boost to their monthly salary. The well-oiled system seemed to be helping all involved.

Worldwide in 2015, 1 in 10 people died prematurely from smoking-related illnesses. Eastern Europe contains some of the smoking-happiest countries in the world. The massive cigarette-smuggling operations are contributing to a global public health nightmare. According to *The Tobacco Atlas,* the illicit tobacco trade has now become more lucrative than drug trafficking.

As we pulled up to the official Romanian border, the grandmas grew quiet. I could tell they were nervous, and this was rubbing off on me.

"Don't worry," Erin reassured me, but even her voice was a little shaky. "I'm sure it will be fine. There's no way all of them would be smuggling the cigarettes this obviously unless they know they aren't going to get caught."

The bus stopped at a customs gate so the Ukrainian border guards could inspect us and our luggage outside the bus. Out on the pavement, we stood in a single-file line. Erin and I clung tight to our backpacks while the smugglers clutched their Hugo Boss bags and smiled. Looking at their bags, there was no way anyone would believe they contained just clothing.

But none of this mattered. The guard glanced at us, lit his own cigarette, smiled, and then waved all of us back onto the bus, whereupon the women checked the cigarettes stashed on their bodies. The protruding packs made weird angles, but they didn't seem too concerned. With a border guard who'd clearly been bribed to let us through, everything was certainly in order. This was just another day in southwestern Ukraine.

What's happening on a regular basis on the Ukrainian border is happening on borders in other parts of the world, too. With 11 percent of cigarette sales worldwide coming through illegal sales of trafficked cigarettes, countries more powerful than Ukraine—and groups more powerful than the smuggling grandmas—play a vital role. In China alone, hundreds of illicit cigarette factories produce a whopping 400 billion cigarettes a year, with fake Marlboros being the most popular brand. Both Hezbollah and the Taliban count on their control of illegal cigarette trade to finance some of their terrorist activities. And even though fines for cigarette companies' role in the illegal trade of their "lost" product have now eclipsed $1 billion, profits from the illegal cigarette trade are still much higher.

Closer to home, in Canada, police believe that there are 105 different groups—most related to organized crime—involved in smuggling cigarettes to and from the United States. In April of 2014 Royal Canadian Mounted Police arrested 25 people in Quebec as part of a smuggling ring that included 40,000 kilograms of illicit cigarettes worth roughly $7 million.

But there's one particular company that seems to defy all sense of decency in the world—even in the shady world of cigarette trafficking. The Baltic Tobacco Company, located in the western Russian enclave of Kaliningrad, has been producing Jin Ling cigarettes since 1997. Jin Ling is known for its labeling and artwork, which are almost identical to the U.S. brand Camel. The packaging is so similar, in fact, that if the cigarettes weren't produced in Russia, I'm guessing Camel could sue for copyright infringement.

Jin Ling cigarettes are churned out at a clip of around 13 billion a year in Kaliningrad. And while this nets Baltic Tobacco an annual profit of about $1 billion, the cigarettes have no legal market. The Jin Ling brand is intentionally manufactured, transported, and sold exclusively by cigarette traffickers. While other cigarette companies might knowingly partake in the illegal cigarette trade on the side, they all rely primarily on legal sales. Baltic just skipped that part.

Perhaps this was a wise business move. In 2008 a container of Jin Lings—one container is 10 million cigarettes—would cost a little over $100,000. In Western Europe, that same container would be worth somewhere between $3 million and $6 million. And with governments all over the world starting to crack down on smuggling, legitimate companies are feeling the heat. The fines are getting steeper and the PR fallout is starting to become more dangerous for business.

But Baltic is based in Kaliningrad, a haven for organized crime, and the Russian government doesn't generally interfere with anything that goes on there. Baltic has yet to be fined, and even if international monitors were to step in, it would be difficult for them to do so. Baltic's headquarters are hidden away with no signage on the building, and there's a good chance that many Kaliningrad residents don't even know the place exists.

Because they aren't sold commercially, Jin Ling cigarettes are not well known in Russia, a country, like Ukraine, that loves its cigarettes. If Baltic Tobacco were to sell its cigarettes legally in Russia, the company would have to play by some of the government's rules, and it has no interest in that. That's because there are plenty of places where Jin Lings can be found all throughout Europe—all on the black market.

Jin Lings are in a perfect position to be trafficked all over Europe. Kaliningrad is geographically separate from the rest of Russia, sandwiched between Lithuania and Poland with a sizable coastline on the Baltic Sea. Jin Ling cigarettes can easily be smuggled on land through Kaliningrad's two former Soviet bloc neighbors. They have made it as far as Britain, and in case anyone needs a highly ironic reminder, all packs of Jin Lings have a duty-free sticker on them. (They also don't include any of the EU-mandated health warnings.) In Britain, it's common for Jin Lings to be sold door-to-door in poorer housing developments or at convenience stores. Less officially, traffickers open their trunks and sell the cigarettes directly from their cars to customers.

In 2007, 258 million Jin Ling cigarettes were seized by European officials. But Baltic Tobacco isn't simply dodging taxes. In 2012 a house burned down due to a woman leaving a cigarette unattended. All legally produced cigarettes must comply with a law requiring a cigarette to self-extinguish if the smoker leaves it unattended. In this case, the unregulated Jin Ling kept smoldering and a 71-year-old woman died in the fire. In 2014, in another raid of Jin Lings, officials discovered some of the cigarettes contained asbestos. But even with all these deterrents, Jin Ling production continues to increase—so much so that the apparent owner of Baltic Tobacco commented that the company is having trouble meeting the demand for its cigarettes. And, one can only assume, since Baltic has little to no interest in the Russian market, the Kremlin doesn't see any need to do anything about this. As far as they're concerned, Baltic Tobacco is a huge success story—a homegrown business that employs Russians and keeps the economy growing.

And in Ukraine and all over the world, there's little doubt that cigarette smuggling is a way of life.

I'm guessing the grandmas would have far more misgivings crossing the Ukrainian border in 2015, no matter how desperate they were to smuggle their cigarettes. With fighting raging on for more than a year now in the eastern part of Ukraine, it's difficult to even ascertain where the borders are anymore.

For all of us on the smuggling bus in the summer of 2008, we knew we'd have to cross the border twice: once on the Ukraine side and then again a few minutes later as we were about to enter Romania. For the Ukrainian grandmas, this second check was the biggest hurdle to clear.

Once we'd reached the Romanian border, the bus driver stopped and called out to the passengers. More hands shuffled and more U.S. dollars were passed forward. A border guard rapped on the door to indicate that we should all exit the bus.

Once again, we all gathered up our luggage and filed off. Unlike the quick Ukrainian border check, however, on the Romanian side, we waited for several minutes. I began to sweat once again, and this time I could see that my fellow smugglers were sweating, too.

The first one to be searched was the bus driver. With the wad of greenbacks protruding from his back pocket—this had to be part of the plan, right?—he stepped forward once the three Romanian border guards showed up. Their black guns seemed to leap out at all of us. But maybe three men on the border patrol just meant that the total bribe money would end up being a little steeper.

When the first guard asked the driver to show him his Hugo Boss bag, I figured we were getting another up-close look at the sham of an international border check.

But the Romanian guard didn't stop at the top of the bag. Removing a single sweater, he revealed the cartons upon cartons of Marlboros beneath it. Furious, the guard started shaking his head. The bus driver started talking to him, pleading with him, but the guard was having none of it. He yelled at the bus driver, who appeared to be trying to plead his case. I wondered if the American money in his back pocket would come into play.

Instead, another guard confiscated the bags and banished the bus driver back to the line. His head down, he retreated as the first woman was summoned forward.

"I don't think this is going well," I whispered to Erin, looking at my own backpack on the pavement and trying to ascertain if my carton of Marlboros was visible from the outside.

More yelling followed from the border patrol. They'd taken the clothes off the top of the grandma's Hugo Boss bag, too. She was berated and then dismissed without her cartons. I could see tears streaming down her wrinkly cheeks.

The border patrol stopped after the third smuggler's bag was searched, and summoned over two more guards. The five of them stood next to the piles of Hugo Boss bags they'd confiscated, seemingly discussing how to handle the situation. They hadn't in-spected any of the women's bodies, but the plastic bags contained the great majority of the cigarettes. Part of me wondered if maybe this was still part of the plan; maybe the guards were using this as a tactic to extract an even larger bribe.

"Please tell me," Erin said quietly, "they're not going to check your bag."

The meeting of the border patrol broke up, and two of them headed right for the middle of the line, where Erin and I were standing with the British man.

They were coming for us.

In the same authoritative tone, the guards pointed at us and roared, *"Bag-gaj! Bag-gaj!"*

Terrified, I looked down to my two bags in front of me and did the only thing I thought might save my skin: I grabbed the smaller, cigarette-free bag and offered it up to the border guard. He inter-rupted me with his booming, irritated voice.

Oh shit, I thought. *I'm screwed.*

But as the guard continued yelling, I could see that he wasn't looking at me anymore; he just kept pointing to the bus.

"Hey," I said, "I think he's telling us we can go back to the bus."

"Are you sure?" Erin countered.

The pointing continued, and the British man chimed in.

"Yeah, I think they're telling us to go—telling us to get our bags and head to the bus."

With this, the guard nodded his head. I grabbed my bags and tried to act like I wasn't about to flee wildly. Once back on the bus, we quietly settled into our seats.

Erin was the first to speak.

"I can't believe what's going on. Can you? What in the world is going to happen to all of them?"

"I have no idea," I responded as I shoved the backpack containing the Marlboros as far under the seat as I could.

Of course they were breaking international laws, but these weren't exactly hardened criminals. Their smuggling was only a drop in the bucket of much larger worldwide operations. The cigarettes they intended to sell in Romania for probably double the price they'd purchased them most likely helped feed their families. And from what I'd seen in Ukraine, there wasn't an abundance of economic opportunities for women like them. While they were clearly committing a crime, knowing that they were in the process of getting caught, I started to wonder if I saw them as the victims.

A few minutes later, the grandmas started to rejoin us on the sweaty bus. The first came flying up the stairs in a huff, peeling away at the layers of clothing on her body, revealing a multitude of Marlboro packs fastened to her arms as she headed to the back.

In all, only seven or eight of them returned. These were the best disguise artists, as far as I could tell. The remainder—at least 30 women—we never saw again.

The last person to reenter the bus was the driver, also looking relieved. He wiped his face and headed straight for me.

"*Cigareta! Cigareta! Cigareta!*"

When I withdrew the Marlboros from my backpack and handed them to the driver, he held them so close to his face that I thought he might kiss the carton. It was the only one of the 500 we'd left Ukraine with to make it across the border. As he marched to the front of the bus, I noticed his pockets no longer contained any U.S. dollars. But he was focused on the glory of his one carton of cigarettes—a carton that might net him $10 of profit in Romania. For a country where the average annual income per person in 2008 was around $3,900 U.S., that one carton of cigarettes certainly meant something to the bus driver. By the time 2015 rolled around, the per capita GDP was exactly the same in a country that's struggling mightily to move forward economically. Every pack of smuggled cigarettes counts.

We had no idea what happened to the rest of the smugglers; were they fined, jailed, warned, barked at, or just left on the side of the road? Perhaps Philip Morris had a shuttle ready to pick them up and take them back to the factory so they could buy more cigarettes. Perhaps they'd dive back into the smuggling ring. This was, after all, a profitable business when you didn't get caught.

The driver started the engine and we rattled along the bumpy Romanian road. As he swerved to avoid potholes, he lit a cigarette and started puffing away. I still didn't understand the appeal; at the age of 29, I'd never even smoked a cigarette.

The green, hilly forests of northern Romania whisked by us as we gazed out the window. We passed a dilapidated farmhouse painted a faded red. In the distance, an older woman was bent over, working in the fields. As she glanced up at us and waved, I wondered which brand of cigarettes she smoked.

What's Left Behind

FROM *The Believer*

IF YOU'RE FROM Seattle, like me, you learn early in life that Montana is spacious, touristy, and full of wayward relatives who knocked off the grid a long time ago. You know about Glacier and Yellowstone and the lax speed limits on the swaths of flat, endless highway beneath limitless skies. And of the few big towns in the state, you know sparse details: Helena is the capital, Missoula is a liberal stronghold, and in Butte a flooded copper mine—the nation's biggest body of toxic water, called the Berkeley Pit—functions as a town monument, a plaguing reminder of the price of industry, and, for some, a lab of curiosity. Montana is a weird, wide-open space—it's the 4th-largest state in the country, but 48th in population density; a place where you can still write personal checks for groceries, where bars feature attractions like live mermaids, and where Americans and mine waste alike are seemingly left alone to do whatever they want.

For years, as you approached Butte along I-90, all-you-can-eat-buffet-style billboards recommended the bizarre detour of the Berkeley Pit, marketing mine waste as historic pollution worth visiting. A massive hole filled with battery-acid-strength water, the signs suggested, isn't a far stretch from picnicking at a battleground or an old fort, retired sites from a different sort of war. Eventually, administrators realized that advertising the pit as a tourist attraction was damning to the town's reputation and took down the enticing signage, but visitors can still pay two dollars and, from a viewing stand, enjoy a recorded history of the town and the breathtaking vista of one of the greatest American copper-mining calamities of the 20th century.

Butte's history has all the heroic and romantic trappings of Wallace Stegner's nostalgic frontier saga *Angle of Repose*. After fortune-seekers panning for gold in Butte in the 1850s couldn't find any, the town was nearly left to return to nature. With only a handful of tacit laws keeping the peace, and without a mother lode, most men moved on. But miners working for one persevering entrepreneur named Marcus Daly, who had the copper version of the Midas touch, discovered a massive vein of the brown metal in 1882 and transformed Butte into the biggest copper-producing city in North America and, at one point, the entire world.

Upon my first visit I knew about the grandiose Butte lore and the pit, and I knew the word "perpetuity," which the Environmental Protection Agency appropriated while deeming the pit a Superfund site under the EPA's remediation program. The word was potent and suggested lifetimes: of scars, of people, of a pit—challenges that come without instructions. Everyone deals with their own disasters in perpetuity, and at the time I had my own: gray teeth and a crisscrossed lip from an accident years ago, a hastily instigated breakup, friendships lost in gulfs of my neglect. This was how the people of Butte would deal with the pit as well: perpetually, for a very long time.

The morning I met Joe Griffin, the state of Montana's Department of Environmental Quality representative, I got into his car without knowing where he was taking me. My Virgil in a dusty Subaru, Griffin led me on a twisting road away from Uptown Butte, through intermittent neighborhoods with boarded-up Craftsman bungalows, rusted-out cars, and the skeletal remains of bars and businesses, their irrelevant signs still dangling from chains with joints that creaked in the light summer breeze.

We came to a final stop in front of the fenced-in Bell Diamond mine, its gate guarded with a heavy chain. The air smelled of hot springs and hard-boiled eggs, and the elemental presence of sulfur clung to my hair and clothes like campfire smoke. Unbeknownst to me, the reason we were at this particular mine wasn't to observe the steel, mantis-shaped headframe that once lowered men and horses nearly a mile underground, nor to marvel at the ground itself, sparkling with feldspar and pyrite like a mirror-ball. Instead, we had come to take in the view of the Berkeley Pit, which, upon first take, surprised me with its similarity to a natural lake that might hold minnows, boats, and swimmers.

Panoramically, Butte doesn't make a whole lot of sense. What most people would consider a downtown area—a space with tall buildings, museums, bars, restaurants, and government complexes —in Butte is called "Uptown" because it's higher than everywhere else. Everywhere else is called "the Flats": a suburban valley populated with big-box stores and car dealerships. Uptown, the metropolitan center, is an art deco masterpiece, a six-square-block area with a cluster of nationally protected buildings that are handsome and important the way Wall Street's once were. But overshadowing its stately and peaceful vista was the treeless pit, looking diamond-cut with its precise edges forming a mile-long, half-mile-wide arrowhead filled with water so brown it looked thick.

The damage of the pit, in its absurd scale relative to the town, signals the historic pillaging of the land. The discovery of copper beneath Butte coincided with the development of the filament light bulb, a product whose mass production necessitated an abundance of copper wiring. Since Montana would not become a state for another decade, copper companies were left to pursue their own interests without regulation. Butte became an ant farm, with mining corporations ultimately digging out 10,000 miles' worth of tunnels under the town, a distance that could comfortably span from New York to Singapore.

Heap roasting was a common technology that used heat to convert sulfides in crushed rock into oxides that could then be smelted and refined into valuable ore. In the process, piles of rock, often the size of city blocks, were set on fire and allowed to burn for days. Smelting was just as noxious, producing excesses of smoke and another form of waste called slag, a muddy slush that would then get dumped from factories into nearby waterways. Silver Bow Creek, which runs through Butte, became a flowing mine-waste disposal site. Smoke from smelting engulfed the town; residents complained about not being able to see across streets. Cattle and other livestock died of arsenic poisoning. Trees ceased to grow.

In 1955 Anaconda Copper, the largest mining company in Butte, adopted the technique of open-pit mining, whereby land is terraced away to create a spiraling hole in the ground. The company proceeded to dig the Berkeley Pit, a hole big enough to accommodate the Eiffel Tower, near the center of Uptown Butte, displacing hundreds of residents and ruining the morale of the blue-collar mining community.

Some geological nuances contributed to the environmental problems developing in Butte. The ground beneath the town is an alluvial aquifer, and consists of a watery porousness similar to the way fish-tank rocks sit loosely together. One of several abundant minerals in this soil is pyrite—fool's gold—which, when exposed to air and water, produces sulfuric acid. For years, companies spent significant time and money pumping groundwater out of mine shafts to accommodate tunneling miners, inadvertently also keeping Butte's pyrite dry. But when the oil company ARCO bought Anaconda in the late 1970s, copper was at its lowest price in years. To save money, ARCO decommissioned the nearly 100-year-old pumps. As the water rose, it reached the pyrite in the porous soil, producing sulfuric acid and mixing with the already existing pollutants. In 1983, once the tunnels flooded, the next thing to fill was the pit.

Catastrophe-wise, the pit falls in the middle of the spectrum. The Bingham Canyon copper mine, outside Salt Lake City, is nearly three times its size. Entire coal towns, like Centralia, Pennsylvania, have been evacuated because inextinguishable fires burn for years in mines beneath their streets. Though Griffin and I gazed out on a scene that was conclusively bad for the environment, I would learn that the pit struggles with a Goldilocks dilemma. While it isn't more disturbing than other sites, it remains the biggest body of contaminated water in the United States, and is essentially a walkable mile from Uptown—so close you could run errands to it on a lunch break. A sense of urgency also distinguishes the pit from those other sites: the contaminated water here is rising. If it reaches what the EPA has designated the "critical water level," which it is expected to do by 2023 without intervention, it will reverse its course and flow back into the water table. To prevent this, the plan put in place via Superfund is to pump and treat the pit water in perpetuity.

The Berkeley Pit is not likely to evacuate Butte. But to keep it safe and contained will drain money—millions of dollars—and attention, for whichever exists longer, the pit or us. All of southwest Montana is one big environmental liability in this sense: the region is infested with abandoned mines, an estimated 20,000 of them, each coming with its own hazardous idiosyncrasies and resting above the same watershed, which rushes out to the Pacific.

"If we all intend to keep going as a civilization, as a society, we still need copper. You're not going to stop progress. Nobody wants to give anything up, even environmentalists. It's a dilemma, really," Griffin mused. Even as we spoke, the Pebble Mine, in Bristol Bay, Alaska, one of the last unharmed watersheds in our country and the spawning ground of multiple endangered salmon breeds, was being proposed as a new copper venture.

"Obviously this isn't going anywhere. I mean, even if you thought, Let's take it somewhere, where the hell would you take it? So this will be here forever," Griffin said. The summer heat pushed down on us as the silent pit, an accident whose full resonance is still unknown, stretched far off to the edges of Butte.

I wanted to make sure I had heard Griffin right, that he had actually used the word "forever" in our conversation, so I consulted a hydrogeologist. Nick Tucci, who worked on the Berkeley Pit for nearly a decade, clarified some details. Tucci moved to Butte in 2003 to get a master's degree in geoscience from Montana Tech, an outpost of the University of Montana and one of the nation's preeminent mining colleges. For Tucci, Butte, with its flooded pit mine, was the perfect place to study. Tucci is articulate and sincere, and bends your ear about complicated subjects in a way that makes you feel like you are discussing something as accessible as the weather.

"There's no proven technology out there that we have right now to stop the water from infiltrating the pit," he told me. "I think whatever technology you use that exists right now, you are going to be pumping and treating forever. Right now, we just don't have the ability to clean up the Berkeley Pit."

But that hasn't been for lack of trying. In his time working at the Montana Bureau of Mines and Geology, Tucci had given out samples of pit water to varying types of scientists (some self-declared) eager to try to solve the problem. Tucci witnessed ideas that varied from snake oil to brilliant. "There was a guy who brought in crystals and thought he could arrange them in such a way that it wouldn't take the contaminants out of the water but would rearrange the molecules to the extent where they were no longer toxic. He was convinced it would work and he was going to show us by drinking it."

Other ideas involved evaporating the pit water with mirrors or sprinkler heads spraying the water over fields where it would evaporate, a method that has worked with other pit lakes (though there would still be the conundrum of water quality to address). One idea that Tucci liked, but wasn't sure was feasible because of its cost, was to fill the pit with mine tailings, a type of mine waste that's like dirt. Groundwater would still have to be pumped in perpetuity, but at least the surface area of the pit could be used for something.

Even without the end goal of remediation, the pit has served as a laboratory for diverse experimentation. Andrea and Don Stierle, organic chemists and old friends of both Griffin's and Tucci's, grew interested in the pit water when they moved to Butte from San Diego. While Don taught at Montana Tech, Andrea, who had originally planned to be a marine natural products chemist, decided to explore Butte's largest body of water, toxic or not. It's not uncommon for scientists to pursue bacteria growth in mine waste —anything thriving in a toxic spot could hold the key to its own cleanup—but no one had really looked into acidic mine water as something that could support life. To Andrea, life in the pit didn't seem too far-fetched. It posed a risky but thrilling challenge. She doesn't dumb things down, so here's how she explained it: "Nobody had looked in toxic waste for a bacterium or a fungus that could produce secondary metabolites that had biological activity that could be helpful. It seemed like a great idea!" It did.

The Stierles weren't initially able to isolate any sort of living organism in the water—until a flock of snow geese spent a perilous night floating on the pit's surface, resting their wings after flying directly into a storm. A black yeast that hadn't been there before started to grow in the water. Andrea sent the culture to a lab for identification and learned something unexpected: the yeast was associated with goose rectums. For years, scientists had been unsuccessfully throwing organic matter, like hay or horse manure, into the pit to see if it would yield new life. The night of the storm, when the party of geese realized that what they were treading wasn't exactly water, they fled the toxic pond. When birds take flight they evacuate their bowels to lighten their load and ease the process of takeoff. In this instance, an entire flock evacuated simultaneously and filled the pit with biological matter. Goose poop had made the pit come alive.

Prior to the discovery of the yeast, Andrea Stierle had already had many successes in her career. While in San Diego, she held a postdoctoral position at the Scripps Institution of Oceanography, and in the 1990s she discovered a fungus that is used to produce Taxol, a cancer-fighting drug, in the bark of the Pacific yew tree. Her focus was trained on the minuscule, and her process has always been to reduce her subjects to microscopic proportions and see what biological activity she could find.

In the pit, the Stierles had set out to find biological life with medicinal properties, similar to Taxol's cancer-fighting capabilities. In fact, the yeast was showing promise as having an effect on two types of ovarian cancer cell lines. But the yeast had another exciting attribute: it pulled metals out of Berkeley Pit water.

Acid-generating rock in the ground beneath Butte creates metal finds—or clusters—that clog filters and amass in wells. In the case of the pit, the finds are high in iron, which is responsible for the water's blood-red color. And as Andrea learned through her studies, the slime liked to eat, or sorb, iron. "This is one of the things this little yeast does exquisitely. It takes these finds, and if you add a drop of the yeast when we grow it in liquid solution and add it to a big flask of pit water with the finds, this yeast will take all the finds, drop them out of solution, and just form this little blob," she explained. "It's amazing. It quickly adsorbs up to 87 percent of a lot of the metals that are present, and that happens within five to ten seconds. It's almost magical."

In her lab, Andrea held a pipette with the yeast cocked over a beaker filled with Berkeley Pit water and dripped its viscous contents into the beaker. "Let's go, baby!" she encouraged the yeast. She swirled the beaker like a lowball glass of whiskey, the yeast twining in dark, wispy tentacles. In the midst of the swishing, the water's cloudiness diminished and a black, marble-sized ball formed in the beaker's center. The yeast had sorbed the metals that once polluted the water, which now did look clean enough to drink. Her slime was a glimpse of refreshing innovation, a repurposing of disaster.

*

Since grant money for people like the Stierles is scarce and there's a dearth of sustaining jobs in Butte, I wanted to know who was young and brave enough to commit the burgeoning parts of their career to a town that is, for all intents and purposes, extremely economically depressed. Griffin pointed me in the direction of Julia Crain, the special projects planner for the Butte–Silver Bow consolidated city-county government, and who is also involved in the Superfund program. Crain is a third-generation Butte resident —her grandfather helped build one of the town's first railroads— and holds a graduate degree in urban and regional planning from Portland State University.

Crain is ambitious and devoted to Butte, and Griffin, Tucci, and Stierle all agree that if Butte has one good thing going for it, it's Julia. She inexhaustibly writes grants for things that residents don't even realize they deserve. In its risk, hard-rock mining once represented the pinnacle of manhood, with miners working hard in the wretched conditions underground and living hard in the bars and brothels above. Butte is still a tough town, and this attitude can stand in the way of progressive change. But Crain is undeterred, and has been awarded millions of dollars to build recreational trails through Butte's public greenspaces and plant trees along Uptown streets, amenities the town didn't know it missed until it had them. Butte's been "taken hostage by its perception of itself," Crain says, in regard to its proud reputation as an overbold frontier town—which can cause her work, along with elements of the cleanup, to be met with occasional hostility.

But that's not necessarily a bad thing. "We know that dialogue here is really healthy and that people are really engaged, because every issue has contention surrounding it, and it's because people are holding fast to something they love. I don't think they're saying no to ushering in a new era; I think they want to be confident there's someone there to really carry it forward into the forever." Change needs gentle coaxing in Butte, but Crain knows that blooming late is better than never blooming at all. "We are playing catch-up. We had to spend thirty years cleaning up a bunch of contamination and figuring out how to protect the people that live here so they could stay. So it's not as though we aren't progressing; it's just that we had to take a different approach to [progress] because of the situation we found ourselves in."

Despite opportunity existing all around in subtle forms, no one was moving to Butte or staying in Butte for it. Instead, one might stay for the town's sense of everlasting potential and the belief systems built around it—just like in the days when Montana was still a frontier. "I think everybody here has their own romances, and maybe some people don't have the words to express it, but I know that Andrea Stierle was completely enraptured by the Berkeley Pit, and her research is the result of that," Crain explained. "You have to be capable of seeing something more, and that's how people can get through here. I'm not saying it's that hard; I'm just saying it's a diamond in the rough."

Thirty-five hundred feet above Butte, along one of the Continental Divide's arched ridges, stands a surprising, 90-foot statue called Our Lady of the Rockies. Our Lady took six years to construct, from the initial plans in 1979 to the final portion, her head, which was airlifted by helicopter to the top of the mountain in the winter of 1985. She looms protectively over Butte, arms outstretched in a come-gimme-a-hug pose. She is impossible to miss from the streets of Butte. During one of the city's economic downturns, miners designed and welded her out of donated steel to serve as a symbol of workers everywhere. She is as strange and Herculean as everything else in Butte: the patron saint of toughness. As the third-tallest statue in the United States, and painted a scorching white, Our Lady is Butte's very own Christ the Redeemer. And you can visit her, twice a day, by way of a shuttle bus departing from the Butte Plaza Mall.

I took the morning tour to Our Lady to avoid the hot July sun. The narrow, unpaved road, the retiree bus driver, and the bus that should've been retired were a nerve-wracking combination during the 45 minutes we spent laboring up the mountain. At the top, I scurried around the base of Our Lady, taking pictures that never managed to get her full figure in the frame. Around me, kids kicked at bushes and people put quarters into mounted binoculars, but the majority of the tourists kneeled and touched Our Lady, seemingly in prayer. The few people I spoke to on the bus weren't from Butte, or even from Montana, but were on vacation, and, as people who were either still working or had worked blue-collar jobs, had a reason to be on that bus: they were paying homage to a town whose culture revolved around self-reliance and whose entire workforce had operated around hard, hazardous, thankless work for generations.

Without realizing it, I had begun to fancy myself a pilgrim, too. Being engulfed in the wilds of national parks still fills me with the awe I first experienced out on Washington's Olympic Peninsula, where I spent summers growing up. There, the land is safe, and nature has the right of way. And it was in a national park, in my late 20s, that I realized that some of my favorite sensory perceptions, like the bitter smell of ferns after rain and the sounds of creatures scurrying through dried leaves, exist largely in places that are now protected by the government.

The lines between what is nature and what is natural have become blurred in my lifetime. Other mammals also consume the land: in Butte, enterprising beavers have depleted floodplains all around the valley with their dams. In getting what you want as a species, it sometimes seems impossible not to leave some sort of mark, but it is the remnants that have become my main concern. Since the damage has already been done, I want to know what we are doing with the damage—how we are transforming our destruction into creation.

During one of our conversations, Tucci, the hydrogeologist, said something to me that I had been thinking all along but had been afraid to say out loud, which was that the pit was beautiful. At first I had wanted to say that it was hideous, sinister even, but the pit's engineered tiers, industrialized terra-cotta complexion, and crimson water have a hard-won refinement, like western art scenes of dusty cavalcades and buffalo runs. "I think the research value of the Berkeley Pit is not quantifiable and the lessons that can be learned from the Berkeley Pit are not quantifiable," Tucci said. "People are going to come here, look at the Berkeley Pit, and know what we are capable of, and people will be cautious, hopefully."

Though on the morning of my visit to Our Lady I felt as though I didn't deserve a seat on the bus, by midafternoon I had decided the miners who built her would want me to believe she belonged to me, too, and that I was welcome to join my fellow tourists in praying at the folds of her steel robes if I liked. Even when it doesn't seem like it, there is a lot of connectivity in towns like Butte that masquerade as the edge of the universe but are really its center. Had I known at the time that we were all there because embracing our scars as they amass is difficult, and loving hard-to-love things is alienating, maybe I would've rested my forehead against her cool steel siding, too.

HELEN MACDONALD

Hiding from Animals

FROM *The New York Times Magazine*

I'M WALKING BESIDE a hedge of tangled dog roses in a nature preserve in eastern England, toward a hide, a building whose purpose is to make me disappear. This one is a rustic box with bench seats and narrow slits in the wall. Half-hidden by branches, it looks like a small, weather-beaten wooden shed. I've made myself disappear in hides for as long as I can remember; structures like this are found in nature preserves all over the world, and they seem as natural here as trees and open water. Even so, a familiar, nervous apprehension flares up as I reach for the door, so I pause for a few seconds before opening it and walk inside, where the air is hot and dark and smells of dust and wood preservative.

Alone, I sit on a bench and lower a wooden window blind to make a bright rectangle in the darkness; as my eyes adjust, I can see through it to a shallow lagoon under cumulus clouds. I scan the scene with binoculars, ticking off species—three shoveler ducks, two little egrets, a common tern—but my mind is elsewhere, puzzling over that odd sense of apprehension, trying to work out what causes it.

Perhaps it is partly the knowledge that wildlife hides are not innocent of history. They evolved from photographic blinds, which in turn were based on structures designed to put people closer to animals in order to kill them: duck blinds, deer stands, tree platforms for shooting big cats. Hunters have shaped modern nature appreciation in myriad unacknowledged ways, even down to the tactics used to bring animals into view. As hunters bait deer and decoy ducks, so preserve managers create shallow feeding pools that concentrate wading birds near hides, or set up feeding stations for wary nocturnal mammals. In the Highlands of Scotland, one celebrated hide gives visitors a 95 percent chance of seeing rare pine martens—lithe, tree-climbing predators—munching on piles of peanuts.

What you see from hides is supposed to be true reality: animals behaving perfectly naturally because they do not know they are being observed. But turning yourself into a pair of eyes in a darkened box distances you from the all-encompassing landscape around the hide, reinforcing a divide between human and natural worlds, encouraging us to think that animals and plants should be looked at, not interacted with. Sometimes the window in front of me resembles nothing so much as a television screen.

To witness wild animals behaving naturally, you don't need to be invisible. As scientists studying meerkats and chimps have shown, with time you can habituate them to your presence. But hiding is a habit that is hard to break. There is a dubious satisfaction in the subterfuge of watching things that cannot see you, and it's deeply embedded in our culture. When wild animals unexpectedly appear close by and seem unbothered by our presence, we can feel as flustered and unsure about how to behave as teenagers at a dance.

Two years ago, I was walking with my friend Christina through a park in a small English town when characters I've only ever seen in bird hides began to appear: camouflage-clad photographers with 300-millimeter lenses and expressions of urgent concentration. We looked to where the cameras were pointed, and were astonished. Three meters away, two of Britain's most elusive mammals were swimming in the shallow river running through the park. Otters! They didn't seem to see us; they certainly didn't care.

Their wet flanks gleamed like tar as they rolled in the water. They broke the surface to crunch fish in their sharp white teeth, showering droplets from their stiff whiskers, then slipped back beneath the surface to swim down the river, the photographers chasing them like paparazzi and intermittently running backward because the lenses they'd brought were the wrong ones for such close views. It was thrilling. We followed the otters downstream and stopped by a woman with a toddler and a baby in a stroller, who were watching them, too. She told me she loved these otters. They were part of her town. Part of her local community. They'd eaten all the expensive carp from the fishpond in the big house, she said, amused. Then she tilted her head at the photographers. "Aren't they weird?" she asked. Outside the hide, they looked faintly ridiculous, so accustomed to their binoculars, camouflage, and high-zoom lenses that they felt compelled to use them even when they were unnecessary.

Hides are places designed for watching wildlife, but they are equally rewarding places to watch people who watch wildlife and to study their strange social behavior. One reason I hesitated before entering the little hide is that I was worried there would be other people in it: walking into a crowded hide is rather like arriving late at a live theatrical performance and trying to find your seat. There are unspoken rules in hides. As in a theater or a library, you are required to be silent, or to speak in a low murmur. Some rules are to prevent animals' detecting your presence—a general prohibition on telephone calls, slamming the door, extending hands out the window. But others are more curious, stemming from a particular problem: your job in a hide is to pretend you are not there, and when there is more than one person in the hide, the sense of disembodiment that the trick relies on is threatened. Regular visitors to hides often solve this conundrum spatially. When she started visiting hides for the first time, my friend Christina wondered why people chose to sit at the far edges, leaving the seats with the best view unoccupied. "I thought it was self-sacrificing English etiquette," she said, "before I realized that people sat at the far sides of the hide because they wanted to be as far from everyone else as possible."

In the hide, there is a constant monitoring of others' expertise as the inhabitants listen to one another's muttered conversations about the things outside—and it can be agonizing when they get things wrong. I remember the chill in the air one spring day in Suffolk after a man confidently told his companion that what he was watching was a water vole. Everyone else in the hide knew this lumbering creature with a long tail was a large brown rat. No one said anything. One man coughed. Another snorted. The tension was unbearable. With true British reserve, no one was comfortable correcting his mistake and lessening him in the eyes of his friend. A few people couldn't bear the atmosphere and left the hide. It is always a relief when you open a hide door and find you are alone.

The uses of hides are as various as their inhabitants. You can sit with a camera hoping for the perfect shot of a passing marsh hawk or owl. You can sit with a proficient naturalist and hear whispered identification tips, or use it as a place to sit down midway through a long walk. Most people sit and scan the view with binoculars for a few minutes before deciding there is nothing of sufficient interest or rarity to keep them there. But there is another kind of hide-watching that I am increasingly learning to love. It is when you embrace the possibility that you will see little or nothing of interest. You literally wait and see. Sitting in the dark for an hour or two and looking at the world through a hole in a wall requires a meditative patience. You have given yourself time to watch clouds drift from one side of the sky to the other and cast moving shadows across 90 minutes of open water. A sleeping snipe, its long bill tucked into pale-tipped scapular feathers and its body pressed against rushes striped with patterns of light and shade, wakes, raises its wings, and stretches. A heron as motionless as a marble statue for minutes on end makes a cobra-strike to catch a fish. The longer you sit there, the more you become abstracted from this place, and yet fixed to it. The sudden appearance of a deer at the lake's shore, or a flight of ducks tipping and whiffling down to splash on sunlit water, becomes treasure, through the simple fact of the passing of time.

About Face

FROM *The New Yorker*

IF YOU WANT to feel bad about your looks, spend some time in Seoul. An eerily high number of women there—and men, too —look like anime princesses. Subway riders primp in front of full-length mirrors installed throughout the stations for that purpose. Job applicants are typically required to attach photographs to their resumés. Remarks from relatives, such as "You would be a lot prettier if you just had your jaw tapered," are considered no more insulting than "You'd get a lot more for your apartment if you redid the kitchen."

South Koreans do not merely brood about their physiognomy. They put their money where their mouths—and eyes and noses —used to be. By some estimates, the country has the highest rate of plastic surgery per capita in the world. (Brazil, if you want the title you're going to have to lift a few more rear ends.) The United States has sagged to No. 6, though we still have the greatest total number of procedures. It has been estimated that between one-fifth and one-third of women in Seoul have gone under the knife, and one poll reported by the BBC puts the figure at 50 percent or higher for women in their 20s. Men, by one account, make up 15 percent of the market, including a former president of the country, who underwent double-eyelid surgery while in office. Statistics in this field are iffy because the industry is not regulated and there are no official records, but we'll get to that in a grimmer paragraph.

In January I spent a couple of weeks in Seoul's so-called Improvement Quarter. This area is in the high-end Gangnam Dis-

trict, the Beverly Hills of Seoul. I realized that getting stuck in traffic would give me more worry lines, so my translator and I took the
subway, which is equipped with Wi-Fi, heated seats, and instruc-
tional videos about what to do in the event of a biological or chemical attack. The walls of the stations are plastered with giant ads for
plastic surgery clinics, many picturing twinkly cheerleader types,
sometimes wearing jeweled tiaras and sleeveless party dresses, and
often standing next to former versions of themselves ("before" pictures) —dour wallflowers with droopy eyes, low-bridged noses, and
jawlines shaped like C-clamps. "This is the reason celebrities are
confident even without their makeup," one caption read. "Everyone but you has done it," another said.

You know you are in the right neighborhood by the prepon-
derance of slightly bruised and swollen-faced men and women
in their 20s and 30s going about their business, despite the ban-
dages. Another clue: there are between 400 and 500 clinics and
hospitals within a square mile. They are packed into boxy concrete
buildings that look as if they were all built on the same day. (The
area consisted largely of pear and cabbage farms and straw-roofed
houses until it was treated to its own speedy face-lift in preparation
for the 1988 Seoul Olympics.) Some clinics occupy as many as 16
floors, and the largest encompass several high-rises. Most are more
modest. Tall vertical signs in Korean jut from the buildings and
overhang the sidewalk like unwrapped rolls of surgical tape. They
advertise the names of the clinics, several of which my Korean
friends translated for me: Small Face, Magic Nose, Dr. 4 Nose, Her
She, Before and After, Reborn, Top Class, Wannabe, 4 Ever, Cinderella, Center for Human Appearance, and April 31 Aesthetic
Plastic Surgery. There is also a maternity clinic that specializes in
beauty enhancement for brand-new mothers and mothers-to-be.

My translator, Kim Kibum, agreed to pose as a potential patient,
and I tagged along with him as we went from one clinic to another,
conferring with doctors about possible ways to remodel ourselves.
Kibum, a professor at Sotheby's Institute of Art, visiting his family
in Seoul, is 31. He is not considered young for cosmetic surgery,
which, like computer coding, competitive gymnastics, and Trix ce-
real, is for kids. A typical high school graduation gift for a Korean
teenager is either a nose job or a blepharoplasty, also called a double-eyelid surgery (the insertion of a crease in the eyelid to make

the eye look bigger), which is by far the most common procedure performed in Korea.

"When you're nineteen, all the girls get plastic surgery, so if you don't do it, after a few years, your friends will all look better, but you will look like your unimproved you," a college student who'd had a double-eyelid procedure told me. "We want to have surgeries while we are young so we can have our new faces for a long time," another young woman said. That is no longer a possibility for me, I'm afraid.

"Let's ask if they can make us look alike," Kibum whispered, at Small Face Plastic Surgery, a hospital that specializes in facial contouring, before we met with a consultant to discuss surgical options and to haggle over the price. (The cost of procedures and services in South Korea varies tremendously, but it is not uncommon to pay a third of what it would cost in the United States. As with Bloomingdale's towels and sheets, it's impossible not to get a discount.) Kibum has monolid eyes, a sculpted nose, a perfectly M-shaped upper-lip line, and chin stubble. I have none of those things, nor am I as handsome as Kibum. We were seated on a leather sofa in a purple-lit reception area that looked like the Starship *Enterprise,* redecorated by Virgin Atlantic. The women who work there—as in all the clinics that I visited—wear uniforms of short skirts, high heels, and tight tops. Their bodies and faces, aside from the occasional nose shaped too much like a ski jump, are advertisements for the handiwork of the Korean medical profession. Everyone is female, except most of the doctors and the barista at the coffee bar (complimentary cappuccino!) in the waiting room of ID Hospital.

I asked Kibum to explain the name Small Face. "Koreans, and Asians in general, are self-conscious about having big heads," he said. "This is why in group photos a girl will try to stand far in the back to make her face relatively smaller. This is also why jaw-slimming surgery"—sometimes called V-line surgery—"is so popular." The desirable, narrow jawline can be achieved by shaving the mandible using oscillating saws or by breaking and then realigning both jaws, an operation that originated as a treatment for severe congenital deformities. (Last year, a clinic was fined for exhibiting on its premises more than 2,000 jaw fragments in two vitrines, each bone labeled with the name of the patient from whom it was carved.)

Kibum and I paged through the "Look Book" of testimonials and photographs of former patients. (From a similar binder at Grand Plastic Hospital: "Pain for a short moment! Living as a perfect, beautiful woman for the rest of my life!" "I used to look like I had been starving for a while, with no hint of luxury. My eyes were sunken, my forehead was flat . . ." "Now I'm good-looking even from the back!") "When I was growing up, in the eighties, the ideal look was Western—sculpted, well-defined faces with big eyes," Kibum told me. "I would argue that that has changed as a result of the plastic surgery culture. Everyone started looking alike, so 'quirky' and 'different' came to be prized." Many dispute the notion that Korean plastic surgery today emulates a Western aesthetic, pointing out, for example, that big eyes are universally considered appealing and that pale skin connotes affluence. Still, just about everyone I talked to in Seoul confirmed the trend toward a baby-faced appearance. The Bagel Girl look (short for "baby-faced and glamorous"), a voluptuous body with a schoolgirl face, was all the rage. Another popular procedure is *aegyo sal,* meaning "eye smiles" or "cute skin." It entails injecting fat under the eyes, which gives you the mug of an adorable toddler.

In the Small Face reception area, a TV was showing a program called *The Birth of a Beauty.* The episode was about a woman who had always wanted to be an actress but, because of her looks, had had to settle for being an extra, until . . . you guessed it. Meanwhile, Kibum answered a new-patient questionnaire. Here are a few of the questions:

Reason you want surgery?
[ ] Preparing for job
[ ] Wedding
[ ] Regaining self-confidence
[ ] Suggestions from people

What kind of a look do you want?
[ ] Natural
[ ] Very different
[ ] Completely different

Which entertainer do you most want to resemble? _____

Do you have other friends who are considering plastic surgery? How
many?
[ ] 1
[ ] 2–3
[ ] 3–5
[ ] Many

If you get the result you want from plastic surgery, what's the thing you
want most to do?
[ ] Upload a selfie without using Photoshop
[ ] Get a lover
[ ] Find a job
[ ] Enter a competition for face beauty

We visited three clinics that day, including one that featured a
plastic surgery museum (complete with, among other oddments,
deformed skulls, postoperative shampoo, and a fun-house mirror)
and a flashy medical center (white leather sofas and marble floors)
that was investigated last year after photographs turned up on In-
stagram showing staff members whooping it up in an operating
room—blowing out birthday candles, eating hamburgers, posing
with a pair of breast implants—while the killjoy patient lay unconscious on the table. We met with three consultants and two doctors. The protocol often involves talking to a consultant, who then
briefs a doctor, who then looks you over and draws lines on your
face before you meet again with the consultant, who closes the
deal. In most of the offices, there was a skull on the table for educational purposes.

When Kibum asked the practitioners what they thought he
should have done, most asked, "Do you really need anything
done?" When I asked what procedures I might need, I was told
that, in addition to laser therapy and a forehead pull ("Asians
don't have wrinkles there, because raising your eyebrows is rude,"
a doctor told me), I should get a face-lift or, at least, a thread-lift—
a subcutaneous web of fiber implanted in the face to hoist my skin
upward, like a Calatrava suspension bridge—except that, because
I'm Caucasian, my skin is too thin for a thread-lift. I also heard so
many tut-tuts about the bags under my eyes that I started to worry
that Korean Air wouldn't let me take them aboard as carry-ons on
the flight home.

One doctor, as he talked to me, made a broad, swiping hand gesture that suggested that a lot of erasing was in order. Kibum translated: "He thinks you should get Botox around your eyes and forehead, and reposition the fat under your eyes."

Me: Does he think I should put filler in my cheeks?

Kibum: He doesn't recommend filler, because it's gone in eight months and you'd need a shitload of it.

Kibum and I didn't have the nerve to request that we be turned into a matching pair, but it wouldn't have been much of a stretch. Every doctor I interviewed said that he had patients who'd brought in photographs of celebrities, asking to be remade in their likenesses; or, for instance, with Kim Tae-hee's nose and Lee Min-jung's eyes. One doctor told me that he had a patient who showed him a cartoon that she wanted to resemble. (He said no.) Also, an increasing number of women are having procedures at the same time as their daughters, arranging for matching operations so that the daughters' looks are attributed to nature rather than to suture.

"Surgery tourists" from abroad make up about a third of the business in South Korea, and, of those, most come from China. One reason is that, throughout Asia, the "Korean wave" of pop culture (called *hallyu*) shapes not only what music you should listen to but what you should look like while listening to it. Cosmetic transformations can be so radical that some of the hospitals offer certificates of identity to foreign patients, who might need help convincing immigration officers that they're not in the Witness Protection Program.

We all want to look our best, but not since seventh grade had I been in the company of people for whom appearance mattered so much. In search of a clearer understanding of why South Koreans are such lookists, I stopped by the book-cluttered office of Eunkook Suh, a psychology professor at Yonsei University, in Seoul. "One factor is that, in contrast to Western cultures, the external aspects of self (your social status, clothes, gestures, and appearance) versus the inner aspects (thoughts and feelings) matter more here," he explained. Suh described an experiment he did in which he gave students, both at Yonsei University and at the University of California at Irvine (where he once taught) a photograph and a written description of the same person. Which format, he asked the students, gives you a better understanding of this person? The

Koreans chose the photograph, and the Americans chose the description. Suh, like others, partially attributes the Korean mindset to Confucianism, which teaches that behavior toward others is all-important. He elaborated, "In Korea, we don't care what you think about yourself. Other people's evaluations of you matter more."

Suh went on to explain that the two societies also have different ideas about personal change: "In Asian societies like Korea, a lot of people hold an incremental theory versus an entity theory about a person's potential." If you subscribe to the latter, as Suh claims we do in the United States, you believe that a person's essence is fixed and that there is only a limited potential for change. "If your American ten-year-old is a born musician and not a soccer player, you're not going to force her to play soccer," Suh said. "In Korea, they think that if you put in effort you're going to improve, so you'd force your kid to play soccer." So, in Korea, not only can you grow up to be David Beckham; you can—with a lot of work—grow up to look like David Beckham, too.

This is not a country that gives up. Surely one of the most bullied nations on earth, Korea, some historians believe, has been invaded more than 400 times through the years, without once being the aggressor, if you don't count the Vietnam War. After the Korean War, the country's GDP per capita ($64) was less than that of Somalia, and its citizens lived under an oppressive regime. Today, South Korea has the 14th-highest GDP in the world. Is it really surprising, then, that a country that had the resilience to make itself over so thoroughly is also the capital of cosmetic about-faces?

The national fixation on plastic surgery began in the aftermath of the Korean War, triggered by the offer made by the American occupational forces to provide free reconstructive surgery to maimed war victims. Particular credit or blame—you choose—goes to David Ralph Millard, the chief plastic surgeon for the U.S. Marine Corps, who, in response to requests from Korean citizens wishing to change their Asian eyes to Occidental ones, perfected the blepharoplasty. As Millard wrote in a 1955 monograph, the Asian eye's "absence of the palpebral fold produces a passive expression which seems to epitomize the stoical and unemotional manner of the Oriental." The procedure was a hit, and caught on fast, especially with Korean prostitutes, who wanted to attract American GIs. "It was indeed a plastic surgeon's paradise," Millard wrote.

There is a word you hear a lot in Korea: *woori*. It means "we" or "us" or "we-ness," but, as explained by Kihyoung Choi in his book *A Pedagogy of Spiraling*, it blurs into a collective "I." Choi writes, "When one refers to one's spouse, one does not say 'my husband' or 'my wife' but 'our husband' or 'our wife.'" (The divorce rate in Korea tripled in 2014.) "It is very important to be part of the *woori* group, to be part of your coalition or clique," Eugene Yun, a private-equity fund manager, told me. "This is the antithesis of individualism. If we go to a restaurant in a group, we'll all order the same thing. If we go into a shop, we'll often ask, 'What is the most popular item?' and just purchase that. The feeling is, if you can look better, you should. Not to do so would be complacent and lazy and reflect badly on your group." He went on, "It's not that you're trying to stand out and look good. It's that you're trying not to look bad." He continued, "This is a very competitive society. In the old days, if your neighbor bought a new TV or new car you would need to buy a new TV or car. Now we all have these basic things, so the competition has moved up to comparing one's looks, health, and spiritual things as well."

For the good of all, then, let's get back to the hospitals. Options offered at various establishments we visited included Barbie-Nose Rhinoplasty ("Let it up to have doll-like sharp nose!"), Forehead Volumization ("Your beauty will increase!"), Hip-Up surgery (to achieve "a feminine and beautiful Latino-like body line"), arm-lifts, calf reductions, dimple creation, whitening injections (called Beyoncé injections by one clinic), eye-corner lowering (so you don't look fierce), smile-lifts that curl the corners of your lips and chisel an indentation into the crooks so that your now permanently happy mouth looks as if it were drawn by a six-year-old (this operation is popular with flight attendants), and "cat surgery," to fix your floppy philtrum.

But most of the surgery performed in South Korea isn't usually too drastic, and seems technically superb. The blepharoplasty can take as little as 15 minutes ("Less serious than getting a tooth pulled," one man I talked to said). Unlike in America, where the goal is to have the biggest you-know-whats, the desired aesthetic in Seoul is understated—"A slight variation on what everyone else has" is the way Kibum put it. "Koreans are still very conservative," Kyuhee Baik, an anthropology graduate student, told me. "It would be a disaster for a girl to show cleavage—it would make you look shallow," a 19-year-old who'd had her eyes and jaw done told me. "You don't want to stand out," Baik went on. "That goes back to our Confucian foundations. It's a very conformist society."

"I never thought about doing plastic surgery," said Stella Ahn, whom I met at a coffee bar with her friends Jen Park and Sun Lee, all college sophomores." But then my father told me, 'You have my eyes, so I spoke to a plastic surgeon who'll make you more beautiful.' Afterward, I regretted it a lot. I felt: I'm not me, I lost my true self. My eyes were bruised at first, so they seemed smaller." When the swelling went down, Ahn came to like her eyes. Lee also had her eyes done at her father's urging. "He told me that beauty could be a big advantage for girls. For instance, when you go on a job interview if the interviewer saw two women who had similar abilities, of course he'd go with the better-looking one." It bears mentioning that, among the 27 countries in the Organization for Economic Cooperation and Development, Korea, where the pressure to get married is significant, ranks last where gender equality is concerned.

Ahn continued, "Before I got double eyelids, the boys didn't appreciate me so much." Lee concurred. I asked if they were ever tempted to lie and say that they hadn't had surgery. "These days, the trend is to be open," Park said. "The reason girls don't lie is that we don't feel guilty," Lee explained. "We are congratulated for having plastic surgery."

Remember *Queen for a Day*, the TV show in which a jeweled crown and prizes, such as a washer-dryer, were awarded to the woeful housewife contestant who could convince the studio audience that she was the most woeful of all the other housewife contestants? A version of that show, *Let Me In*, is among the most widely viewed programs in South Korea. Each contestant on the show—given a nickname like Girl Who Looks Like Frankenstein, Woman Who Cannot Laugh, Flat-Chested Mother, Monkey—makes a case to a panel of beauty experts that his or her physical features have made it so impossible to live a normal life that a total surgical revamping is called for. The contestants' parents are brought onstage, too, to apologize to their offspring not only for endowing them with crummy genes but also for being too poor to afford plastic surgery. At the end of every show, the surgically reborn contestant is revealed to the audience, which oohs and aahs and claps and cries.

There are a number of plastic surgery reality shows in Korea along these lines, but one, *Back to My Face,* has taken a different approach. I met with Siwon Paek, the producer of the show's pilot. In the pilot, contestants who had had at least 10 surgeries compete to win a final operation that promises to undo all the previous reconstructions. Paek emphasized that the aim is to help plastic surgery addicts come to terms psychologically with their appearance. Those with lower incomes, she said, tend to be the most compulsive about plastic surgery. "They feel they have no other way to prove themselves to people and lift themselves socially and economically," she said. Although the *Back to My Face* pilot was popular, Paek said that she will produce no more episodes. "I didn't have the strength to continue," she told me. The responsibility of changing people's lives weighed too heavily on her, she said, and finding contestants was hard. "For one month, I stood outside a dance club," she told me. "I solicited two hundred people. Most didn't want to go back to the way they looked before."

In recent years, a new Korean word, *sung-gui,* began to surface online. It means "plastic surgery monster." A college student I spoke to defined the term for me as a person who has had so much cosmetic alteration that he or she "looks unnatural and arouses repulsion." Not long ago, the Korea Consumer Agency reported that a third of all plastic surgery patients were dissatisfied with the results, and 17 percent claimed to have suffered at least one negative side effect. The agency keeps no official records of accidents or botched surgeries, but every few months there is a story in the newspaper about someone not waking up from the anesthetic after a procedure.

Amazingly, this does not seem to hurt business. Hyon-Ho Shin, who heads the malpractice branch of the Korean lawyers' association, told me, over tea in his office, "These days, there are so many accidents, and nearly every hospital has had a serious incident, so it doesn't matter so much. People who are having plastic surgery accept that it's a risk they take." Just before I arrived in Korea, a college student who had gone in for eyelid surgery died. Before the anesthetic was administered, the doctor offered to give her a bonus jaw operation free of charge if she allowed the hospital to use her before-and-after photographs. It was later reported that the doctor was actually a dentist. Shin estimates that as many as 80 percent of doctors doing plastic surgery are not certified in the field; these are known as "ghost doctors." A 2005 BBC report mentioned radiologists performing double-eyelid surgeries and psychiatrists operating the liposuction machine. Shin believes that nurses and untrained assistants are wielding the scalpel, too. Sometimes a hotshot doctor with a recognizable name will be there to greet the patient, but after the anesthetic kicks in it's hello, Doogie Howser!

Another surgeon, Dr. Ha, told me, "The larger hospitals have become factories. One hospital even sets timers in the operating room so that, for instance, each doctor has to finish an eyelid surgery in under thirty minutes, or a nose job in under an hour and a half. If they go over, there are financial consequences and verbal reprimands." These lapses have become an issue of national concern. Last year, a Korean lawmaker complained to parliament that 77 percent of plastic surgery clinics were not equipped with mandatory defibrillators or ventilators.

When the mother of South Korea's former president Chun Doo Hwan was trying to conceive a child, in the 1920s, she met a wandering monk who told her that she had the face of someone who would be the mother of a great man—unless her buckteeth got in the way of destiny. With dispatch, she knocked out her front teeth using a log. (Some accounts say that she used a rock.) Her son ruled Korea from 1980 to 1988 as a brutal and repressive dictator.

If it worked for Mrs. Hwan, it could work for you. It is not uncommon for a Korean who is considering face alteration to seek the opinion of a professional face reader—i.e., someone who offers advice on which nips and tucks will do the most good. The occupation grew in prominence after the financial crisis of 1997–98, when competition for jobs became fierce.

On my last day in Seoul, I decided to pay $50 to consult a face reader. "Should I smile?" I asked my translator, who communicated the question to a squat old man in a quilted Chinese-style jacket, who was, like so many others I met that week, gazing critically at my countenance. "Just be natural" came the answer. We were in the face reader's dark, tiny office, which was crammed with oil paintings, an old TV, drawings of the body segmented as if they were cuts of beef, and lots of tchotchkes (a Manchester United paperweight, a small Buddha, a piggy bank).

After asking me when my birthday was, the face reader offered some general truths. "He says if there is a scar between your eyes it makes you desolate from all your wishes and hopes. Then totally, yes. One should have plastic surgery," my translator said. "He says if there's a nose bridge that isn't straight enough, it disconnects you from your family."

But, I asked, what about me?

"He says your eyebrows look like you have a lot of friends," the translator said. "And your nose indicates that you are going to be wealthy."

Should I change anything?

"He doesn't have a bad thing to say about you. But your teeth might be a little weak. And you should eat a lot more beef."

D. T. MAX

A Cave with a View

FROM *The New Yorker*

TAKE ANY ROAD in Italy, look up, and you'll see a lovely hilltop town: a *campanile*, a *castèllo*, a few newer buildings spilling down the slope, as if expelled for the crime of ugliness. But even amid this bounty there is something exceptional about Matera. It clings to a denuded peak in the extreme south of the country, in the Basilicata region—the instep of Italy's boot. Travelers are often shocked by the starkness of Matera. It's a claustrophobic outcropping of cave dwellings carved into limestone, like scrimshaw, with hardly a tree or a blade of grass to be seen. In the afternoon sun, Matera looks like a pile of tarnished gold thrown down by a careless giant. Its severe beauty is as much a tribute to human resilience as to the rugged landscape where it is situated. Most places in Italy encourage you to celebrate the prettiness that wealth bestows: exquisite iron grillwork, festive marble fountains. Matera is more visceral —a monument to endurance and thrift, to hard lives lived without waste.

Matera may look inhospitable, but people have been settling here for a long time: it is often cited as one of the oldest continuously inhabited cities in the world, in a league with Aleppo and Byblos. There is something inherently alluring about this natural fortress, which towers above fertile plains and the Gravina River. A cave near Matera contains the remains of a 150,000-year-old hominid; another has tools and bones from 10,000 years ago, and dozens of Neolithic sites dot the surrounding ridges. Matera was already a significant settlement in the Bronze Age.

Because of Matera's narrow confines, rebuilding has been con-

stant, making the city a palimpsest in stone. A dig in 1906, near
the Duomo, in the town center, went 35 feet below the surface
and found Christian coffins and the remains of a Saracen invasion
from around A.D. 800. The scientists kept going, and below that
they discovered statues, broken columns, and money from the Byzantine occupation, of around A.D. 400. Farther down, they uncovered ancient Greek and Roman coins and, under that layer, bits
of ceramics from 3,000 years ago. Matera stands at what has long
been a crossroads between East and West. As Anne Parmly Toxey
points out in her comprehensive 2011 study, *Materan Contradictions*, Greeks, Romans, Longobards, Byzantines, Saracens, Swabi-
ans, Angevins, Aragonese, and Bourbons all passed through the
town. Man came here and never left—that's the local boast. Given
this history, it is jarring to learn that 50 years ago the government
tried to make Matera go extinct.

In the middle of the 18th century, Giuseppe Antonini, a baron
from Salerno, praised Matera for its "highly cultivated" citizens
and "its vast and extremely fertile countryside." The Roman abbot
Giovanni Battista Pacichelli, a contemporary of his, was likewise
impressed. The town, Pacichelli noted, was divided into three sections, as it is today. The main section, the Civita, contains grand
churches and picturesque palazzi; it is flanked on both sides by the
Sassi, or the Rocks—steeply graded districts where mostly peasants
lived. The pileup of the Sassi disconcerted Pacichelli: the roof of
a house, he wrote, could well be the floor of a church, "confusing
the places of the living and the dead." But he, too, admired what
was then a thriving ecclesiastical hub. The town was the seat of
an archbishop and, at the time of Antonini's and Pacichelli's accounts, a regional capital. From Matera, Spanish occupiers oversaw
part of the Italian Peninsula, eventually giving way to the French.

   Matera's status began declining in 1806, when Joseph Bonaparte
moved the seat of the region's government to Potenza, 60 miles to
the west. Over time, Matera became known as "the capital of peasant civilization." Rulers came and went, but the locals endured in
their cave homes, or *grotte*. Each morning, they descended long,
narrow trails into the valley, and worked in fields that were often
miles away. At dusk, they returned to the mountain. Much of the
communal life of the town was lived outdoors, in small courtyards
called *vicinati*.

Materans were tough and self-sufficient. They had their own rituals and songs, their own demons and dialect. Many of their traditions developed as ways of preventing waste. Using shared ovens, they produced a unique horn-shaped bread that was leavened and baked slowly, yielding large pores that helped it stay fresh for a week. Rainwater was captured by a complex network of stone basins and underground ceramic pipes. Resourceful as the Materans were, however, their lifestyle increasingly lagged behind that of the rest of the world. The better-off citizens of Matera began departing for the Piano—a more recently settled, flatter section of the hilltop—and the townspeople who remained in the Sassi were almost exclusively poor. In the caves, plumbing, electricity, and telephones were practically nonexistent. And until the 1930s you couldn't take a wagon drawn by a donkey into the Sassi, only a hand-pulled cart.

Within Italy, Matera came to be seen as just another out-of-the-way town in the impoverished south; among foreigners, it had a reputation as a picturesque troglodytic locale. But, as the world modernized, curiosity gave way to repulsion. It seemed grotesque for people to live in lightless dwellings alongside their animals. In 1853 John Murray's *Handbook for Travellers in Southern Italy* declared Matera "a dirty city" and noted that "its lower classes are said to be the most uncivilized in the whole province of Basilicata." Its problems seemed intractable: poor sanitation, brutal work conditions, malaria. Yet the population continued to grow, reaching 15,000 by the early 20th century. Half a dozen family members often crowded into a cave; residents used basins for toilets and burned the waste on the cliffs. Italy was falling behind the other nations of Europe, Basilicata was falling behind Italy, and Matera seemed to be last of all.

In 1902 Prime Minister Giuseppe Zanardelli visited the Sassi and reported that it awoke in him "not just amazement but deep pity." He proposed new railways, which weren't completed, and land redistribution, which didn't happen. In 1926 the archaeologist and social activist Umberto Zanotti Bianco called Matera "a Dantean horror."

By this time, the Fascists were in power, and Benito Mussolini was determined to bring his humiliated country up to date. Matera was an obvious candidate for modernization. He connected the town to the Apulian aqueduct, providing the Sassi with running water, but the Fascists were stymied by the prospect of overhauling the caves. One solution, they decided, was to depopulate the Sassi and transfer the residents to houses near their fields.

Mussolini was ousted in 1943, and, paradoxically, it was one of his opponents, the leftist Carlo Levi, who fulfilled the Fascist agenda for Matera. Levi, a doctor and a painter from Turin's upper class, had been arrested for anti-Fascist activities in 1935 and exiled to Aliano, south of Matera. He spent a year there, amid poverty that he would not have seen otherwise. In his 1945 autobiographical novel, *Christ Stopped at Eboli,* he described the peasants of Italy's extreme south as living "in a world that rolls on independent of their will, where man is in no way separate from his sun, his beast, his malaria." During his exile, Levi visited Matera only briefly, but his sister, also a doctor, passed through on her way to see him, and his book incorporated her observations of children "sitting on the doorsteps, in the dirt, while the sun beat down on them, with their eyes half-closed and their eyelids red and swollen" from trachoma. She described boys and girls trailing her down a path, begging for quinine.

Levi was a gifted polemicist, and his concise retelling of his sister's experience changed Matera's destiny. *Christ Stopped at Eboli* was widely translated, and the Sassi became notorious. Italian newspapers started calling Matera a national embarrassment. There were many villages in bad shape across southern Italy, but, as Toxey notes, the "mere idea of a cave, with its subhuman associations, offended the progressive mentality of the designers and leaders of the postwar world."

In 1950 Alcide De Gasperi, the head of the Christian Democrats, visited the Sassi and declared that "this sad remnant of past centuries should disappear." Two years later, the party passed the first bill for the *risanamento,* or cleanup, of the Sassi. Materans living in the worst caves would be moved; the more habitable *grotte* would be renovated.

At the time, the United States was funding the rebuilding of Europe through the Marshall Plan. With money flowing in, the Materan *risanamento* could be done with style. Italian architects were filled with modernist ideas for creating ideal communities. Problems of economic inequality that had never been solved politically might, they believed, be solved aesthetically. Materans would not be forced into generic new apartments; rather, they would be immersed in communities that reproduced the nurturing aspects of Sassi life—the courtyards where people met and gossiped, the communal ovens where they baked their special bread.

The Italian planners had in mind the ambitious example of the Tennessee Valley Authority, which had resettled thousands of Appalachian families. An American sociologist, Friedrich Friedmann, led a team of researchers—including a historian, a doctor, a geographer, and a psychologist—who assessed conditions in the Sassi. After architects devised several potential resettlement schemes, Friedmann's team asked the peasants which design they thought was best. In the new rural development of La Martella, four miles west of the Sassi, the architect Ludovico Quaroni attempted to recreate the open-air *vicinati* that the Materans had used as their plazas and drawing rooms. Each resettled family was given a house with an adjoining barn for animals; the bedroom windows looked out on the stables, so that residents could keep an eye on the beasts at night, as they had in the Sassi. The first families were moved to La Martella in 1954. The *Giornale del Mezzogiorno* declared that Materans had traveled "from the darkness of the Sassi to cottages in the green countryside!" Italian newspapers continued to support the cause, and the government began encouraging residents whose caves had originally been thought salvageable to move.

The process of moving the peasants, though, did not go as planned. Not enough land was made available for farming. The new *vicinati* did not feel like the courtyards of Matera—they were not placed at the juncture of several houses, so residents did not naturally spill into them. Ambitions flagged, and builders began putting up ordinary apartment complexes.

In 1961 a reporter for *La Stampa* found the Sassi empty but for a man and his lonely mule, which had been "made melancholy," its owner speculated, by the disappearance of the people it had known. In the article, the director of local tourism suggested, hopefully, that the Sassi should become a museum. The newspaper later reported that locals wanted to use cement to bury the Sassi—or dynamite to blow up the area. Such radical measures turned out not to be necessary. Long before the caves were empty, the oldest ones began crumbling, and the government began fencing them off. Matera's ancient settlement appeared to be coming to an end.

*

In fact, the Sassi was about to be reborn. Squatters began occupying some of the caves, and others were used for drugs and prostitution. Then Raffaello De Ruggieri, a lawyer who considered the depopulation campaign a grievous mistake, moved in. "People felt I was crazy to subject my wife to the desolation and emptiness of the Sassi," he recalls. The De Ruggieris were relieved to discover, however, that they had some friendly neighbors. Local artisans used the caves as workshops for making *cucù*—ceramic rooster whistles that are a town tradition.

Other young Italians began seeing the Sassi's potential, and they became homesteaders. Roofs were buttressed, and modern plumbing was installed. In 1986 the Italian government encouraged the Sassi's revival by offering subsidies that cut the cost of restoration work in half. Small shops began to appear, and in 1992 La Traccia, a software company, opened. "We came here because everyone else was boycotting it," Franco Petrella, one of the owners, told an Italian newspaper.

For a time, the new Sassi and the old butted heads. When a pioneering restaurant, the Caffè del Cavaliere, opened, someone set off a small bomb in its entryway. The *Corriere della Sera* reported that some new residents felt as if they were living in the Wild West, and were thinking of buying guns to fend off "harassment, requests for money, and acts of intimidation."

But order was established, and as the limestone hilltop was restored its rough simplicity found new admirers. In 1993 UNESCO named the Sassi a World Heritage site, and with that designation "tourism really began," according to Nicola Rizzi, a retired high school teacher who was born in the Sassi. Cave dwellings were combined to form restaurants and boutique hotels.

Materan culture, once thought backward, was now admired for its warmth and its precocious commitment to sustainability. By the turn of the millennium, the Sassi had a popular jazz club, and artisanal winemakers were storing their grapes in the limestone warrens. A candlelit cave set on a hilltop turns out to be an ideal spot for a holistic spa.

In February I flew to Bari, a port city on Italy's southeastern coast, and drove 40 miles, to the hilltop. To enter the Sassi now, you have to park on the edge of sprawling modern Matera, which sits along the western side of the old cave town, and go the final hundred yards on foot. The modern quarter was built on a plain above the cliffs, so you walk down a winding road to reach the Sassi. It was night when I arrived at my bed-and-breakfast, the Casa nei Sassi, which opened a few years ago. Light from street lamps installed in the 1990s reflected off the paving stones. Cats prowled alleys that glistened in a light rain. For centuries, the street where I was staying had been an open sewer; the Fascists had paved it over. In the 2000s, the strip became crowded with clubs and restaurants. It can get noisy during the summer, but is tranquil in the middle of winter. My room was at the top of a dozen twisting steps, in a converted hayloft, and it overlooked a bar where I sampled Padre Peppe, a Southern Italian liqueur made from green walnuts. From my balcony, I had a view of hundreds of irregular terraces, odd abutments, incidental buttresses, and half-hidden alleys.

The next morning, when the sun came up over the plateau that faces Matera to the east, I set out for a walk. You can get anywhere in town by way of the mazelike steps, but I took another road built by the Fascists, Via Madonna delle Virtù, which follows the edge of a thousand-foot cliff. Soon I stood on an outcropping—slabs of stone ending in a low wall. Behind me were the *grotte*, hunched and worn, one on top of the other. In the oldest part of the city, there are almost no stores, bars, or restaurants. Laundry fluttered from an occasional balcony, but most of the structures were unoccupied. Rows of vacant caves looked like giant skulls, with the empty doorways as eyes. The limestone walls were pockmarked, rain-streaked, and sun-bleached, and they varied in hue, from gray to yellow, as the light moved across them.

To see the new Matera emerging from the old, you have to look up the hillside. These residences have the best light and, being closest to the modern city, were the easiest to renovate. They first drew architects and other creative people, then arts professionals and Web designers, and, finally, wealthier types. It's like a tiny Tribeca. Many of the cave interiors have been playfully reimagined; in some, ceilings have been knocked out, creating three-story aeries.

On my walk, I came upon a four-star hotel, Casa di Lucio, which opened in 2001. In the hotel's windowless dining room, white laminate moderno tables were neatly aligned, and recessed wall lighting emphasized the pebbly nap and the roseate color of the limestone. A deep cistern was on display under glass. The hotel, whose rooms are spread out over several caves, had the one-of-a-kind glamour of the paradors that occupy former monasteries and fortresses in Spain. Nearby, in the basement of the Palazzo Gattini, whose owner was assassinated by brigands in 1860, there is a luxury spa offering hot-stone massages for 90 euros. An old cistern had been turned into a small swimming pool.

The new residents of Matera don't always seem imbued with the communal spirit of the old days: some property owners have fenced off *vicinati,* making the most public part of the Sassi private. As I went around the Sassi, I was relieved when I came upon a buzzing marketplace where apples filled straw baskets and smoked fish dangled from wooden trestles. An energetic young woman was currying a donkey and chatting with a young man and woman in rough clothes. A dusty wooden cart was leaning against a cobbled wall. But when the carter smiled her teeth were perfect, and the way the cart leaned against the wall was archly jaunty. This hive of activity turned out to be a movie set: a Hollywood crew was filming a new version of *Ben-Hur,* starring Morgan Freeman. Next to a 13th-century church, San Pietro Caveoso, a Roman eagle had been placed atop a newly constructed arch—the scaffolding in back gave it away. A crew had installed klieg lights above the ancient buildings. I discovered that *Christ the Lord,* an adaptation of the Anne Rice novel, had been filmed in Matera a few months earlier. When I went into a *grotta* covered with a bed of straw, I joked to a production assistant, "Is this where Christ was born?"

"No," he answered. "It's just a typical Roman stable."

Matera has played a prominent role in several biblical films, serving as a stand-in for ancient Jerusalem. Christ has walked the town's streets at least four times, most famously in Pasolini's *The Gospel According to St. Matthew,* released in 1964. I became used to men going up and down the stairways in tunics, skullcaps, and neon sneakers.

Visitors armed with new guidebooks that praise the Sassi's artisanal traditions sometimes know more about the town's history than locals whose families were transferred to the modern quarter. I walked by a handsome Renaissance structure with a precipitous view over a low stone wall, and asked a local policeman the building's name. "Convento di Santa Lucia," he said, adding that he'd learned it only recently, from Japanese tourists.

At the end of my walk, I looked across the valley, past a stream that had carved out the mountain on which the Sassi clustered, toward terraces of olive and fig trees. They were once cultivated, but now grew wild and unpruned. Across the gorge were weathered limestone caves that had sheltered shepherds since Neolithic times. Not so different from the refurbished *grotte* behind me, they seemed to mock the idea of human progress.

And yet Matera has an affable commitment to the young and the new. The town increasingly has the feel of a small Bologna. It has a branch of the University of Basilicata and a classical conservatory, whose students' music pours out as you walk under its windows. This winter there was an exhibit on Pasolini. Each September a women's-fiction festival takes place. A jazz festival, Gezziamoci, runs nearly the whole year, with performances in and around the Sassi, and a national archaeological museum, in a former convent, displays the riches of local digs. You can play minigolf in an underground cistern, and the new restaurants of Matera produce extraordinarily good food, turning what was once shameful into a source of pride. Matera's *cucina povera* contains a lot of chickpeas, fava beans, and crushed peppers. An especially delicious dish is called *ciallèdd*, which, in Matera, traditionally combines eggs, the springy town bread, and flowers that grow in the nearby Murgia. (Yellow asphodels are considered the sweetest.) Restaurants proudly announce their local sourcing, and waiters are happy to tell you the story of your dish, as if a parcel of Northern California had dropped into Basilicata.

This past October the European Commission named Matera one of its two capitals of European culture for 2019. (The other is Plovdiv, Bulgaria, a city that also traces its history to the Bronze Age.) Previous cultural capitals have included Istanbul and Marseilles, so the recognition is noteworthy for a small town in a region without an airport. The European Union has offered Matera 50 million euros for investment, and tourism will surely rise further.

The organizers of Matera 2019 have designed an official logo, a horn-shaped tube with six extrusions. Depending on which resident you ask, the image is meant to symbolize either the old communal courtyards of the town or its intricate water system. The town's pride in the coming celebration was evident: as I walked around the Sassi, the symbol showed up with Pynchonian frequency.

The EC designation is seen, in part, as an acknowledgment of

Matera's fraught history. No official apology has ever been given for the forced exodus. Half a century after the depopulation campaign, few cultural historians support the decision. It is now a shameful memory of a more desperate time in Italian history, after the trauma of the Second World War, when the country was intent on erasing its past. The transfer of Materans is seen as one of many patronizing attempts by elites to save indigenous people from themselves.

The town's mayor, Salvatore Adduce, told me that the depopulation of the Sassi was "a laceration." Despite the best efforts of Italy's modernists, Materan culture did not flourish outside the caves. Some former Sassi residents abandoned farming and became construction workers, building homes for other émigrés. When that work ran out, they moved north, to work in factories. Many Materans eventually lost their dialect, their customs, their trades, and —most of all—their sense of community. A number of those who stayed behind joined the Italian bureaucracy and contributed to the demise of their town's way of life. As Toxey, the author of *Materan Contradictions,* has written:

> In the space of twenty-five years, the government transformed the populace from a dialect-speaking, land-working, troglodyte peasant culture that largely existed outside the Italian nation into wage-earning, tax-paying, Italian-speaking state employees and blue-collar consumers . . . dependent upon the government for work, wages, housing (rented from the government).

Locals were excited when Matera was named a capital of European culture—the mayor cried on national TV—but the accolade raised difficult questions. How do you commemorate a disastrous social experiment? What should Matera become? What should the town do with all those empty *grotte?* And how should Basilicata handle the influx of tourists?

Materans agreed that they did not want the Sassi to become just another afternoon tourist stop. "We don't want busloads of barbarians setting up tents," Mayor Adduce told me. "We want people who, above all, can know what Matera is."

The artistic director of Matera 2019 is Joseph Grima, a former editor of *Domus,* the European design magazine. Grima's approach might be called anti–Olympic City: he wants to avoid monumental gestures. The only thing that he plans to add to the Materan landscape is a portable concert hall, by the architect Renzo Piano, that Grima found in a warehouse in Milan several years ago. The structure, made of interlocking curved wooden ribs, can be brought to Matera, used for a year, and then taken down again. It fits with the town's sustainable aesthetic, and is properly modest. Grima told me that he had thought hard about the EU award. "It certainly brings wealth, but it has also killed so many cities," he said, as tourists and destinations catering to them hollow out the real life of a place. He said of Matera that it would be particularly cruel to kill a city that has just come back from the dead.

Italy is constantly being confronted with challenges from its past: the palazzo too big to heat, the metro dig upended by a Roman ruin. At the same time, Italians like to say "Si fa"—It works out. Lately, though, things have not been working out in Basilicata. It is one of the poorest regions in Italy, and the unemployment rate is 14.7 percent. Its manufacturing jobs are being lost at a rapid pace, and between 2008 and 2013 the economy contracted by 13.6 percent.

One of Basilicata's few bright spots is the Sassi. Not only does it draw tourist dollars; the Italians who now fill the caves are better educated and better paid than the people who left them. They are part of the generation that is succeeding the failed industrial one. Alberto Cottica, a Web entrepreneur who was a consultant to the Matera 2019 committee, told me, "The people who moved in were hipster central." The Sassi has a lot of digital businesses—broadband is available—and it can seem as if every ounce of Matera's patrimony were being presented on local websites. Last year, part of a prominent ancient building was loaned to a millennial-led organization called unMonastery—a group of self-described "civic hackers" who run a "social clinic" that embeds "skilled individuals within communities that could benefit from their presence." (The group, now thriving, recently decamped for Athens.) Everything produced by Matera 2019 will be digitally accessible and copyright-free.

Grima champions Matera's new digital ethic, and notes proudly that there is no plan to build a conventional new museum or exhibit space. To collect the artistic riches from the region and put them on display in the Sassi would deracinate them, he argues. Instead, curators in Matera will construct an online database that can guide visitors to various local collections. "The region has an extraordinary abundance—much of it in private hands," Grima said. Matera plans to open a reading room to help visitors appreciate the region's cultural treasures, but the objects will remain where they are. Matera's vibrant virtual community, it is hoped, can replace the traditional one that the government destroyed.

One day I took a tour of the Sassi with a man named Vito Festa, who grew up in the district in the 1950s. He is unusually open about his past: many older Materans still refuse to visit the Sassi or even talk about it. Some of those who built new homes overlooking the caves made sure that there were no windows facing their old dwellings. They found it humiliating to confront the way they had lived before the government rescued them. They had been told they were filthy so many times that they had internalized the sentiment.

Festa had spent several years in the north of Italy, working as a technician in a chemical lab, but he was not embarrassed about his southern past. Now 67, he looked like many older Materans, with an orangey skin tone that resulted from spending so much time outdoors when he was young. Marching with him up the hill, I could see that he enjoyed revisiting scenes of his boyhood: the steep path where he had carried water jugs home to his family, the place where he and some friends had accidentally kicked a soccer ball off a cliff. He showed me the outlines of old cisterns and called up the names of farmers who had cultivated the olive and fig trees that now grew wild. Many of his memories were about struggling to get enough to eat: he pointed to a parapet where he had put down bird traps ("I never caught any"), and to the roofs where his family had left almonds to dry. "No one worried about us back then," he said. "Those were different times." It had been a community, he remembered, where everyone helped everyone else. As we walked, he bumped into old friends and joked with them in the traditional Materan dialect, which is spoken slowly, with open vowels.

Festa had a comfortable pension; the Italian system had done right by him in the end. We walked past the Duomo—where he and his 10 siblings and half siblings had been baptized—and past the town's one outdoor postcard vendor, then followed the narrow path to the Sasso Caveoso, the poorest part of the town, where he had grown up. He had no trouble finding his *grotta,* now abandoned and exposed to the weather. Mold grew on the walls, and some of the stone facing had flaked off. Archaeologists had dug into the floor, then covered their holes with straw. He remembered that the cave had two functioning lights, installed by the Fascists. Wires still dangled from the cave roof. His parents and his grandparents slept in the front, and he and his siblings slept in the back. Smiling, he said, "Una pazzia totale!"—What madness! He remembered that he and a brother had walked the family pig every evening before putting it in a stall behind their bed.

Festa's family left the Sassi in 1959, when he was 11, for Spine Bianche, one of the nearby developments built by the modernists. "We were so happy we jumped on the bed!" he recalled. He now owns his own house, in the north of town. As we drove to see it, I got my first good look at modern Matera. Given the economic difficulties of Basilicata, I was surprised by how vital the place seemed. It was a midsize city, with busy trattorias, a *via nazionale* that backed up at rush hour, and a dog-shit problem. We drove past a 10-foot-high statue of De Gasperi, the man who had emptied out the Sassi; his hand pointed upward, as if in benediction.

Festa's house is about two miles from the Sassi, on a street of flat-roofed two-story buildings that seem to pay homage to the old *grotte*. The interiors, though, could not be more different. Festa proudly went through his garage to unlock the main door. He showed me pear and grapefruit trees that he was cultivating in a tiny enclosed garden in back, the shiny marble floors, and the two kitchens—one in the basement for days when it was too hot to cook near the living room. Everything sparkled. The Sassi caves are celebrated for their lack of right angles; Festa's home was a series of perfect squares. Nothing had any history to it, except for one red rotary-dial phone, which was meant to be decorative. "I like pretty things," Festa explained.

Around every corner in Matera, it seemed, I came across clusters of new residents—the prime engines of revitalization in the Sassi. Many of the men had two-day stubble and wore jackets that kept them warm inside the caves. Bit by bit, these locals were reviving the city, with Web services, excavations, renovations, or small artisanal stores.

Some of them were members of Circolo La Scaletta, a volunteer organization cofounded by Raffaello De Ruggieri, the lawyer who helped lead the charge back into the Sassi. During Matera's dark time, La Scaletta had functioned like the Guardian Angels, watching over the town's patrimony; its members had saved rare frescoes and uncovered various cavern churches in the Murgia. "We had to choose between being the children of misery or the children of a proud history," De Ruggieri recalls. "We chose the proud history." Over time, La Scaletta expanded to include an organization called Fondazione Zètema. One evening, the Zètema group took me to a museum it had just opened, showcasing the work of José Ortega, a Spanish artist who died in 1990 and spent years working in the Sassi. The museum contained several papier-mâché works inspired by local artisans. The house had been beautifully restored, but it felt clammy; to warm up, I opened some wooden doors and went out onto a balcony. Matera is labyrinthine in the manner of Venice: you never know which direction you're facing. I was stunned to be met by the panoramic expanse of the Murgia, all empty blackness. Standing there felt almost like falling.

The members of Zètema suggested that I visit some of the rural cave churches in the area. In Matera, they pointed out, there was a confluence of Eastern and Western Christianity. Some of the town's Renaissance churches were deliberately built on top of the more Eastern cave churches of an earlier age. In Matera, the new has always covered up the old.

I decided to seek out a local "rock church" that is nicknamed the Crypt of Original Sin. It can be visited only by appointment, and is situated just outside Matera, along the Appian Way. Above the church is an enormous railroad bridge that connects to nothing—it was part of a failed attempt to link Matera to the main national railway lines. Approaching the cave in a car, I didn't see anything special. This was no accident: the monks who lived here, 1,200 years ago, did not want to be noticed.

A small group of Italians were also visiting the church, and so we all descended into a low underground chapel. When the group's guide turned the lights up, we found ourselves in the presence of half a dozen surprising frescoes. They were in the stilted Byzantine style, but they seemed imbued with an extraordinary modern sensibility: the flat figures looked at you with rounded, lively eyes, as if they might say hello to you on the street. The images, which depicted scenes from the Bible, were the least didactic series of church frescoes I'd ever seen. Mary was a warm, brown-eyed mother holding a baby in her arms. Saint Peter had a beard and mustache, like a Levantine patriarch. The joy of being alive seemed more potent than worries about the Fall. Eve held out to Adam a wonderfully suggestive fig, instead of the usual apple. In an adjoining fresco, Adam raised his arms toward God as Eve emerged robustly from his rib. God was invisible except for his hand; long and delicate, it was the hand of an artist, not that of the muscular world-maker depicted on Michelangelo's Sistine Chapel ceiling. Amazingly, the rock church had been entirely forgotten during the war and the years of the Sassi's depopulation. Now, like so much of Matera, it was found.

Born to Travel

FROM *AFAR*

I'M WAIST DEEP in water that's brisk only in contrast to the sultry air of a 90-degree day. The sea is the color of the sky, a pale wash of blue, and clear to the sandy bottom. But I can't see my feet. They're obscured by my pregnant belly, which is round and taut and frighteningly large. As I stand, acclimating to the faint chill of the Panamanian Pacific, a school of tiny, transparent fish moves toward me like a stampede of Pamplona bulls. Thousands of see-through fish in a see-through sea. I slowly lower myself into the shifting, undulating cloud of marine life, letting the buoyancy of my belly pull me to the surface, where I bob like an apple in a barrel.

From sea level, I look up at the nearby hillside—steep and cluttered with small, Easter egg–hued homes—and imagine my mother here, in this water, on this island, 35 years ago. At the time, she was 28 and several months pregnant with me, her first child. Her hazy accounts of traveling in Central and South America before I was born—"with you in my belly," as she invariably puts it— were among the defining origin stories of my childhood. And Isla Taboga, a 50-minute ferry ride from Panama City, was her first stop on a spontaneous, multimonth journey that shaped my perception of travel as much as any of the family trips we would later take. I'm now six years older than my mother was then, a travel writer by profession, and seven months pregnant with my own daughter, who is the size of a papaya, according to my smartphone app.

When my mom learned she was pregnant, a casual late-'70s encounter morphing into a lifelong commitment, my dad was not immediately enthusiastic. It was unexpected, and it took him a while to get used to the idea. Never one to sit around waiting for a man, my mom bought a plane ticket: first from the Bay Area to New York City, then to Panama, then to Ecuador. I've always assumed the trip was a simple escape—a sun-seeking last hurrah before single-motherdom, a way to show my dad that she didn't need him.

But during my own pregnancy, I've thought often about her months traveling in Latin America as a young, pregnant hippie and wondered what that time might have meant to her. A beautiful and creative but intensely volatile woman, Mom struggled with motherhood. The extreme highs and lows that define her temperament were not easy for me or my brother, who is three years younger and has a different father. My relationship with her has been one of the challenges of my life. It is this messiness that has made identifying with my mom now, as I prepare for motherhood myself, feel all the more urgent.

Though Mom talked about her trip often when I was a kid, it is now more than half her lifetime ago. Her memories, understandably, have become fuzzy and unreliable. My two days on Taboga were less a re-creation of her travels than an extrapolation, an exercise in empathy.

My parents never did become a couple, but my dad soon devoted himself to fatherhood, and the two of them raised me together-but-separate in rural Northern California. Both were travelers. My mom loved road trips through the American West with unplanned stops at kitschy roadside attractions, Native American powwows, and undeveloped riverside hot springs. Dad's adventures were fewer, farther between, and more ambitious. When I was 11, he and I spent more than two months traveling in Southeast Asia. Later, during my sophomore year of high school, he bought a sailboat, took me and my brother—who needed a father, so my dad treated him as a son—out of school, and cruised from San Francisco to the Panama Canal with us in tow.

In the 20 years since, my dad has spent half of each year on that same 44-foot sailboat, *Coyote*. Having circumnavigated the Caribbean, he is now—coincidentally—back on the Atlantic coast of Panama, in Bocas del Toro. So in addition to retracing my mom's steps, I've come to see him.

The trip began with a two-leg flight from San Francisco to Panama City via Atlanta. Tucked into my passport was an official-looking midwife's note scrawled on a prescription pad: "Freda Moon is pregnant and healthy. She is able to fly without problems." But on six flights in two countries over 10 days, my permission slip was never needed. What was needed, though, was a sense of humor.

At the SFO security check, I zeroed in on the closet-size cylindrical scanning device, eyeing it with a skepticism and concern I'd never had before. When the machines first appeared post-9/11, I'd been interested in their safety, long enough to do a Google search and never think of them again. Suddenly, I felt insufficiently informed. Erring on the side of extreme caution, I asked for a patdown and waited for a "female assist." When the middle-aged screener finally waved me over, she briefly examined my belly and announced, "You're having a boy!" She'd had three. She could tell.

"A girl, actually."

The screener's face turned sour. "But you're so . . ." She trailed off, shaking her head in disbelief as she slid the back of her hands over my breasts, pausing at the seam of my bra, scrutinizing the wires below my armpit. "Is that your bra?"

"Yeah," I nodded.

"I don't think you need that much support," she said, giving me flashbacks to my flat-chested adolescence.

She moved down, patting at my growing middle.

"Are those maternity pants?"

"No," I said. "They're just stretchy and rest low on . . ." I stopped midsentence. How did I end up here, I thought, justifying my wardrobe to a stranger as she gropes my crotch?

Fourteen hours later, I arrived in Panama City, where I was greeted with a simple but glorious sign: a stick figure with a bowling ball belly and an arrow pointing toward an empty lane. I was entitled, it seems, to bypass the snaking customs line—to stroll past the elderly couples with onerous luggage, the exhausted-looking families with small children—and enter a special aisle reserved for diplomats, the disabled, and pregnant women. As I slipped through international immigration and out of Tocumen International Airport in under five minutes, I felt like I was getting away with something.

*

When I stepped off the ferry in Taboga the next morning, it was barely 9:00 a.m., but the sun was already pulsing overhead. I was greeted at the dock by a sullen young man in a glorified golf cart. Taboga's only town, San Pedro, is patterned with a web of paved footpaths, and only a few are wide enough for these comically compact vehicles. After a silent 15-minute ride, I was deposited at Villa Caprichosa, an Italianesque seven-room inn incongruously terraced into the hillside above a tangle of clapboard homes.

My driver handed me his cell phone. On the line was a woman named Margaret, who explained that she was a friend of the owner, who had to go away unexpectedly. I was given the Wi-Fi password and told there would be no other guests that night, and I was welcome to use the private pool in the upstairs suite. I had the place to myself. It was thrilling, as if I'd stumbled upon an abandoned chateau, front door ajar. But I felt something else too—something out of character and embarrassing: I felt vulnerable. What if I go into early labor, I thought, flashing on a "Signs of Pre-Term Labor" checklist my midwife gave me during my most recent visit. There wasn't a landline in the room, and my cell didn't have service. If I shouted for help, would anyone hear? Would someone come?

Mostly, though, what I felt was hunger. Other than an energy bar I had brought from home, I'd barely eaten since the day before. It was the Monday of Semana Santa, the Holy Week preceding Easter, and San Pedro was sedate. I opted for food at the first open restaurant I saw, the bougainvillea-draped Vereda Tropical, where I had the dining room to myself and was served a tortilla-less rendition of huevos rancheros. Afterward I climbed back uphill to Caprichosa. It was almost noon. The sun scorched, and each concrete step felt like a hurdle. By the time I made it to my room, all I could do was change into a bikini, guzzle water from the mini-fridge, and collapse on the bed beneath a ceiling fan. Two hours later, I woke without having realized I'd fallen asleep. It was my first taste of the tropics as a pregnant woman, and I'd been defeated by a 10-minute walk in the midday heat. I spent the rest of the afternoon alternating between a miniature faux infinity pool and the shade of a red umbrella. From the heights of Caprichosa's plant- and sculpture-filled terrace, I could see the beach, a narrow shard of sand that at low tide joins Taboga with El Morro, a small, rocky mound just offshore.

I made my way down to the ocean and am now bobbing like an apple. In the distance, there is a field of freighters that recall childhood games of Battleship. Hulking, rusted beasts with stark paint jobs—black, white, red, and blue—the ships look like floating factories, wrapped in industrial pipes and chugging exhaust. Beyond them, the skyline of Panama City is a metropolitan landscape of jagged jack-o'-lantern teeth. Though Taboga's beaches are immaculate, it is hard not to think of that field of working ships, that ugly urban runoff. The pool, I tell myself, poses no such risks, and I return to my aerie.

I wouldn't say I'm lazy on Taboga so much as purposeless. Twice a day, I walk to one end of town and back again. I stroll the paths and climb the stairs and sit on the beach and register the details of the place: the Catholic altars embedded in concrete walls, the large frogs that startle at my feet, the particular way the evening wind off the water rattles the bougainvillea vines. They're the kinds of things you notice when you're alone. Then I think, *This is probably the last time I will be alone for a very long time.*

But I don't feel alone. Not in the way I used to. I now understand why every story of my mom's time in Central and South America included me, as if I were a companion, a fellow traveler. What I'd always seen as one of her many eccentricities has revealed itself to be a bond I didn't know we had. Not the bond of mother and daughter, but the bond of mothers who travel—who insist on traveling even when we are told again and again that having children means our days of travel are behind us.

As a rule, I don't think men should receive special praise for being parents to their children. But my dad was an unusual father. A single dad in the late 1970s, before it was cool, he shared me with my mom—an equal parent, by his telling, caring for an infant by himself for days at a time. We've always been close, but in recent years we'd lived on opposite sides of the country and I'd seen him less. My pregnancy, and his impending grandparenthood, compelled me to close that gap. Spending more time together became a priority. All the better if I could see him while also being weightless in a warm ocean, drinking *maracuyá* (passion fruit) juice, eating just-caught fish, and revisiting a place, Panama, that has played a recurring role in my life since before I was born.

By the time I step off the prop plane and onto the blazing runway in Bocas del Toro, my dad has been here for two months, working on getting *Coyote* ready for another Canal crossing and its next ambitious passage: a single-handed transpacific sail to Hawaii, perhaps. At 70, he is recovering from his fourth hip replacement. Meanwhile, his dinghy, the small inflatable motorboat that is a cruising sailor's primary local transportation, was stolen last year and has yet to be replaced. In every way that matters to him, my dad is less mobile than he'd like. When I arrive, he seems restless but eager to introduce me to his friends at the marina, excited by the prospect of me planning and being in charge of our adventures for once.

Bocas Marina is separated from town by mangroves and saltwater channels and is accessible only by boat. Dad relies on water taxis, which charge a dollar per person, to get him back and forth. But, he tells me, he rarely makes the trip to town. I can see why. In recent years, Bocas has become a stop on the international backpacking-and-partying circuit. Its waterfront is lined with stilted buildings in Caribbean-pastel tints: hotels, tour companies, and dance clubs that advertise "Nasty Monday" specials ($1 beer bong and $1 tequila shots) and Organic Trance, a genre of music that apparently makes heavy use of the didgeridoo. Restaurants have slogans like "No Place Like Om" (at an Indian vegetarian spot) and "Store in a Cool Place" (at the Super Gourmet kosher deli). Between the dreadlocked travelers selling handmade jewelry and the blond revelers in short shorts dancing on hostel balconies, Bocas could just as easily be Thailand or India or anywhere else on the sun, surf, and cheap drugs itinerary.

None of that is my father, but not because he's 70 or because he's stuffy. A believer in the enduring power of the counterculture, Dad is not uncomfortable with eccentricity or queasy at the spectacle of youth. But he's also not overly enthused about spending time in a crowd of strangers. While I travel for culture—for food and architecture, history and art—Dad travels, above all else, for nature. Sailing, and seeing the world at eight knots per hour, appeals to him because it means experiencing places that aren't accessible to most of us. Dad doesn't dislike Bocas, but for him it is a means to an end. That end is the hundreds of largely uninhabited islands that lie just southeast of here, in the San Blas archipelago.

For me, on the other hand, this trip has taken on a weight and meaning beyond its scope. After years of being told that having children will change everything (a truism that, when spoken by people with kids to those without them, can sound like a threat), this is my last chance to travel as the person I've been.

Being my father's daughter hasn't been my primary identity for decades. But as I prepare to become a parent myself, I'm acutely aware of the anchor he has been in my life. My dad becoming a grandfather makes him mortal for me in a way that he has somehow escaped until now. He's not a religious man, and when he talks about having a grandchild, he seems more at ease with aging —and with death—than I can ever remember him being. "It's a total trip," he tells me. "Becoming a grandfather puts me in touch with something cosmic—something beyond my everyday life. It plugs me into something greater and beyond any of us."

My first full day in Bocas is Good Friday, which the mayor has declared a dry holiday. There is to be no alcohol sold anywhere, and the sailors of Bocas Marina are not happy. But they have a plan. A small group arranges for two *pangas* to shuttle them to the Blue Coconut, a bar-restaurant built above the water off Solarte, one of the outlying islands. Dad and I decide to join—though more for the company and the easy access to a clean, swimmable bay than for the bar's signature curaçao cocktail. We sit for hours that afternoon beneath the thatched roof as a half-dozen sailors drink Balboa beers and trade stories. At one point, Dad rolls out one of his favorites from Southeast Asia: the time I befriended a small, cheerful monkey, spending every moment I could with it over the course of weeks, only to have it turn one day and bite me.

When I was a kid, our adventures were big. I snorkeled with sharks in Palau, stumbled upon massive anti-American protests in the Philippines, and stepped up as a vital crew member as we sailed into drenching, violent rain. But our four days together in Bocas are made up of smaller, sweeter moments.

In that short span, we hit more "sights" than Dad has likely visited in his months on the island. We go to Playa Estrella, where the Semana Santa fiesta is in full swing. There are DJ booths, banana boats, wasted tourists, and large local families celebrating despite a drizzle. Someone in the crowd calls, "Oye, mamá, ¡baile!" and I give a quick shimmy. Dad and I find the quietest piece of sand we can and spend a couple of hours wading into the water, out of place among the throng. We go on a snorkeling excursion, where we swim among platter-shaped fish and Seussian corals. We visit the botanical garden and search for snakes, sloths, and monkeys among the foliage, but find only plants—common U.S. house-plants supersized by the near-equatorial climate. I know the pack-aged nature is underwhelming for Dad. But his spirits are high. He seems to relish his role as a father, talking me up to anyone who will listen. When we meet parents traveling with young kids, it takes him back. "Remember when . . . ," he says. Or, "Where was that?" Or simply, "That was such a great trip." Will I have the guts to take my kid out of school to go sailing?

This, I realize, is what I had come to Panama for. I wasn't here for the beauty of the place, though it is stunning. I'd come for the concentrated time with my dad. Just him and me. The last time we'd traveled alone together was 14 years before, when I was in college and had just met my now-husband, Tim—and any travel-ing we do together from now on will almost certainly be as a larger, noisier family. For me, this trip was a bookend. But it was also a much-needed reminder of the joy Dad took in traveling as a par-ent and, therefore, what I might hope for—and aspire to—myself.

One morning, we take a water taxi into town, curious to see what tours might be within reach of a very pregnant woman and a soon-to-be-grandfather recovering from major surgery. We walk up and down the main drag, but I'm irritated by the hustling sales-men, and, since taking a tour was my idea, I feel the pressure of choosing the right one. So I procrastinate, and instead of buying tickets, Dad and I end up at the Super Gourmet, where we find our favorite ice cream, Häagen-Dazs coffee, buried deep at the bottom of the freezer case. As we sit on the sidewalk outside, the Doors' "Hello, I Love You" hums through the market's speakers. Plastic spoons in hand, barely saying a word, we devour the entire carton.

The Reddest Carpet

FROM *GQ*

KIM JONG-IL LOVED the movies. After a hard day running the world's most oppressive regime, the jumpsuit-clad dictator would, according to local lore, repair to his private cinema deep inside a Pyongyang bunker, where he'd select his entertainment from a collection of 20,000 videos. The Dear Leader, who ruled North Korea from 1994 to 2011, was reputed to worship *Rambo*, and it requires little imagination to picture him chortling at the explosions, the macho dialogue, the buxom actresses, the sheer charisma of the vigilante.

Comrade Kim—whose official titles included Iron-Willed Brilliant Commander and Guiding Star of the 21st Century—died in 2011, and yet he attends the movies still, in a manner of speaking. Here he is now, in a sprawling mural on the wall of the Ponghwa Art Theatre lobby, standing alongside his father, the Great Leader and Eternal President Kim Il-sung, surrounded by smiling soldiers and dancing women and cheering masses. Together they welcome guests and delegates to a very special event: the opening ceremony of the biennial Pyongyang International Film Festival.

I'm standing below the mural, staring gape-jawed at the Kims as attendees file into the auditorium. Swirling around me are military men in olive uniforms and half-moon hats, high-ranking government officials with jet-black hair, and hardworking citizens of the capital decked out in fine suits and traditional dresses that look like Christmas trees. There's also an oddball assortment of foreign delegates from countries as far-flung as Myanmar and Iran.

The communist government of Kim Jong-il's apple-cheeked son, Kim Jong-un, has allowed exactly eight tourists to attend the festival. I am one of them. We're a collection of curious film buffs who have paid a group called Koryo Tours about $2,000, on top of airfare to and from Beijing, for the privilege of visiting the secretive Democratic People's Republic of Korea.

It's a strange time to be in the country: just three days ago, a 25-year-old American named Matthew Miller was sentenced to six years of hard labor for tearing up his tourist visa upon arrival because of a "wild ambition," he supposedly said, to see a North Korean prison. Meanwhile, two other Americans are languishing in the country's penal system for alleged Christian proselytizing. This is all while Seth Rogen and James Franco are preparing to promote *The Interview,* the Kim Jong-un assassination comedy that will ultimately provoke North Korean sympathizers to launch an epic cyberattack on Sony Pictures, nearly forcing the studio to abort the film's release—which shouldn't have been surprising, for this is a country that treats cinema as a matter of life and death.

"Let's go!" says Miss P, our petite headmistress of a guide, trying to usher us to our seats in the auditorium. We're lingering in the lobby. Miss P is wearing cat-eye glasses and a no-nonsense skirt and blouse, and making clear on our first full day in the country that she disapproves of lingering. *"Let's go!"*

Miss P leads us past two young women in flight-attendant outfits offering cups of a sugary carbonated apple drink, and past a bustling concession stand selling cans of coffee, bags of dried banana slices, and mystery-meat wieners. Meanwhile our other local guide, Mr. O, a 30-something man with square glasses, a dimpled smile, and frizzy hair that perpetually looks like it's just been towel-dried, corrals a few members of the group who've wandered off to take photos. Miss P looks like she's about to burst a blood vessel. "Come on," she says. "The ceremony will begin."

The eight of us take our seats together in a row. I'm sitting beside Koryo's tour leader, Vicky, a sardonic Scottish expat who lives in Beijing and is on her 10th trip to the DPRK. On my right is Andrew, a friendly man with a peppery gray beard who is the No. 1 Tupperware salesman in the United Kingdom. Farther down is Roman, a dreadlocked Polish DJ who's writing his master's thesis on North Korean cinema, and Hyae-shook, a Korean Canadian housewife whose parents fled from the North before the war. In the aisle in front of us is the photo crew: Yuri, from Moscow, secretly shooting for *GQ*, and Mark, a bon vivant from Los Angeles.

Koryo's representatives have told us we'll be safe as long as we don't do anything stupid. But I can't help wondering what happens if the North Koreans find out I'm a journalist. Does reporting on the film fest qualify as "something stupid"?

The festival's hosts—two women and a man—appear onstage to light cheering. They welcome guests in Korean and awkward English. The ceremony's vibe is Eurovision meets grade-school pageant.

Above the stage is a suspended plastic dove that looks like it's pooping out a rainbow-colored film reel. A sunrise graphic playing on a screen in the back appears to have been made on Windows 95. The hosts call to the stage the minister of culture, a squat, bullet-shaped man. "During the festival, you will be able to witness with your own eyes the reality of Korea," he says in the halting monotone of a career bureaucrat. "In which the beautiful dream and ideal of the people come into full bloom, as well as the confidence and optimism of the Korean people, who are making a dynamic struggle to build a thriving nation under the wise leadership of the dear respected Kim Jong-un."

After a few more speeches and song-and-dance performances, the hosts announce the opening picture: *Fast Girls*, a low-budget 2012 British drama about female track-and-field hopefuls, whose rippling muscles and nubile buns get enough screen time to become characters unto themselves. The story centers on a sprinter recruited to the national relay squad. At first her rebellious streak makes her an awkward fit, but—in a common North Korean movie trope—she ultimately learns the value of teamwork and cooperation.

We sit back and take in the movie, oblivious and numb. That's the power of film, of course, and a clue as to why the dictatorship would allow it. And the local film crews scattered throughout the auditorium, whose cameras are often pointed in our direction, provide a clue as to why the regime would allow *us*.

As the credits roll, the audience politely applauds. "And the crowd goes wild!" Vicky says drily. "That was pretty shite."

It almost doesn't matter. The world's most unlikely film festival is under way.

*

The Yanggakdo International Hotel—aka Festival HQ and our home for the duration of the trip—looms like a spectral fortress in the middle of Pyongyang. It's situated on a small island halfway across the moat-like Taedong River, which conveniently prevents mischievous tourists from giving their guides the slip. The place is basically Alcatraz with a pool—and a bowling alley, brewpub, billiards room, Egyptian-themed casino, revolving rooftop restaurant, and a "full body" massage parlor in the basement.

Visitors often compare Pyongyang to a movie set. More specifically, it's like *The Truman Show*. It's as if every person, every object, has been placed there especially for you. There's something costumey about the way people dress, and something dialoguey about the way they talk. You can also learn a lot by what's unseen: garbage, pets, glowing restaurant signs, shopping malls. Look closely and everything seems cheap and staged.

In this respect, the city makes a natural setting for a film festival —a celebration of the imagination. PIFF was launched in 1987 as the Pyongyang Film Festival of Non-Aligned and Other Developing Countries. This was toward the end of North Korean cinema's golden age, a real thing that existed almost entirely due to the unbridled enthusiasm of Kim Jong-il, who served as minister of culture before grabbing North Korea's unsteady reins after his father's death.

The Dear Leader still casts a girthy shadow over North Korean cinema. He wrote not one but two treatises on film—*On the Art of the Cinema* (1973) and *The Cinema and Directing* (1987)—that continue to steer the country's movie industry. The books are filled with weirdly precise directives about how film can serve the country's *juche* (loosely, "self-reliant") ideology. A pretty standard example: "A writer who is to serve the people must naturally have a deep interest in their lives, and be quick to recognize the urgent problems which can be used to raise the level of their class consciousness and to advance society, and must strive to solve them in the interests of the revolution."

In the decades after the DPRK's founding in 1948, movies were used to reinforce and perpetuate the national myths: the fatherly wisdom of the leaders, the virtue of sacrifice to the nation, the importance of the collective over the individual. (Schoolchildren and workers attended mandatory film screenings as a means of ideological training even as the country struggled to feed its own people.) Though fewer in number than in the heyday of the 1970s and '80s, most films produced in recent years follow the same formula.

Kim is said to have dabbled behind the camera himself, supposedly producing such films as 1969's *Sea of Blood,* a black-and-white epic set during the Japanese occupation. In 1978 he allegedly ordered the kidnapping of the South Korean director Shin Sang-ok, who served four years in a prison camp—surviving, Shin later said, on "grass, rice, and salt"—before finally agreeing to make movies alongside the Dear Leader. By then Kim had grown despondent about the state of the North Korean film industry. Unbothered by more pressing issues facing his country, Kim sent filmmakers to East Germany, Czechoslovakia, and the Soviet Union to learn the latest techniques, but North Korean movies still paled compared with those made overseas. "I have been struggling with this problem for five years," Kim told Shin in 1983. "We have to know that we are lagging behind and make efforts to raise a new generation of filmmakers."

Kim and Shin embarked on a mission to create a new type of North Korean movie, one that both entertained and indoctrinated. The duo made seven films together, the best-known of which is 1985's *Pulgasari,* a $3 million monster movie often called North Korea's *Godzilla.* The director escaped in 1986 while on a film junket in Vienna, fleeing to the U.S. embassy. The film lives on, however, on YouTube.

PIFF now receives around 500 submissions from more than 50 countries. This year, 29 movies are screening in three competitive categories—features, documentaries, and shorts and animation —with another 63 shown out of competition. (Still, the delegates I speak with during my stay view PIFF more as a novelty than as a serious stop on the festival circuit.) The festival's lineup is stocked with pictures that will never reach a theater in the United States: Myanmar's *The Moon Lotus,* for example, alongside India's *Singh Saab the Great* and an Egyptian documentary called *I'm Tremendously Happy That I'm Going to Play Golf.*

If nothing else, the festival allows some basic interaction between North Korea and the outside world. Dozens of delegates are here screening films from all over the globe, and that qualifies as cultural exchange, even if those movies aren't *12 Years a Slave.* It's about baby steps. But there's a flip side: Hosting an international film fest is also a chance for the regime to say, *Citizens, look at how open we are! Witness these many foreigners flocking here to show us their movies!* "Of course, it's a big propaganda event," says Johannes Schönherr, author of *North Korean Cinema: A History* and a festival delegate in 2000. "And of course, foreigners who attend the event become extras in the big propaganda show."

The morning after the opening ceremony, after a breakfast of eggs and "rice gruel" from the hotel buffet, we're taken on a tour of the sprawling Pyongyang Film Studio, which is sometimes called North Korea's Hollywood. It's a peculiar moniker, considering no films are actually being shot here during our visit. The studio puts out just a handful of movies a year, a distant cry from the days when Kim Jong-il was an on-set fixture. It's now essentially a propaganda tool, like the movies it once pumped out, suggesting a booming industry that doesn't really exist.

Today the lot is crawling with school groups. We walk through empty sets made to look like ancient times and others resembling midcentury Europe and China. South Korea Street, as it's called, portrays the "puppet" state on the other side of the DMZ as debauched and morally bankrupt. There's bar after fake bar, ads for Suntory Brandy, and a hand-painted poster for Marilyn Monroe's *The Seven Year Itch.*

In the afternoon, we're taken to Pyongyang International Cinema House, one of the festival's main screening locations, on the same lot as our hotel. Its vast interior is lit only by skylights and strung Christmas lights. Our group, along with a couple of dozen locals, is ushered into a 100-seat cinema that smells like an old couch for a screening of 1972's *Flower Girl*, one of North Korea's most treasured movies. It tells the story of a peasant girl forced to sell flowers to afford medicine for her ailing mother, who has toiled for years in the service of a cruel family that collaborates with Japanese imperialists. In the end, the common people rise up to rid the nation of "landlords and capitalists." North Korean legend has it that Kim Il-sung wrote the script.

In the audience is the film's star, Hong Young-hee. Just 17 years old when the movie was made, she's now middle-aged, with a gentle, motherly face and a perm—the Sally Field of the Hermit Kingdom. Before the screening, she reads a speech titled "Past, Present, and Future of *Juche* Film Art," dishing about Kim Jong-il's presence on set, where he offered wide-ranging advice on acting, costuming, and props. The Dear Leader "wisely led filmmakers to make ideologically and artistically excellent films," she reads into the microphone. Kim couldn't have said it better himself.

Unless treated as a historical artifact, *Flower Girl* is tough to watch. Lacking nuance of any form, it consists of three main components: weeping, crying, and sobbing. The acting is wooden, the pace painfully slow. I attempt to sleep several times, but the theater is too hot, the seats too uncomfortable. During the screening, North Korean TV cameras, there to capture festival footage, focus on us eight outsiders, blinding us with their lights.

Afterward, outside in the afternoon sun, Hong politely poses for photos with a few fans. When I ask through Miss P whether the actress still makes movies, Hong laughs quietly and says no, she's just an "old lady." Then she leaves, and that's that. This is celebrity in North Korea.

On the bus, I make the mistake of asking Mr. O if he thought the movie was boring. He answers gravely, "No." I immediately regret asking the question and tell him I found it interesting, though there was too much crying.

He nods. "A green nation cannot be happy."

"Green?"

"Greeeive."

"Grieving?"

"Yes. Cannot be happy."

We watch movies. Some are North Korean—*The Other Side of the Mountain, A Traffic Controller on the Crossroads*—and others are foreign. We see *Good Fellows,* which is not a Scorsese remake but a gentle Iranian morality tale set in an elementary school. We also catch Bollywood superhero flick *Krrish 3* in a 2,000-seat theater so oversold that people are seated in the aisles. The movie's dance sequences allow for gratuitous shots of the hero's oiled pecs and feathered mullet; in one musical interlude, Krrish dry-humps a female villain against a canyon wall. The audience loves it.

When we're not watching movies, we talk about them. Every night, Roman, the Polish DJ, views a North Korean movie on a laptop as research for his master's thesis, and he gives us plot rundowns the next day. I ask our guides about their favorite films.

Mr. O is all about *Nation and Destiny*, the longest-running film series in North Korean history. Miss P says she doesn't have a favorite, she's seen too many. What about foreign movies? I ask. She leans in and whispers, "*Titanic*. It's very romantic."

Throughout the festival I take notes as discreetly as possible. Reporting is tricky in that I'm not technically allowed to report anything or talk to regular North Koreans about anything remotely substantial; in fact, before leaving Beijing I'd been made to sign a form that assured I wasn't a journalist. (The pretend job title on my visa application was "independent travel promoter.") Yuri is periodically forced to delete photos from his camera of soldiers or anything Mr. O deems "dirty." At one point, Mr. O sees me scribbling in a notebook and asks, "Are you reporter?" He doesn't look scared or angry, more like perturbed. I mumble that I'm just writing down my thoughts, and he makes a face like he's smelled something foul. "Reporter!" he says, before climbing onto the bus. I stick to writing in my phone after that.

After a few days of moviegoing, Miss P and Mr. O take us to North Korea's holy place: the Kumsusan Palace of the Sun, where Kim Il-sung and Kim Jong-il lie in state. On the bus over, Miss P briefs us on the palace's many formalities: Empty your pockets of everything; don't cross your arms; don't hold your hands behind your back or in your pockets; bow on each side of the leaders' bodies; etc.

Once inside the Sun Palace, visitors are made to stand on a moving walkway and examine several decades' worth of framed pictures of the leaders. Most depict them delivering the family's patented field guidance—basically, pointing at stuff. Many have clearly been Photoshopped. Some are so absurd you're tempted to laugh, if it weren't for the risk of being scolded. In one, Kim Jong-il, dressed in a tan jumpsuit, is standing on a cliff overlooking an emerald sea, a big smile revealing cigarette-yellowed teeth, hips slightly askew in a pose inspired by a 1950s starlet.

The leaders are kept in separate rooms. They are both in glass boxes, covered in blankets and lit in faint red light. The rooms are cold. Well-dressed Koreans weep and dry their eyes with hankies. We stand in rows of four, walk slowly around the boxes, bow awkwardly on each side, and move on. Each crypt is followed by a room containing framed awards, medals, and honorary degrees, most of which come from leaders of long-gone Third World dictatorships: Pinochet, Sese Seko, Idi Amin.

We step outside into the palace's vast courtyard. It's drizzling and cool. "I like the rain. Washing off the crazy," Andrew the Tupperware Man says. "That was like some crazy interactive theater."

On the bus heading to the next must-see monument, I keep thinking about Kim Jong-il's preserved corpse. That was weird. Kim Jong-il, he's the despot we grew up with, the ornery bad guy in *Team America: World Police*. Hollywood could not have created a more perfect dictator for the outside world to mock. The tinted glasses, the bouffant, the wee pointed shoes.

But seeing with my own eyes his shriveled, blanket-covered body, looking like a sleeping raisin in a room resembling a Shanghai cocktail lounge, I felt kind of sad. Not sad for the man, but sad about the whole thing. It's easy to laugh at North Korea, but it's a lot tougher to understand it—the people, the history, the ideology. It's impossible, really. I could watch a hundred North Korean movies, squirming with boredom every time, and still not get them. Because the movies speak to feelings—deep, complex feelings—that you and I will never know. And what became crystal clear as we walked through the Sun Palace is that those emotions are not funny or ironic to North Koreans. They are real, and they hurt. We could see them all in Miss P's dampened eyes. If she was acting, she deserves an Oscar.

Our guides tell us to look nice. Tuck in your shirt, that kind of thing. Tonight's the big night, when the prestigious Grand Prix gets awarded to the festival's top film. The closing ceremony is back at Ponghwa theater, and the scene feels much like the opening. This time, though, there are more cameras, and they are very much focused on our gang of eight as we enter the auditorium and find our seats. We wonder if we're going to be on North Korean TV.

Onstage are the same pooping dove and female host struggling with her English. There are speeches and performances, and I soon stop paying attention. I flip through a program and drift off thinking about how surreal and surprising the festival has been. One film from the Philippines featured a gay protagonist—this in a country where the government claims homosexuality doesn't exist within its borders. The Judi Dench vehicle *Philomena* was on the program, along with shorts from Canada and Australia, a gesture toward the West that runs contrary to our prevailing assumptions about the DPRK.

In fact, while our visit has largely reinforced some North Korean stereotypes, the country itself has been, in many ways, a surprise. Foreigners can purchase 3G SIM cards for their cell phones. NGOs work here, and Christian tour groups are allowed to pass through, as long as they don't try to convert anyone. (And those three incarcerated Americans were ultimately released after negotiations with Washington.) Though the government perpetually denounces capitalist America, you can buy Coke imported from China. Pyongyang has a Viennese café and a pizza restaurant where a performer belts out "My Heart Will Go On." I saw a boy in a Steve Nash Phoenix Suns jersey and a girl in fresh New Balance sneakers. This place isn't as cut off from the world as the rest of us think.

This is a good thing, I muse to myself. Yes, this festival is a benevolent force, a much-needed way of bringing the world to North Korea and vice versa. Through film we can understand each other. Movies can help make the world a better place . . .

And just then a thin Swedish delegate named Henrik Nydqvist takes the stage, and all those noble ideals dissolve like vaporizer mist. Fifteen minutes before the ceremony, Nydqvist's Korean minders had handed him sheets of paper and told him it was too late to deliver the speech he'd prepared on his own—a personal message, on behalf of all the foreign delegates, about the virtues of cultural exchange through film—which he'd been assured he could present. Instead, he must read this one:

"To your esteemed excellency, Kim Jong-un," Nydqvist begins, addressing the absent leader, his accented words echoing throughout the auditorium. "We express our heartfelt thanks to your excellency for the meticulous care you have shown to the success of the festival from the beginning to the end . . . People admire, and will remember in their hearts, the undying exploits and greatness of your excellency, who pursues the policy of love for the people, true to the noble intention of the great generalissimos Kim Il-sung and Kim Jong-il, the eternal suns of *Juche* . . ."

His speech done, Nydqvist exits the stage and we settle in for one last movie: the German film *My Beautiful Country,* a tale of forbidden love between a wounded Albanian soldier and a Serbian widow during Kosovo's civil war. The story adheres to another common North Korean movie theme—the pain of separation—and thus earns *My Beautiful Country* the Grand Prix.

As the theater darkens, I sit next to Mr. O and watch my final movie on the North Korean big screen. It seems like a pretty good film, though I wouldn't really know, since it's not subtitled.

The movie isn't meant for me, anyway. The entire festival, from beginning to end, is for the North Koreans in the theater: the soldiers, the party members, the people. The rest of us, we're just extras.

JUSTIN NOBEL

Growing Old with the Inuit

FROM *Nowhere*

THE FLIGHT TO Cape Dorset, an Inuit community on a small island in the Canadian Arctic, was due to depart in minutes, but Inuit elders were still checking in with battered suitcases, swollen duffels, and giant black trash bags filled with frozen and bloody caribou legs. Once aboard, I snacked on Oreos and ginger ale as the turboprop plane hummed west across Baffin Island—a treeless brown expanse fractured by gleaming blue streams. Taking off in Iqaluit, capital of the vast Inuit territory of Nunavut, skies were clear, but as we approached the Hudson Strait a bright wall of clouds swallowed our plane. This foggy shield had prevented aircraft from landing in Dorset for seven days. Our pilot found a hole and down we went, skidding to a stop on the gravel runway.

Outside was an eerie Arctic world. Dark hills surrounded the town. The mountains looked like crude piles of rock, flung down by a primordial god who then stopped time, petrifying the landscape in buckles and cleaves. The waiting room was a crush of people clamoring for essentials like milk, bread, and booze, which had run dry in the fog. Royal Canadian Mounted Police in tight beige uniforms with guns strapped to their hips monitored the crowd. A banner indicated the reason I was there: WELCOME TO THE ELDERS' GATHERING IN CAPE DORSET, AUGUST 15–19, 2011.

There is not much material out there about how different cultures once killed their elderly, a practice called senicide, but there is some. In rural Japan, upon reaching age 70, sons carried their mothers and fathers up a holy peak called Obasute-yama, or Granny-Dump Mountain, and left them on top to die of exposure and starvation. The Bactrians, who inhabited present-day northern Afghanistan, threw the old and sick to specially trained dogs called undertakers. Streets were littered with human bones. In North Africa, troglodyte elders no longer able to tend to their flocks asphyxiated themselves by fastening the tail of an ox around their necks. East of the Caspian Sea, the Derbiccae murdered males at age 70 and ate them. Women were merely strangled and buried. Among the Massagetae, who lived around the Aral Sea, relatives sacrificed old men and stewed them together with wild beasts, while the Iazyges of Sarmatia, who roamed lands north of the Black Sea, were slain by their children with swords.

Closer to home, on the rocky Diomede Islands in the storm-thrashed Bering Strait between Siberia and Alaska, the Iñupiat ritualistically murdered elders with knives, guns, and nooses. Those who wanted to die would explain their wishes to a relative, who would try to dissuade them. If minds could not be changed, the killing went forth. The person to die turned their clothing inside out, and relatives carried them on a seat of caribou skin to the destroying place at the edge of the village. The one who did the killing was called the executioner, usually the victim's eldest son. One story, reported in a 1955 *Southwestern Journal of Anthropology* article, tells of a 12-year-old boy who killed his father with a large hunting knife: "He indicated the vulnerable spot over his heart, where his son should stab him. The boy plunged the knife deep, but the stroke failed to take effect. The old father suggested with dignity and resignation, 'Try it a little higher, my son.' The second stab was effective."

From the Canadian Arctic comes the story of Charles Francis Hall, a Cincinnati newspaper publisher who in 1860 abandoned his wife and children to explore the frozen north. On southern Baffin Island, not far from present-day Iqaluit, he visited the igloo of a dying old woman named Nukertou, only to find the community had barricaded her home with bricks of snow. Thinking it unchristian to let her die alone, Hall forced his way in. "One, two, three, four, five, six, seven did I slowly count in the intervals of her breathing," he wrote in his journal. "At last I could count nineteen between her inspirations but her respirations were short and prolonged—irregular. At length Nukertou ceased to live."

About 60 years later, in the early 1920s, Knud Rasmussen, an explorer and anthropologist, reported senicide among the Netsilik Inuit of King William's Land. "For our custom up here," he noted, "is that all old people who can do no more, and whom death will not take, help death to take them." During long winter marches between hunting grounds, elders were left behind on ice floes to die. A decade later, the French adventurer Gontran de Poncins lived among the Netsilik and described a son who abandoned his mother in a blizzard, one of the last known accounts of senicide.

De Poncins marked the end of the explorer-anthropologist. Anthropology became a profession thereafter, with guidelines and degrees. Some questions were deemed relevant, others ridiculed. Modern anthropologists are more concerned about how things like Christianity and television and climate change affect the Inuit. Rather than being locked in igloos, Inuit elders are now confined to elder homes, which have popped up across the territory. No one thinks much about senicide, and if they think anything, they think it is a lie. "Over the last three centuries, white explorers and adventurers, police officers, missionaries, traders, and especially anthropologists, sociologists, and other scholars have spun many a twisted story about the Inuit," wrote Canadian anthropologist John Steckley in his 2007 book *White Lies About the Inuit*. But when I dialed Steckley by phone at Humber College in Toronto, I was surprised to learn that he had written his entire book from the university library. The man had never been to the Arctic.

It was at about that time that my grandparents, who had traveled the world in their 70s with nothing much more than a beat-up green rucksack, staying in hostels, taking local buses, and sending me postcards from remote villages in India and China—missives that surely helped spawn my own wanderlust—were being transferred by their sons from their rustic South Jersey home to a fancy nursing home in the suburbs of New York City. The questions of how best to deal with the aging, the inevitable frailty of the body, and the transition to death we all face seemed more important than ever. And the Inuit, at a crossroads between the violent elderly deaths of the past and the sleepy elderly deaths of the present, promised answers. Around the same time, an opportunity to investigate those answers presented itself: elderly Inuit from across Baffin Island and Nunavik, an Inuit region in Arctic Quebec where I once spent a summer reporting for the local newspaper, were meeting in Cape Dorset for an elders' gathering. In the summer of 2011, with my grandparents safely squirreled away in their new living quarters, I returned to the Arctic.

To communicate with the elders, most of whom spoke only Inuktitut, I needed a translator. On my first night in Dorset, the mayor introduced me to just the man: Black. We chatted outside the Sam Pudlat School, where events for the elders' gathering were to be held. Children played on swings as the sun slowly dropped. Black wore a black hoodie, black sweatpants, and black boots without laces. He had black hair that was going white and a wispy goatee that had already gone. He spoke perfect English and was sarcastic in a way one seldom sees among the Inuit, fond of phrases like "Holy Eskimo!" A sloppy tattoo on his left arm depicting a knife stabbing a rose suggested he had been to prison. I liked him immediately.

Black's real name was Pootoogoo, which means "big toe" and is a very popular Inuit name. Of 14 kids in his elementary school class, five were named Pootoogoo. One student started calling him Black and it stuck. Black now worked as a translator when journalists and scientists came to town. He also worked as a pseudo parole officer for the police, coordinating releases when Inuit were tossed in the drunk tank. With no planes for a week, there had been no booze and the drunk tank was empty. "This is perfect for me," said Black, lighting a cigarette. "I've got no work right now."

I explained that I was looking for elders who knew stories of senicide. Black said he had someone in mind and asked for an advance. I gave him 60 bucks. He quickly passed it to his mousey wife, who headed for the grocery store. I mentioned taking a walk that evening to the dark hills outside town, but Black said not to; there was a polar bear on the loose. He relayed a story I would hear several times: A hunter camped outside town was recently dragged by his head from his tent. The man broke free, but couldn't see a thing; his scalp had been ripped away and was dangling in front of his eyes.

I skipped the walk and instead joined a barefoot Inuit man on his porch for swigs of Smirnoff and thin silver cans of high-octane Molson's. "More strong, less weight," one woozy female drinker explained, referring to the fact that lighter cans were cheaper to ship north. Other Inuit dropped by; everyone seemed to be blind drunk. Just one year before, a teenager named Peter Kingwatsiak had stabbed his sleeping uncle in the head, then shot and killed his slumbering stepbrother. Shortly after that, a 19-year-old named Elee shot a dog, then a raven, then his brother Jamesie in what was reportedly a fight over an iPod. Three days after that incident, two 15-year-old boys roamed the town with rifles, firing at will, an escapade that ended in a police standoff in which one boy was shot in the torso. The town was still on edge from these events, and with the influx of alcohol the entire community was throbbing with a dangerous energy. Sure enough, later that night everything exploded on cue. No one died, but a handful of fights broke out, including one involving Black's son. The drunk tank was packed, which meant my translator had to return to his other job.

On opening day of the elders' gathering, I joined a group of old ladies from Iqaluit who were watching a potbellied Inuit with a guitar named Nowdlak Oshuituk. Oshuituk played folk songs introduced by Scottish whalers. "He's a self-taught musician from Cape Dorset," whispered Napatchie, chaperone of the Iqaluit ladies. "His name means 'man without a penis.'" Napatchie's mother, a stoic 82-year-old named Enoapik who wore sealskin boots and a floral dress, stood up and motioned for me to dance with her. I'm a terrible dancer, but with much of the crowd watching me, turning down one of the gathering's VIPs seemed foolish. We did a sort of jitterbug. Then came the World's Smallest Clothes competition.

Five elderly women paraded across the gym floor in ridiculous outfits. One wore Spiderman tights, a too-small Spiderman top, and a child's Spiderman cap. Another had on jean capris and a lacy top, not necessarily that small, though her sunglasses still made her something to look at: tiny, vintage, dusted in glitter. The clear winner in my opinion, though I don't think one was ever declared, was an obese woman in sweatpants and a tube top. As contestants posed for pictures, one of her breasts slipped out of the tube top. With the whole gym in hysterics, the ladies retired to the locker room and a big bucket of cookies was passed around.

"There's evil amongst us, sicknesses the health system can't do anything about," a pastor named Udjualuk Etidloie announced the following day at a church opening in the Valley—a stretch of trailerlike homes bordered by a gravel pit, a metal dump (where the polar bear had last been seen), and a cemetery. His church was part of a homegrown religious movement gathering steam across

the Arctic. Inuit pastors, bored of the vanilla Christianity of Angli-
canism and Catholicism, preached their own brands. Services featured rolling around on the floor and speaking in tongues. Some
scholars believed these new churches signaled the reemergence
of shamanism. The spark for the movement occurred in 1999 in
the Baffin Island community of Pond Inlet. Plagued by suicide,
alcoholism, and domestic violence, community leaders decided to
torch pornographic magazines and heavy-metal CDs in a bonfire.
But sin remained. Then one cold February morning a mysterious
booming interrupted a church service. "There was a mighty rush-
ing fire, and tongues of wind," an Irish missionary in Dorset told
me. Those present were convinced they had witnessed the Second
Coming, or at least the coming of the Second Coming. The event
was thereafter referred to as the Revival. There is a YouTube video
about it.

After Pastor Etidloie finished his sermon, an elder snipped a
piece of red yarn, then held the scissors triumphantly above her
head. Church was open. The animated group marched back up
the hill to the Sam Pudlat gymnasium, where the pastor donned a
saxophone and took the stage with an Inuit Christian-rock group
called the Kingait Band. The elders' gathering was beginning to
feel like a hokey family reunion, and I began to tire of it. One evening, as elders posed for photos in traditional white bead-studded
jackets with capacious hoods for carrying toddlers—called *amautis*
—I slipped out the back door of the gymnasium. A trio of youths
were climbing on a shipping container, smoking cigarettes and
looking bored. I introduced myself.

Numa, 13, was a chatterer with a backwards New York ball
cap and braces. Willie, 14, wore black jeans and had acne on his
forehead. The leader of the pack was Tiggy, who was only 10 and
looked like a lost pup, with untied shoelaces, patched jeans, and
an oversized green hoodie. He carried a slingshot made from a
scrap of rubber and was continuously picking up stones and shooting them into the tundra. I suggested we walk to the dark hills
outside town. They said OK. There was a waterfall there that they
wanted to show me. I asked if we needed to worry about the polar
bear. They said no.

The sun fell and the kids fired questions at me.

"Do you wanna go party?" asked Willie.

"You like Katy Perry?" asked Numa.

"Is your father still alive?" asked Willie.

"You should live here," said Numa.

All the while, Tiggy gathered rocks and loaded them into a slingshot. He seemed malnourished.

"Guess what?" said Willie, pointing at Tiggy. "His mom smokes weed with him."

"He's kinda poor," said Numa.

"Look!" Tiggy shouted, pointing into the sky. A delicate line fluttered against the blue, barely visible, like sewing thread fluttering in the stratosphere. It was a skein of snow geese.

"Koola kook!" Willie called to the birds, his hands cupped to his mouth. "Koola kook! Koola kook! Koola kook!"

We circled a still lake on a road sticky with orange mud. The farther we got from town, the more the kids spilled.

"The last couple days lots of people were drunken," Willie said.

"I live with my grandmother because my mother doesn't like me," said Numa. "Some of the people hurt little kids. They get angry, and . . . I don't know."

"You know a lot of people who commit suicide?" asked Willie. I knew some, I said, but not a lot.

"I knew another Willie," said Willie. "He committed suicide."

Willie pointed to one of the dark hills, which we were now approaching. "You see that mountain?" he said. "Some girl saw the devil there, with a tail."

"There are ghosts there," added Numa. "They're dark, black, and small, kinda like smoke."

The waterfall was a lathery current pressed flat against slick rocks, like a giant's unfurled tongue. Tiggy ran up its sheer face as if it were a ladder. I was sure he'd fall, but he made it to the top. He didn't raise his arms above his head in victory as kids sometimes do, but dashed off. Behind us the sun was fiery red above the town. In the other direction the sea was dusky blue with a strip of gray between it and the sky. Then the moon, a white sphere, three-quarters full and rising. It was hard to believe I was still in the same universe as the elders. The gathering had made them doe-eyed and merry, like children. Meanwhile, the children were the ones who had been abandoned.

Suddenly Tiggy reappeared. His green hoodie was striped with wet marks. It was just water, but it looked like he had taken part in a strange ritual, as if he really had become a tiggy.

One afternoon I ran into Black outside Northmart. He looked frazzled. "I've been looking everywhere," he said. "Have you been shot?" I'm not sure why, but I examined my torso. No, I hadn't been. "Phew," Black said. "A woman who lives next to you was arrested last night for trying to shoot her children; she was firing her gun into the air." He had other news, also sour. With the town still sunk in drunkenness, Black was too busy to arrange interviews. But a few days later, he called to say the man he had in mind was ready to talk, a brawny 72-year-old with neatly combed silver hair named Atsiaq Alasuaq. We spoke at Black's home, a small yellow house in the Valley. Atsiaq sat in a swivel chair by a window that looked out on a cemetery of cockeyed white wood crosses. Behind them rose a steep ridge—an ancient polar-bear pathway, Black said.

Atsiaq grew up in a hunting camp, where he lived in a sort of igloo condominium. Three igloos, each belonging to a different family, were connected by passageways. To minimize heat loss, there was only one door to the outside. A system of knocks let families communicate between igloos. There were knocks for mealtime, knocks for heading out hunting, and knocks for just passing through. Atsiaq's camp was near a spot where walrus liked to haul up. I asked him if he ever hunted them. "Of course I've hunted walrus," he said. "When I was a kid I was the one who harpooned the walrus, because I was the strongest." They killed the 2,000-pound beasts as they napped on the sea ice.

Still, famine was common. "Families that went hungry would have to eat their dogs," said Atsiaq. "I've also heard of actual cannibalism, but that was way before I was born." He swiveled his chair to face the window and began pointing. I thought he was indicating the graves, but he was referring to the ankle-high Arctic plants. When he was younger they would mix the roots with seal fat to stave off hunger. "Nowadays," lamented Atsiaq, "no one eats the roots."

He confirmed elderly had indeed been left to die on ice floes, but the practice stopped about a decade before he was born. When he was younger, after someone died their body was surrounded by a ring of rocks—"so the bones, when they disintegrated, wouldn't blow away." A person's favorite tool was put outside the ring. If

someone were to die alone on the land, they placed their tool
outside the ring themselves, then crawled inside to die. I asked
Atsiaq what his tool would be. "My knife," he replied immediately.
"It is made of ivory with a wood handle, and mainly used to hunt
walrus."

Atsiaq left and I heard a commotion outside. Kids were shouting and I could see people running. The polar bear! Black and I
rushed into the street. A crowd had gathered around a neighbor's
house. One boy pointed to a marble-sized black lump on the wall.
"Holy Eskimo!" said Black. "We never see those in the North." It
was a fly.

The elders' gathering ended with a flurry of exciting events. There
was a soccer game, played with a ball made of sealskin, followed
by a feast of raw caribou, bowhead whale, and baby seal. I saw
one woman snatch something from a bloody slit in the seal's neck.
When I asked her later what it was, she replied cheerfully, "The
brain." On the final night, we gathered again in the Sam Pudlat
School gymnasium. It was announced that the next elders' gathering would be in Aupaluk, a 174-person Nunavik community on
Ungava Bay where the United Arab Emirates recently made plans
to construct an iron mine that would employ 10,000 people. Select
elders gave closing words. Enoapik, still wearing her trademark
sealskin boots and floral dress, was among them. "You have to help
the elders, share with them your small food," she said. "You'll all
be old too."

My flight back to Iqaluit was delayed for two days because of
fog, then delayed again because of a deadly plane crash in the central Arctic, then delayed another five days because of fog. On the
evening I finally left Cape Dorset, the turboprop plane climbed
quickly into a lavender sky. Below, the community was a button
of light in a welt of black. And then there was only black. A stew-
ardess passed around drinks; I got a ginger ale. Just before I left
Nunavut for good, I visited an elder home in Iqaluit, the territory's
largest one. Manager Elisapee Gordon greeted me wearing polka-
dot galoshes, a cell phone clipped to her tight jeans. She showed
me the washroom, the laundry room, the rooms that were more
like apartments, where elders had a measure of autonomy. Then
she showed me rooms that were more like hospital rooms, where
elders had access to 24-hour care. Some things remained tradi-

tional: boiling away in giant steel pots for lunch was polar bear stew.

A few days later I returned with a translator and met one of the tenants, an 83-year-old woman in a wheelchair named Udloriaq Ineak. She was a shrunken, toothless thing in fuzzy magenta slippers and teal sweatpants. Her eyes were watery blue and her arms were bruised and swollen from diabetes. Jars of jam decorated her nightstand, and completed puzzles hung on the walls: a parrot, dogs of the world, and Christie Brinkley, sitting on her haunches in a field of flowers.

Udloriaq was born in the Baffin Island community of Kimmirut, but at age 4 moved to a hunting camp outside town, living more like the Inuit always had. At 14 she married, not for love or because her family wanted a dowry, but for food. "I used to go hungry," she said. "After I got married, I never went hungry." Her husband hunted by dogsled. One day while he was gone, a polar bear came by the tent. She had two young girls at the time, and although she had a gun, she didn't try to shoot the bear; she just watched it. "I had no fear," said Udloriaq. She had been through too much. In the early 1950s famine and disease struck, and Udloriaq was one of the few people who remained healthy. She became a nurse to the entire community, helping the dying die with dignity, helping the almost dead back to life.

"Are you afraid to die?" I asked Udloriaq.

"I'm not afraid of death at all," she said. "I've seen death around myself a lot, more than once, in the days when there was famine and there were people freezing. I believe once a soul passes away it goes to heaven, and those who are not believers go to that other place."

Unlike explorers such as Hall, who wrote about the North as outsiders, Knud Rasmussen was born in Ilulissat, Greenland. He grew up with the Inuit, spoke perfect Inuktitut, and by age eight was running his own dog team. In 1921 he embarked on a 20,000-mile journey across the Arctic, from Baffin Island to Siberia, observing the Inuit just before contact with fur traders and missionaries changed them forever. He recorded senicide among the Netsilik Inuit of King William's Land and was one of the few explorers who succeeded in communicating with shamans—hermetic, mercurial men who spoke only Inuktitut. During a blizzard in a swampy section of the central Arctic called the Barren Grounds, Rasmussen took refuge in the igloo of a shaman named Aua. After a meal of raw walrus, talk turned to the netherworld.

Those who die slowly, like from a withering sickness, go to a purgatory called the Narrow Land located at the bottom of the ocean, Aua explained. Those who die quick, violent deaths go to the Land of Day, located in the sky. It is "a land of glad and happy souls," Rasmussen recorded in his journal, "with many caribou, and the people there live only for pleasure. They play ball most of the time . . . with the skull of a walrus, and laughing and singing as they play." It's possible to get from the Narrow Land to the Land of Day, but first you must confess your sins to a sea goddess named Takanaluk Arnaluk, who was flung from a boat by her father in a storm to lighten the load. Takanaluk clung to the side, but her father chopped off her fingers.

"I wonder about it too," said Laval University anthropologist Frédéric Laugrand, coauthor of the 2010 book *Inuit Shamanism and Christianity: Transitions and Transformations in the Twentieth Century*. I had asked him by phone why Inuit who died quickly were rewarded. He believed it had to do with the body's desire to free its soul. A slow death held up a soul on its way to the afterlife, whereas a violent death let the soul leave the body swiftly and go straight to heaven. Laugrand thought Inuit senicide made sense within this context, and believed that the elderly were once left to die on ice floes. In fact, he imagined that for those who actually lived to be old, it was common practice. "There was no scandal of death; that is a Western idea," said Laugrand. "For an Inuit elder, there came a moment when he or she would think life was too much, and that it is better to fall from the sledge and freeze to death."

Once every month or two, I buy a loaf of uncut sourdough bread and a cranberry muffin and take the train from Grand Central Station north, getting off in Harrison. I walk half a mile through leafy suburbs to a majestic neo-Georgian estate called the Osborn. I give the muffin to the nurse and the bread to my grandmother, whose eyes tear with joy. Then I walk to the couch where my grandfather seems to be forever resting, flat on his back. He isn't so much dying as disintegrating, hurtling through space like a meteorite, with flecks and pieces flying off—his hearing, his back, his vision. But the thing is not dead until the core is dead, and so onward he hurtles.

He was born Joseph R. Knobel in Łódź, Poland, in 1917. His father went to America in search of work and a few years later sent back four tickets. Only Joe and his mother came. His older brother and a twin brother had both died of malnutrition. Once in America, the family settled in Patterson, New Jersey, where Joe's father ran a small factory that made silk cloth. In the Depression he went bankrupt. Joe graduated high school and hitchhiked to New Orleans, looking for work as a cabin boy on an around-the-world steamer. But there was no work. He tramped to Louisiana State University in Baton Rouge, camped in an old stadium, fell in love with Francis Seligman while waiting for a ride, got a degree in chemistry, worked at a sugar plant deep in the bayou, married Fran. They reared six children, traveled the world with their green knapsack, sent postcards to their 18 grandchildren, hundreds of postcards, thousands of miles, millions of breaths, heartbeats, seconds, time, lives burning away under azure skies, foreign skies, broiling away, boiling away, living away, familiar skies. No answer to the answerless question that is the thing called our lives.

"Joey," my grandmother calls from the kitchen, "your grandson Justin has brought you some bread."

We are holding hands on the couch. I want to carry him up a holy mountain, abandon him on an ice floe, stab him in the heart, but I don't have the guts. Those days are indeed over. There will be no ring of rocks, and everyone has forgotten their favorite tool. These days, the world over, we die on couches.

STEPHANIE PEARSON

The Green Heaven

FROM *Outside*

EACH AUTUMN THE residents of Kerala, a lush southern Indian state bordering the Arabian Sea, go all out to celebrate their secular 10-day harvest festival. It commemorates the return of the legendary King Mahabali, who is said to have given every Keralan —whether Hindu, Muslim, Christian, Sikh, Buddhist, Jew, Jain, or other—equal rights and total prosperity. Over the centuries, Mahabali has morphed into an Indian version of Santa Claus, and you'll find him everywhere—on billboards hawking new cars and in the flesh, twirling parasols in parades.

I bumped into Mahabali while attempting to cross the street in the city of Vaikom. I was so preoccupied with buying a sari for the festival that I didn't notice a parade of hundreds following a bejeweled man with a giant belly and wearing a crown. Being Mahabali, he handed me a piece of candy as he passed, while a TV news reporter stuck a mike in my face and asked: "What do you think of Onam?"

"It's a happy time!" I stammered, trying to sum up ancient history in a sound bite.

After a few days of exuberance, I can attest that Keralans know how to celebrate. Yesterday, on Lake Vembanad, I feasted on the traditional Onam meal, known as *sadya,* at an ecoresort called Coconut Lagoon. The 26 vegetarian servings included ash gourd, masala curry, sambar, papadams, mango pickles, and pressed rice flakes with jaggery, a pure form of sugar, which were served on a banana leaf and eaten by hand. This morning I'm on my way to the festival's last event, the Aranmula Boat Race, a 700-year-old, nearly one-mile contest that starts at the Aranmula Temple on the River Pamba. According to legend, Lord Krishna, one of the most venerated of Hinduism's many deities, designed the boats. The race, in which 120-foot-long *palliyodams,* or snake boats, from 48 villages go head-to-head in front of thousands of spectators, has the pomp and circumstance of the Olympics and seems a fitting end to the celebration.

On the bank of a stream, there are two snake boats, handcrafted from wild jackwood and with sterns shaped like cobras' heads, being prepared for the event. The boats are draped with marigolds and filled with racks of bananas to fuel the dozens of shirtless men in each. The men have sandalwood marks on their foreheads and are wearing white loincloths and headscarves; some have already dipped into toddy, a fermented coconut alcohol, and are starting to get a little rowdy.

"Are you going to win the race?" I ask one of the men.

"It all depends on God," he replies, before they paddle off toward the start line in perfect synchronicity.

The race is mayhem. One of the boats capsizes, and the revelers let out a collective gasp as the paddlers swim toward the opposite shore. A motorboat packed with costumed men wearing devil masks and impersonating foreign tourists, complete with fake boobs and blond wigs, speeds past. If this raucous festival is an accurate representation of life in the state famously known as God's Own Country, then, I decide, God must thrive on chaos and like to have fun.

"In Kerala, many things make sense and many things don't," says my guide, Rajesh "Raj" Padmanabha Iyer Ramakrishnan, a 36-year-old Hindu priest and yoga instructor. Since the beginning of our 600-mile car and train journey across the state, he's been chanting the Mahamrityunjaya, a melodic devotion to Lord Shiva, the many-powered creator and destroyer whom Hindus worship as one of the primary forms of God.

"It boils down to a plea for victory over death," he says of the prayer. Which makes sense—I don't have a seat belt, so I'm trusting Shiva for safe passage through the rolling countryside of rubber tree and banana plantations, Hindu and Christian shrines, towering coconut palms, and goats, cows, people, and tuk-tuks as we pass a sign that reads SPEED THRILLS, BUT KILLS.

Kerala, one of the smallest states in India, is roughly the size of Maryland and Delaware combined but has a population of 35 million—about the same number of people in the entire country of Canada. Despite the masses, Kerala is intensely beautiful. In the west, 360 miles of palm-fringed, sandy coastline hugs the Arabian Sea. To the east, the mountainous Western Ghats, one of India's seven UNESCO World Heritage natural sites, rise up to the 8,842-foot summit of Anamudi, the highest point in the country outside of the Himalayas. Herds of wild elephants and solitary tigers roam the Ghats through the sprawling Nilgiri Biosphere Reserve, a wildlife corridor that extends into the neighboring states of Tamil Nadu and Karnataka.

Numerous wild rivers flow from the Ghats' peaks, many of them into the "backwaters," an interconnected inland waterway of lagoons, canals, and lakes near the Arabian Sea. Plant anything here and it will grow, from coconuts to mangos to ginger, which is why the food is so fresh and healthy. Add forests full of medicinal herbs, spices, and flowers and it's no wonder Keralans have been practicing the healing art of Ayurveda for centuries. Ayurvedic hospitals and spas treat 90-year-old farmers with arthritis and stressed-out Western execs who fly in on private jets for month-long treatments.

"Kerala, the green heaven, can not only be a great recuperation place after a big Himalayan trek or expedition, but a destination in itself," says Mandip Soin, a pioneering mountaineer who made the first Indian ascent of 21,162-foot Meru North. In 2008 Soin founded the Ecotourism Society of India, a national body driving the country's responsible-tourism agenda. He's also the owner of Ibex Expeditions, the company that arranged my trip.

"One can easily spend days trekking in the Western Ghats, mountain-biking over the rolling coffee plantations, kayaking in the backwater lagoons, and looking for the tiger on foot," he told me as we mapped out an itinerary between Kerala's five national parks, 17 wildlife sanctuaries, hundreds of miles of forest, and endless beaches.

As the epicenter of the world's spice trade, Kerala has also endured as a largely independent, multicultural society for centuries. It's a mind-boggling amalgam of cultures and beliefs. "Kerala is perhaps the only place in the world that is able to produce both a practicing Catholic and an agitated Communist," Jose Dominic, the managing director of CGH Earth hotels, a group of sustainable ecoresorts and properties in southern India, told me.

Yes, Kerala has Communists. In 1957, 10 years after India gained independence from Britain, the state became the first in the world to democratically elect a Communist government. The Communists successfully pushed through land reform in 1970, making Kerala one of the first states in India to end the feudal system. Drawing on a long history of enlightened Hindu rulers and Christian missionaries, the Communists and successive parties (which continue to trade power in any given election) made it a priority to educate the masses. Today, 93 percent of Kerala's population is literate, which is perhaps why everyone always seems to be reading one of the state's 31 Malayalam newspapers. Kerala also has affordable universal health care, the lowest infant mortality rate in India, and an average life expectancy of 73, seven years higher than the national average. In almost every quality-of-life indicator, Kerala is off the charts.

"Kerala is a breath of fresh air for Mother India," Dominic said. "It's much safer than the north, and travelers aren't as shocked here. The fear of communism kept industrial investors out, and eventually local entrepreneurs navigated through the political minefields. Now small, high-value, and local has become the flavor of Kerala's growth. Nothing will be permitted here if it is at the cost of the community."

Which isn't to say that Kerala is without struggles, including occasional outbursts of violence between feuding political parties, strikes, and one of the highest rates of alcoholism in India. And in a state where there are 2,200 people per square mile, my Western notions of rugged individualism and wide-open spaces may need a little adjusting.

"When you look at this, you can feel destination infinity," says Raj. We're just north of Alleppey, a backwater hub, paddling sit-on-top kayaks on Meenapally Kayal, a wide, beautiful lake and an important link to the numerous channels in the 297-mile backwater ecosystem. It's also one of the most popular backdrops for Mollywood blockbusters (Malayalam-language movies filmed in Kerala), because of its impressive expanse and uncluttered shoreline ringed with coconut palms.

Known as "the rice bowl of Kerala," the backwaters are one of the only places in the world outside of Holland where land is cultivated below sea level. Small villages line the canals and are surrounded by a chlorophyll heaven of rice paddies, banana leaves, and gardens of spinach, long beans, and curry. Lavender houses, indigo pet peacocks, women in brightly colored saris, and men in plaid dhotis pop out of the foliage in brilliant relief. This is the land of Arundhati Roy, who spent part of her childhood in the village of Aymanam, where she set her haunting novel *The God of Small Things*.

With a shock of white hair, a master's degree in philosophy and religion, years logged teaching yoga in an ashram, and a serious Facebook addiction, Raj has led dozens of trips through the backwaters, but those have been on *kettuvallams,* the famous houseboats that were used in the days of the spice trade and are now motorized party barges for tourists. At last count, 800 *kettuvallams* plied the waterways near Alleppey, and the government is keeping tabs on licensing. Some of the boats are luxurious cruisers outfitted with air-conditioned staterooms. But to reach the remote channels a kayak is required, which is why we're with Binu Joseph, a 26-year-old local whose mother loaned him her gold to buy six kayaks from new Zealand to start his own motorless tours.

"I see everyone in the houseboats, and they are not experiencing the backwaters," Binu tells me as we paddle past honking *kettuvallams* belching diesel fumes. "So I search the Google for a flat boat. When I started the trips, there was only me doing it, but now there are three others."

Binu grew up near here and knows his way through these labyrinthine waters. We stop along a major canal at an open-air restaurant for a breakfast of *appam,* which is like a coconut pancake, accompanied by a *sambar* and some fresh toddy that a "toddy tapper" had just collected from a tree. It's a little sweet, a little tangy, a lot less sour than I expect, and it goes down smoothly. We hop in the boats and paddle past a Hindu marriage hall and temple and the local Communist Party headquarters before paddling into a smaller canal that will take us deep into peaceful Muslim, Christian, and Hindu neighborhoods, where orchids grow with abandon, kids race our boats in wooden canoes, and kingfishers, egrets, and cormorants dart.

The ubiquitous wooden canoes are like cars, and most everything needed to sustain life can be found along the waterways, including a floating medical clinic, churches, schools, mosques, temples, and supermarkets that sell rice powder, paper, soap, and oil. At one point the small canal, called a *thode,* is so narrow and choked with water hyacinths that it feels like we're turning down a path of no return. But after a few hundred yards, the channel widens and spits us back into the lake, where Binu's driver is waiting for us in his colorfully roofed outboard *shikara.*

Binu, who has a stocky build, got married a few months ago and has a bachelor's degree in business from Kerala University. His family has high hopes that he'll go to law school. He's preparing for his entrance exams, but, he tells me, "I don't want to go to the court. I like my life."

I can see why. I felt the pull of the backwaters a few mornings ago when I awoke, at a family-run inn called Philipkutty's Farm, to a driving, predawn monsoon. The crickets, frogs, and roosters chirped, croaked, and crowed the world to life. Minutes later their wild cries were drowned out by the staccato blast of hundreds of firecrackers, a classic Hindu offering, especially popular during the Onam festival. By 6:00 a.m., a melodious hymn wafted over the water via a loudspeaker at St. Mary's Church in Kudavechoor, where believers were already celebrating mass and spreading the word.

"Do you see this? It's Spanish lady, we use it to treat kidney stones," says Renjith Hadlee, a wiry 28-year-old in an elephant T-shirt and a baseball hat over curly dark hair. "And this is camphor basil. We use it to treat cold and flu. This is an African tulip. The bark is good for treating malaria. This? Wild nutmeg. It tastes good. And this is a poinsettia tree. It's just pretty," he says.

To understand how integrated Keralans are with their natural surroundings, take a stroll with one through the forest in the Western Ghats. It's hard to believe that this steep mountain landscape, with its bald granite peaks, plunging Class 5 rivers, and cool climate, is in the same state as the backwaters.

I'm at 5,000 feet near the hill station of Munnar to hike among emerald-green tea and cardamom plantations in west-central Kerala. It's peaceful to be in the quiet abundance of the forest, a welcome reprieve from the honking cars and inquiring eyes of Kerala's cities. Hadlee, who cofounded a trekking and mountain-biking company called Kestrel Adventures three years ago, is leading me up and down a rock path covered in luminescent green moss through a *shola,* or tropical mountain forest. More than 1,200 endemic species live among the commercially planted cardamom, which is an ideal crop at this altitude because it needs little sunlight and requires a lot of moisture. There's no rain today, but the trees are dripping with a mist that settles in like a shroud. Between the dense fog, the wild pharmaceuticals, and the exotic-bird sightings, it feels like an enchanted forest.

Hadlee's family has lived in Munnar for five generations, which is why he sees this *shola* as a medicine chest for Ayurveda, an Indian practice that dates back 5,000 years. I have yet to experience a treatment, but it's evident that these hills are alive with healing powers.

Over the next few days I visited three more hill stations, including one near Periyar National Park, a 357-square-mile tiger and elephant sanctuary that was named the 2012 United Nations Development Programme's best-conserved biodiversity park in India, and Karnataka's Nagarhole National Park, in the foothills of the Western Ghats and part of the tristate Nilgiri Biosphere Reserve, which has one of the highest tiger densities in the world. The big cats evaded me at both, which isn't surprising—they are solitary and nocturnal, and there was too much foliage when I was there in September. But at Nagarhole, I did see a bull elephant, wild peacocks, a herd of gaur, and a crested hawk-eagle. If I had opted for the predawn walking safari instead of searching for exotic birds along the shore of Kabini Lake, I would also have seen three leopards sprawling across the limbs of a tree.

Between stints at the hill stations, we took a short detour to the beach. It's a stunning coastline but not home to beach life the way you might think of it. With the exception of fishermen, most Keralans seem to have a distant personal relationship with the ocean.

"It is not part of our culture," a Keralan businessman told me later, when I asked why there were so few people on Marari Beach, a long stretch of white sand six miles north of Alleppey. "The ocean means a lot of sun, and we don't need the tan."

Even as temperatures were pushing the high 80s, the beach was nearly empty, save for a woman in a black burqa chasing a toddler, a few Indian honeymooners, and a dozen fishermen launching a panga into the sea. As much as I wanted to shed my long skirt and long sleeves, seeing the burqa reminded me to stay covered in a

conservative culture that doesn't easily tolerate women in bath-
ing suits. Along this part of the coast, the vibe is local and chill,
and guests like Paul McCartney come to tuck into thatch roofed
bungalows for yoga and Ayurvedic treatments. Western-style sports
like surfing and stand-up paddleboarding are just starting to take
root farther south, near the cliff-edged beaches of Varkala and the
more developed Kovalam.

No matter where I was in Kerala, it kept occurring to me that most
of life here is lived outside. It may not always be in the wide open
spaces and solitude that Westerners so jealously guard as their
birthright, but Keralans have an uncanny knack for integrating
with their natural surroundings, no matter how chaotic or peaceful those may be. In God's Own Country, it's difficult to discern
where humanity ends and nature begins.

A few days later, when I returned to the Western Ghats, I made
an early-morning appointment with Sony Sumi, the first woman
in a long family line of male doctors to practice Ayurveda. She
has two offices: one in her house in the city of Thekkady, to treat
locals, and one at Spice Village, a mountain retreat and Ayurvedic
spa on the edge of Periyar National Park, where we stayed.

"How is your bowel movement?" she asked. "How is your appe-
tite? Your immunity power? Do you like sweet or sour? What kind
of dreams do you have?" After the rapid fire Q and A, Sumi, who
was wearing an elegant gold salwar kameez, took my pulse at her
desk. Behind us was an ornate copper lamp with a steady burning
flame, which, Sumi explained, illuminates the presence of God.

"Before and after the treatments, we pray to God. God resides
everywhere. Do you believe in God?" she asked.

Hindus believe that Ayurveda was handed down from Brahma,
the god of creation, to Dhanvantari, the physician of the gods.
Simplified, its premise is that we are a mixture of three *doshas,* or
energies. If our *doshas* are in equilibrium, our body, mind, and
spirit are healthy. If our *doshas* are out of balance, disease, depression, and physical pain set in. To balance the *doshas* requires a
stringent routine of diet, exercise, massage, and meditation, and
often less pleasant detoxifiers.

"In modern medicines, they treat the particular symptom,"
Sumi told me. "In Ayurveda, we treat the disease from its root.
In such an era of stress, pollutants, and climate change, we can

treat and eliminate toxins by decoctions and by sweating, enemas, bloodletting, and vomiting."

A true diagnosis and treatment can take up to three weeks, but I had only a day, so Sumi diagnosed my primary *dosha* as *vata*. "Basically, the quality of *vata* is movement, very fast acting," she said, which is no surprise to me, considering that I'm a restless wanderer and chronic insomniac. She gave me a long list of foods to eat (like maple syrup and avocado) and to avoid (chocolate and raw garlic) and recommended a *sirodhara* Ayurvedic treatment. After receiving a blessing from the therapist, followed by a rigorous scalp and body massage, I lay flat on my back on a traditional teak Ayurvedic treatment bed while a clay pot that swung like a metronome a few feet above me dripped sandalwood-infused sacred oil in a straight line across my forehead, directly over the third eye. The steady drip relaxes the nervous system and relieves migraines, insomnia, stress, and fatigue. It put me in such a relaxed trance that I wondered if Shiva himself was reaching down to erase my worry lines.

Darwin's Forgotten World

FROM *Smithsonian*

MEETING THE GREAT-GREAT-GRANDSON of the great, great naturalist Charles Darwin demands total immersion in Australian nature. The first step is locating Chris Darwin's abode, hidden in the foothills of a vast, rugged labyrinth of gorges and valleys called the Blue Mountains. From the sleepy hamlet of Glenbrook, a narrow paved road descends into lush eucalyptus forest, where, alone apart from the birds, I spotted a tiny mailbox. I slowly edged my rented vehicle down a sloped driveway flanked by raw sandstone outcroppings, wondering how I would ever manage to reverse back out if this turned out to be the wrong address. The driveway finally ended, much to my relief, at a brick house almost engulfed in foliage. Beyond this point lay a string of nature reserves and national parks—2.5 million acres of pristine bush, just 40 miles west of Sydney.

Darwin bounded out of his doorway to greet me with a hearty handshake along with two curly-haired boys. The lanky, 53-year-old Chris is far more the eccentric Englishman than his sober ancestor Charles. Completely barefoot, he sported a crimson tie with a bird pattern, and britches held up by red suspenders—a Tolkien character in mufti, as if the forest-dwelling wizard Radagast the Brown had gone to Oxford.

"Shall we go into the rainforest?" Darwin asked in his cultivated accent, as his sons hung off his arms in the kitchen. "I think we must really talk about Charles Darwin there. He *loved* rainforest. He said it left him intoxicated with wonder."

"Let's go to the vines!" 9-year-old Erasmus cried out.

"No, the waterhole!" chirped Monty, age 7.

Before we could set off, Darwin insisted we pack hot tea and Christmas cake as sustenance. Soon I was stumbling down a steep dirt track, balancing a steaming cup in one hand and a plate in the other, as the brilliant Australian light flickered though the trees. Shafts illuminated the rainforest floor, a succulent carpet of native ferns and fungi. Climbing vines with evocative names like "wonga wonga" and "wombat berry" snaked upward around the trunks.

"Watch out for that jumping jack nest!" Darwin laughed, nodding to a swarming mound of ants. "They give a hell of a sting." After a slow and (to me) precarious descent, we arrived at a natural pool like a black mirror in the ground. We perched on mossy rocks and attempted morning tea, while the boys roared like wild things, throwing boulders into the water to splash us, Chris all the while smiling indulgently.

There is a satisfying historical logic to the fact that one of the most vigorously nature-worshipping of Charles Darwin's 250-odd direct descendants—a man who gave up a successful career in advertising in London to be a climbing guide and environmental activist, not to mention an expert on his ancestor's storied life—ended up living in this particular pocket of the Antipodes. "Charles Darwin thought the Blue Mountains the most beautiful part of Australia," Chris said, gazing at the exotic greenery, thick with coachwoods, sassafras, and the glossy green leaves of the lilly pilly. "And of course, so do I."

Few non-Australians are even aware that the 26-year-old Charles visited the continent in early 1836 on his round-the-world voyage on the HMS *Beagle*. The fresh-faced Cambridge grad had been invited on the *Beagle* because of his passion for natural history, and when he arrived in Australia, after traveling around Cape Horn and up South America's Pacific coast, his radical ideas were as yet unformed. In fact, young Charles had been groomed for a career in the clergy. As had been his custom, he collected specimens in Australia to take back to London for further study over the coming decades.

Most important, it was Darwin's 11-day adventure in the Blue Mountains that kick-started his thinking on evolution, as historians have shown from his diary, letters, and field notes. The visit would prove as influential for his path to *On the Origin of Species*, published 23 years later, as his canonical studies of the Galápagos Islands.

"When I was a child, my father taught me all about Charles Darwin's visit here," Chris said. "Our family always viewed him as a very romantic figure, and Australia was one of the wonderful exotic places he went to. We liked to imagine him on horseback, riding through the summer heat wave, discovering marvelous things."

On that 1836 excursion, Darwin was puzzled by Australia's strange wildlife, including the duck-billed platypus—the furry, semiaquatic mammal whose appearance is so freakish that British biologists thought the first specimens sent to London were a hoax, fabricated from different animals. Darwin was able to observe it in its natural setting, which upset his religious assumptions. "We were told from a very young age about the 'platypus moment,' which was a real epiphany for Darwin," Chris said. Although his conclusions took two decades to reach, the seeds of his revolutionary theories on natural selection were sown only a few miles from where Chris now lived.

"It was here that Charles Darwin questioned creationism for the first time," Chris said suddenly, between sips of tea. "He came out of the closet, basically."

When the 10-gun sailing vessel HMS *Beagle* hove into Sydney's glittering harbor on January 12, 1836, before a light morning air, according to his journals, Darwin was in a fragile mood. The voyage had already lasted four years, twice as long as expected, and he had been seasick all across the Pacific. He was homesick and lovelorn, too, having recently learned that his teenage sweetheart, Fanny Owen, had married another. Still, he was keen to explore the new British outpost, founded as a prison colony only 48 years earlier: "We all on board are looking forward to Sydney, as to a little England," he wrote.

His optimism was shaken by his first glimpse of the Australian landscape, which was suffering from a protracted drought. Despite impressive sandstone cliffs, he found the bush around Sydney Harbor made up of "thin scrubby trees [that] bespoke sterility." Worse, no letters awaited the *Beagle*'s crew. "None of you at home, can imagine what a grief this is," he wrote pitiably to his sister Susan. "I feel much inclined to sit down & have a good cry." Darwin cheered up a little while strolling around Sydney, which boasted a population of 23,000, now mostly free settlers. "My first feeling was to congratulate myself that I was born an Englishman," he wrote in his diary, marveling at the stores full of fashionable goods, the carriages with liveried servants, and the splendid mansions (although there were rather too many pubs for his liking). The apparent industry made a pleasing contrast to the decay of Spain's much older South American colonies. Over the next few days, the colony's democratic character unsettled him. As a scion of England's ruling class, he was disturbed to note that ex-convicts, once they had served their prison term, were now prospering in business and openly "reveling in Wealth."

To plunge into his nature studies, Darwin decided to travel into the nearby Blue Mountains, where mysterious species (many already renowned among the British scientific community) thrived in a geologically unique setting. He hired a guide (whose name is lost) and two horses. A highway had been carved across the rugged landscape two decades earlier, but it was still difficult going. He passed convict chain gangs under redcoat guard, and a party of aboriginals, who for a shilling threw their spears "for my amusement." Having met the indigenous people of Tierra del Fuego as well as the New Zealand Maoris earlier on the voyage, he condescended to find the aboriginals "good-humored & pleasant [and] far from the degraded beings as usually represented." He predicted that aboriginal contact with convicts and rough settlers from British slums, who exposed them to alcohol and diseases, boded ill for their future.

As for the Blue Mountains, Darwin had expected "a bold chain crossing the country," but instead found the scenery "exceedingly monotonous." (The name originates from the bluish tinge, when seen from a distance, created by tiny droplets of evaporated eucalyptus oil in the air.) His opinion improved at Wentworth Falls, where above the roaring cascade he was astonished by sweeping views of the Jamison Valley. Here were the "most stupendous cliffs I have ever seen," he raved, each precipice topped with ancient forests, framing a "grand amphitheatrical depression" dense with untold numbers of eucalyptus trees, whose "class of view was to me quite novel." He speculated that the valleys were carved by ocean currents. In fact, the Blue Mountains are what remains of a dissected plateau, whose bedrock, deposited by the sea some 250 million years ago, has been eroded by wind and rivers over the eons.

Today, visitors can follow Darwin's route, beginning at Sydney's spectacular ferry terminal at Circular Quay, where the *Beagle* weighed anchor in front of today's Opera House, and traveling the Great Western Highway into the crisp mountain air. In the village of Wentworth Falls, the old Weatherboard Inn where Darwin spent the night is long gone, although his bush trail has been preserved as the Charles Darwin Walk, and it still makes the most exhilarating introduction to the Blue Mountains. The two-mile path follows a creek through a waterlogged forest, known as "hanging swamp," that is alive with native birds, including honeyeaters and screeching black cockatoos feasting on banksia trees, whose flowers resemble spiky yellow brushes. It opens up with a flourish above the 614-foot-high waterfall, with untouched views of those golden cliffs.

It's easy to see why Darwin was taken with the primeval view: one almost expects a long-necked dinosaur to lumber into the scene at any moment. Human settlement has always felt tentative here. The region was thinly populated by early aboriginal inhabitants compared with the warmer hunting grounds of the coast, although the people here did leave their mark in cave paintings of animals and handprints. With white settlement, a few roadside pubs and mining outposts took hold, and in the Victorian age, scenic villages such as Katoomba and Blackheath became vacation resorts. Honeymooners from Sydney marveled at the Three Sisters, a trio of sandstone sculptural forms rising from the bush, and the Jenolan Caves, the world's oldest cave complex, its 25 miles of tunnels filled with gleaming white stalactites and stalagmites of unearthly beauty. The American naturalist John Muir stopped by on his 1904 world tour. Today, the Blue Mountains still boast historic hotels like Lilianfels, where you can take tea and scones in rattan chairs, and the Hydro Majestic, a sprawling art deco gem reopened last year after a decade-long renovation.

The real attraction—the wilderness—still has a huge following of devoted Australian bush walkers. Today, seven national parks and an additional reserve are combined into the Greater Blue Mountains World Heritage Area, whose 2.5 million acres encompass underground rivers, spectacular waterfalls, and natural swimming holes. Some of its slot canyons are so steep that they have reportedly never been visited by humans. There is a sense that any-thing can still be found here—a feeling that was proven in 1994, when a young fieldworker for the park service stumbled across a plant species that scientists had believed extinct for two million years.

David Noble was on a weekend hiking trip in a northern park with two friends, rappelling into remote canyons and spelunk-ing. "I wasn't looking for anything new or unusual," he recalled. "We picked a gully off the map at random to explore." As the trio stopped for lunch in a sheltered niche, Noble observed a cluster of unfamiliar trees looming over them 60 to 100 feet tall, and took a clipping back to the park lab. The staff biologist was unable to recognize it, and a more scientific excursion was arranged. It was soon ascertained that the tree, the Wollemi pine, matched fossils from the Jurassic era.

The discovery caused a sensation in scientific circles and among the Australian public, with tabloids calling the pine a "living dino-saur." The original location of the specimens remains undisclosed to deter souvenir hunters and to protect the vulnerable plants from disease. But the tree has since been cultivated; the public can see the pine in botanical gardens around Australia (including the hugely popular Royal Botanic Garden in Sydney), Europe, Tai-wan, and Japan, with one example in North America, at the Kings-brae Garden in New Brunswick, Canada. "Is there anything else out there in the mountains?" Noble mused. "Well, I didn't expect to find the Wollemi pine! If you look at the sheer [enormousness] of the parks, I wouldn't be surprised what turns up."

From the Jamison Valley, Charles Darwin headed to the frayed edges of colonial settlement, descending the western flanks of the mountains via Victoria Pass. The climax of his trip occurred in an unexpected setting, a lonely sheep station (Australian for ranch) called Wallerawang, where he put up for two nights with the super-intendent, an amiable Scot named Andrew Browne. Darwin found the sandstone homestead sorely lacking ("not even one woman resided here"), and the young gent's sensibilities were offended by the convict farmhands—"hardened, profligate men," he judged, heavy-drinking, violent, and "quite impossible to reform." But, in-spired as ever by nature, he made a horseback day trip on January 19 down into the glorious Wolgan Valley, where he collected rock samples. The fauna fired his imagination, as he noted the kangaroo rat (also called a potoroo), electric-hued rosellas (native birds), and sulphur-crested cockatoos.

But his safari became more profound back at the Wallerawang homestead, when Darwin followed a stream in the cool of dusk and "had the good fortune to see several of the famous Platypus," playing in the water. These wildly peculiar monotremes (egg-laying mammals) were behaving exactly like the water rats he knew back home in England. His companion, Browne, helpfully shot one so that Darwin could examine it more closely.

In the waning sun, Darwin sat by the creek and pondered why the animals of Australia were so eccentric in appearance. The kangaroo rats had behaved just like English rabbits, and even as he considered this, a fierce-looking Australian antlion dug the same conical pit before his eyes as the smaller English antlion would do. According to Frank Nicholas, a now-retired animal geneticist and coauthor (with his wife, Jan) of *Charles Darwin in Australia*, this was a key moment: "The obvious question was, if you were an omnipotent creator, why would you bother going to all the trouble of designing two different species to occupy very similar ecological niches?"

Darwin's diary entry for this day has become widely studied: "A Disbeliever in everything beyond his own reason, might exclaim, 'Surely two distinct creators must have been [at] work; their object however has been the same & certainly in each case the end is complete.'" But the radical difference between the species was baffling: "Would any two workmen ever hit on so beautiful, so simple & yet so artificial a contrivance?" The remarks were expressed in cautious terms, Nicholas argues, because Darwin knew his notebooks would be read by Christian relatives back home. (He adds a hasty creationist disclaimer: "I cannot think so. —The one hand has worked over the whole world.") But one thing is certain, Nicholas says: "This was the first time that Darwin put such a question on paper." Only when writing *On the Origin of Species* did he accept the implications of his heretical thought—that different species had in fact evolved from the same origin over millions of years, changing their characteristics to suit their environments.

"It would be one of the great understatements to call this a portentous moment," writes University of Sydney professor Iain Mc-

Calman in *Darwin's Armada*. "At no other time on the *Beagle* voyage did Darwin raise the issue, and afterwards he buried it for a further twenty years." In retrospect, it is as much of a eureka moment as Isaac Newton's storied encounter with an apple. "One thinks of Charles Darwin as a cold scientist," adds Chris Darwin, "but there was real passion there. He could stare for hours at an ant's nest, or a rose in a garden. In Wallerawang, he sat by himself, gazing at the dead platypus for hour after hour, thinking, 'It just doesn't make sense.' Why had God made the water rat for Europe and North America, and the platypus for Australia? It's terrifying, really."

Today, Wallerawang is a drowsy pastoral town with a pub or two. Instead of the farm where Darwin stayed, there is now a muddy dam. It was created in 1979 to supply a power station, sadly submerging the colonial homestead. Since then, local pride in the connection to Charles Darwin has blossomed. An elderly woman living in a caravan tended a small municipal park named after the naturalist, dominated by a sign: PLEASE DO NOT STEAL THE PLANTS. A few rocks have been arranged as an official memorial to the 1836 visit, complete with a bronze platypus statue.

The nearby Wolgan Valley, however, which Darwin saw on his day trip, still offers an unchanged view of the 1836 frontier. It's Australia's answer to Monument Valley, an otherworldly plain surrounded by mesas, like an arena of the gods. The core 4,000 acres are now a nature reserve as part of the luxurious Emirates Wolgan Valley Resort and Spa, where guests have their own bungalows, each with a private swimming pool. The facility was created (surreally enough) by Emirates Group, the parent company of the airlines, to offset the carbon footprint of its aircraft. (It also has a grove of Wollemi pine saplings, not far from a stream where platypuses can sometimes be spotted at dusk.)

My ultimate goal was one of the oldest structures in the Blue Mountains—a farmhouse dating from 1832 still nestled in a pasture with stunning views of the valley. As the only white habitation in the valley at the time of Darwin's trip, the naturalist would almost certainly have visited. One of the tour guides now employed at the property, Nicholas Burrell, wearing an Akubra hat and R. M. Williams work boots, opened up the doors to the empty homestead for me, as wind whistled through the wooden boards, and opened a dark shed that had housed the farm's 10 convicts. "I've got convicts on two sides of my family," Burrell assured me. Most modern Australians take pride in tracing criminal ancestors: convicts were usually deported for petty theft or other minor offenses, and they are now seen as victims of an unfair system, creating a reverse aristocracy. Burrell then showed me the mummified corpse of a rabbit, discovered by archaeologists when the foundations of the homestead were raised during restoration. It had been buried under a corner post, an old Scottish tradition, he says, to protect the house from evil spirits.

In a country that once gave little heed to its past, the homestead is a rare survivor. For me, standing on the creaking porch hung with rusty tools, I could finally imagine the young Darwin gazing out at this same ancient landscape, his imagination racing.

One of the many astute observations Charles Darwin made on his 1836 Australian tour was that the country's native wildlife was in long-term peril. While staying at Wallerawang, he saw English greyhounds easily chase down a potoroo, and noted that, thanks to overhunting, farming, and introduced predators, settled areas around Sydney were already devoid of marsupials and emus. In a startling continuity across the generations, Darwin's great-great-grandson Chris has joined the campaign to halt extinction in Australia. "My ancestor Charles discovered the origin of species," Chris told me. "I want to stop their mass disappearance."

It wasn't always obvious that Chris, who grew up in London, would fulfill his ancestral destiny. "When I failed my school biology exam, it was quite a family crisis," he recalled with a laugh. "My father wondered if the species was devolving!" His teenage nickname became "the Missing Link." But the Darwin name, he admits, opened doors. "People hope to find a spark of Charles Darwin inside me, so there is more curiosity when they meet me as opposed to, say, Peter Smith."

Chris Darwin was also raised to love nature, and in his 20s, he windsurfed around Britain and hosted what was, at the time, the world's "highest-altitude dinner party," on an Andean peak, with climbers in top hat, tails, and ball gowns; the event raised money for charity and gained an entry in the *Guinness Book of World Records*. But he chose a career in advertising, which caused a lot of stress and unhappiness. "I'm not embarrassed to say that I had a dark period in my life," Chris says. In 1991, at age 30, he attempted suicide. He moved to the Blue Mountains to be surrounded by wilderness, and became a rock-climbing guide. He was still a "climbing bum," as he put it, five years later, when his grandmother left him an inheritance. "I thought, here is a real opportunity to do something for others, as Charles would have wanted!" He donated 300,000 Australian dollars (about $175,000 in U.S. dollars at the time) to an organization called Bush Heritage Australia to create a private nature reserve in Charles Darwin's name. In 2003 the 265-square-mile reserve, one of 35 now managed by Bush Heritage, was established some 220 miles northwest of Perth. It's one of the world's remotest environmental hot spots, where scientists have since found dozens of new and endangered plant, insect, and bird species.

Chris is now taking his anti-extinction message to North America in what he is calling a PR campaign for Mother Nature. The project will start next year or the year after. He plans to meet 20 other direct descendants of Charles Darwin in Manhattan, all wearing beards, wigs, and Victorian suits, to promote a regeneration program for an endangered species of moss endemic to New York State. In California there'll be a black-tie dinner party high in the branches of a redwood tree, perhaps on the anniversary of Teddy Roosevelt and John Muir's famous 1903 trek through Yosemite. In Florida, he hopes to convince the Florida Panthers hockey team to adopt its namesake feline, of which only an estimated 70 survive today.

He thinks his peripatetic great-great-grandfather would have approved.

After traveling as far west as Bathurst in the summer of 1836 (he described himself as "certainly alive, but half roasted with the intense heat"), Charles Darwin rode back to Sydney and set sail again on the *Beagle* with crates of specimens and a jaundiced view (he never went to the city of Darwin; the site was named for him during a later *Beagle* voyage, and only settled in 1869). After stopovers in Tasmania and the port of Albany on the southwest coast of the continent, he admitted that Australia was "an admirable place to accumulate pounds & shillings," but he could not feel comfortable there, knowing that half his fellow citizens were "somewhere between a petty rogue & [a] bloodthirsty villain." His verdict: "I leave your shores without sorrow or regret."

Others on the *Beagle* were more open-minded: Darwin's servant and specimen collector, Syms Covington, soon emigrated back to Sydney, where he thrived, gaining property, becoming a postmaster, and running an inn. The pair corresponded for years, and in 1852 Darwin admitted that, "I feel a great interest about Australia, and read every book I can get hold of." A gold rush allowed the colony to prosper more than Darwin had ever imagined, and four years later he even told Covington he felt a touch of envy that he hadn't settled there himself. Although he was by then a wealthy, respected scientist, Darwin thought that Australia might offer his children a brighter future than "old burthened" Britain. (He would eventually have five sons and three daughters who survived beyond infancy.) "Yours is a fine country," he wrote Covington warmly, "and your children will see it a very great one."

Little Things That Kill You

FROM *Outside*

IF THE DOOMSAYERS are right and we are headed toward a zombie apocalypse, I'll have a laugh from the grave about whoever eats me. Unless they cook my flesh to an internal temperature of 160 degrees Fahrenheit, they're going to experience the same torture that I recently endured after enjoying a meal of undercooked black bear meat in central Alaska that was contaminated with the roundworm *Trichinella spiralis.* The parasites bred inside me and sent forth untold thousands of progeny to burrow through the walls of my vascular system and into my muscular tissue. The gastrointestinal issues were horrific, but not nearly so nasty as the muscle pain. It felt like a bad weightlifting accident spread across my entire body. The Pepsi-colored urine that I was passing served as a visual aid to help me understand just how much hard-won muscle I was literally flushing down the toilet.

The worms were just the latest invaders in a series of microscopic parasites and bacteria that have infiltrated my body in recent years. In terms of severity, the highlight of the run was a bout of Lyme disease, caused by bacteria transmitted through a tick bite that manifested with amnesia and concluded a few agonizing months later with a four-week round of intravenous antibiotics administered through a tube that ran from a hole in my arm to my heart. Preceding the Lyme was a complex case of giardia, an intestinal infection from parasites, that landed me in the emergency room twice in one day and then in a hospital bed for four nights. Following the Lyme was the trichinosis. The larvae of those worms now survive in my muscles, protected by calcified cysts. They have no way of harming me again, though they will make life hell for any creature that digests my uncooked flesh and thereby liberates the legions of pests.

Much of this trouble has come as an occupational hazard. I host a television series called *MeatEater* on the Sportsman Channel that explores the world of hunting, wild foods, and adventure. I've also had a lifelong interest in spending as much time outside as I can, and I'm never happier than when I'm off the grid at my tiny cabin in southeast Alaska, filleting halibut and salmon I caught with my brothers. This lifestyle has brought me up against all manner of threats, including a moose attack, a grizzly charge, and a couple of tussles with wild boars. But it's the microscopic critters that have proven most effective at putting me on the ground. Trust me: anyone who ascribes to that old adage about not sweating the small stuff hasn't spent much time outdoors.

Years ago I went to a lecture by a mountaineer who had recently returned from Mount Everest. During his talk, he discussed a famous study from the late 1990s in which researchers instructed subjects to watch a video of six people playing catch with two balls. The subjects were tasked with counting how many times the balls traded hands between the individuals, who were identified by black and white shirts. Meanwhile, in the video, a woman dressed in a gorilla suit walked through the middle of the game. Half of the subjects failed to see the gorilla, thanks to something that researchers describe as inattentional blindness, or a failure to perceive unexpected stimuli that are in plain sight. But the mountaineer offered his own interpretation: those who see the gorilla survive the mountain; those who don't, do not.

I'd take that argument further and say that those of us who turn a blind eye to the little things we come across are also courting disaster. Granted, a giardia cyst is only about one-fiftieth the size of the period at the end of this sentence. The larvae of *Trichinella spiralis* are plenty small, too—you can't detect them with the naked eye. Trichinosis diagnoses must be reported to the local Department of Public Health, which asked me to provide a piece of the bear meat I'd eaten for testing, in order to verify the cause of my infection. It turns out that the meat contained about 360,000 larvae per pound. That it still looked delicious is a testament to the invisibility of the worms.

Microthreats are hardly confined to the wilderness. From the common cold to the Ebola virus, various nasties could be waiting to pounce on you every time you shake someone's hand. But in the outdoors, there's this whole other league of bizarre and miniature predators desperately wanting to make the jump from the animal to the human world. You could go on for hours trying to name them all: Rocky Mountain spotted fever, leishmaniasis, rabies, malaria, cryptosporidium, hantavirus, tularemia, leptospirosis.

I've been around enough to have accumulated a basic understanding of most of these ailments, a fact that my wife, Katie, used against me when I contracted trichinosis. "You should be embarrassed," she said. "I mean, you know about this kind of stuff!" She raised a valid point, which is perhaps the funniest—or maybe the saddest—part of all this: I'd learned about every one of the diseases that I recently caught well in advance of catching them. In the case of trichinosis, I not only knew about the disease, but I had warned others about it through a book, published articles, and several *MeatEater* episodes.

With giardia, I had gone so far as to read academic papers about the protozoa. What's more, I'd already struggled with minor giardia infections on two separate occasions prior to the day that I contracted my most recent case, while filming in Arizona. On that morning, I was standing at the bottom of a canyon in the Galiuro Mountains after spending a waterless night camped on top of a high butte. I dipped a Nalgene bottle into a creek, filled it with some of the most beautiful water on the planet, and dropped in two iodine tablets. You're supposed to wait about 15 minutes, but I gave it an impatient 5 and then chugged away.

About a week later, I was filming a wild-pig hunt in Northern California when things started to go seriously wrong in my gut. I carried on despite the rising discomfort and ended up getting a nice boar. But the pig must have been rolling in poison oak— within two days, I was covered in rashes from the waist up and running a fever, in addition to suffering from a case of giardia-induced diarrhea. A doctor put me on steroids for the rash, which wreaked havoc on my immune system and undoubtedly heightened the giardia's effect on my intestines. Soon I was passing copious amounts of blood in a hospital bed. When I was released four days later, a doctor inquired about any "prevention plans" that I could use on upcoming outdoor adventures. I thought about the gorilla in the study. It wasn't that I didn't see this one coming, however small it was. But rather than move out of the way, I opted to let it walk up and beat me half to death.

One thing I admire about the small stuff is how insidious it is. The delay that separates the infection date from the onset of symptoms can be weeks or months. If you look at things from the perspective of the disease, the time lapse is a shrewd strategy. For one thing, it makes diagnosis extremely tricky. When I got trichinosis, I was shooting an episode of *MeatEater* that involved taking a Navy SEAL officer on his first hunt. He wanted an intense experience, and I figured that hunting and eating bears in the western Alaska Range would suffice. In total, three crew members and I got sick. There are typically fewer than a dozen reported cases of trichinosis in the United States every year; I'm proud to know a significant percentage of this year's victims. We ate the bear meat on June 6, but the symptoms didn't hit until the Fourth of July. If we hadn't been in touch through work emails, I don't think we ever would have put it together. But knowing that we were all having the same experiences helped us narrow down the list of potential causes. Still, just try walking into a doctor's office and explaining that you've self-diagnosed a condition that's about as relevant today as scurvy. Persuading someone to take you seriously is almost as annoying as the worms.

Another result of delayed symptoms is that it makes the condition seem slightly more palatable. When you're faced with a scenario that might cause you to get sick at some point in the future, it's easier to take risks than if you could get sick right away. The day that I contracted Lyme disease, I was with a buddy in New York's Westchester County, about a 45-minute drive from where I was living at the time. It's one of the nation's worst counties for the disease: the majority of the area's black-legged ticks, which transmit the bacterium, are infected. It was June, which is the high season for humans to contract Lyme. I was walking through tall grass on trails made by white-tailed deer, which host the black-legged ticks. Yet I spent the day traipsing around on those trails without taking any meaningful precautions—no deet, no pant legs tucked into socks, no long sleeves—because I was intent on catching some bluegills from a local reservoir to make fish tacos for my family.

Would I have behaved any differently if you had told me that 50 percent of the ticks in those woods were capable of rising up and smacking me on the head with a baseball bat? Absolutely.

A month later, I was sitting in my office and suddenly I had no idea how I'd gotten there. I couldn't remember waking up or leaving my house that day. I couldn't account for the words written on my computer screen. When I tried to get home, I couldn't remember the route. I called my wife, with difficulty, and she took me to the emergency room. Initially I was diagnosed with something called transient global amnesia; however, a continuation of strange defects in my nervous system—most notably a numbness in my legs that made it difficult to walk—eventually led to an accurate diagnosis of Lyme. The five-month recovery process included a $20,000 course of antibiotics. It's worth mentioning that I didn't catch a single bluegill that day in Westchester County.

Not long ago, while filming in the jungles of Bolivia, I was stung on the ankle by a bullet ant—a gargantuan creature compared with the sorts of things I've been talking about. On the Schmidt Pain Index, which rates insect stings, the bullet ant is the only one awarded a four-plus rating, the highest possible score. The entomologist Justin Schmidt, who created the index, aptly describes it as "pure, intense, brilliant pain. Like walking over flaming charcoal with a three-inch nail grinding into your heel." To me it felt like being stung by a chicken-size wasp, with a deep and throbbing ache that ran from my toes to my knee. I squashed the guilty ant within seconds of it stinging me, not out of malice but to ensure it couldn't hit me again. For the rest of the trip, I went out of my way to enjoy the sight of any bullet ant that I happened to encounter in the jungle. The species had earned my admiration.

On the occasions that I've been sick from microscopic tormentors, I've tried to regard them in the same way that I regard dangerous animals and treacherous landscapes. But hard as I try, I can't quite bring myself to love the little guys. I respect them, sure, but it's like how a general respects an opposing force. It's a respect that is tainted by a desire to see them cleansed from the face of the earth.

But at what cost would the annihilation come, however unlikely it is? How differently would we perceive the outdoors if it weren't for that great biodiversity of little bastards hiding in the water we drink, the food we eat, and the bugs that bite us? In the absence of risk, would we find contentment, or would everything taste and feel a little less exciting? In the words of the great conservationist Aldo Leopold, "It must be poor life that achieves freedom from fear."

I think back to that meal of black bear meat in Alaska. I can picture it perfectly: a collection of purplish red hunks of flesh suspended above the coals on willow skewers as smoke wafted from below and rain fell from above. Distracting me from the task of cooking was a large grizzly that had been hanging around south of camp. We'd been reveling in the presence of the big bear, but if he was going to show up for dinner I wanted to know well in advance. As soon as the outer surfaces of the meat achieved a nice mahogany color with charred accents, we all popped a few pieces in our mouths and then started the long hike back to the lake where we'd landed a week before on a float plane. Flying out of there, I was quick to miss the palpable sense of danger that makes me feel so gloriously alive when in the wilderness. But now I realize that such longings are completely unnecessary. There's a good chance that some part of the wild is tagging along, hiding right inside of me.

Swiss Dream

FROM *The Washington Post Magazine*

I HAD BEEN WALKING around for an hour trying to find a street musician—more precisely, a street musician playing a particular instrument—when I heard the buzzy strain of a clarinet. That wasn't what I was looking for, but maybe it was a start.

Here in the crowded foot traffic of Bern's Old Town, it wasn't clear where the sound was coming from. I took a few steps in a couple of directions until I heard the muffled darts of a Middle Eastern drum accompanying the clarinet. I moved past Stauffacher, a bookstore that featured in its window not one but two books on the pop group Abba, past Magic X, an erotic megastore. At the end of the narrow alley was the clarinetist and a much taller man playing a small darbuka with a stick as thin as a baton.

I leaned against a wall, waiting for the song to end. I pulled out my laminated picture of the hang—an elusive musical instrument, introduced in 2000, which I'd come all the way to Switzerland to find. Under the picture I'd typed a caption: HAVE YOU SEEN THIS MUSICAL INSTRUMENT? Every time I thought the musicians were winding down a tune, they segued into another. After 20 minutes, they'd gone from smiling at me (*Hey, this guy really likes us!*) to looking annoyed (*This guy is creepy, right?*). Finally I stopped them midtune. The pair looked at my picture, then at me. They wore the stony expressions of prison guards.

"Dutch," the drummer said. They didn't speak English.

The hang is a percussion instrument. It resembles a large wok with indentions on the sides and a bubble on top—all of which you strike with your hands to produce the notes. There's an echo

of the steel drum in the sound, but the hang is richer, more reso-
nant. Thousands of people all over the world want one.

In my desperation I mimed playing it, as if that might clarify the
situation, though it must have looked to them as if I was warding
off bees. They shook their heads again and glanced at each other.
I sulked away, but not before the drummer pointed with his toe
toward the basket in front of them.

I fished out two francs.

As I walked away, they started up "Over the Rainbow." The skies
were blue, with the clouds far behind me—that was true—but
my troubles weren't exactly melting like lemon drops. Yes, I was
here in beautiful Switzerland, on a musical crusade of sorts. I had,
though, a sinking feeling that my troubles were just beginning.

Before I bought my plane ticket, my editor had said, "Wait—do
you know it really exists?"

I've been playing the drums since seventh grade and collecting
world percussion instruments my whole adult life. I have a dumbek
from Pakistan, an angklung from Bali, a balafon from Mali, bao
gongs from China, a kalimba from South Africa, a rain stick from
Brazil, and tongue drums, a talking drum, an udu drum, bongos,
a djembe. I have a drum set so elaborate that it's like climbing into
a helicopter cockpit to play it.

I also surf the Internet for drumming videos, and a couple of
years ago I came across an instrument I'd never seen. A blond man
in Rasta dreadlocks—the way Oliver Twist might have turned out
if he'd moved to Jamaica—was playing the hang on a street. His
hands over the instrument were like flowing water, and the melody
was like a message from outer space. I was spellbound.

It was called "the hang" (pronounced "hong"), or "hand" in
the Bernese German dialect, and was created by Felix Rohner and
his partner, Sabina Schärer. The only way you could get one, I
learned, was to write a letter—no emails—and make a case as to
why you were worthy of owning this instrument. Most applications
were denied. The lucky recipient, though, had to fly to Bern to
pick up the hang in person—and pay about $3,000. But not right
away; there was a waiting list of a year or longer.

With two sons still to send off to college, I was no more likely to
pay that than I was to start driving a German tank, but my want was
modest: I was seeking a single encounter.

Felix had cowritten papers for the International Symposium on Musical Acoustics, and sometimes the name Uwe Hansen was attached. I called him to see if he could put me in touch with Felix.

These guys didn't play around. Back in 1966, Uwe's PhD dissertation in physics was titled "Dielectric Anomalies in the Cyclotron Absorption Spectrum of Lead Telluride."

"He's sort of a part-musician, part-scientist, and part-theological philosopher," Uwe said of Felix.

He forwarded an email to Felix for me: "I would travel all the way to Bern for the chance to play a Hang even for five minutes," I wrote.

In his email reply, Felix wrote: "It seems you were touched by the virus of the Hang. This virus is rather strong, and people travel around the world to get touched again . . ."

He also wrote, "The Hang chapter is closed, and we turned the page." His company, PANArt, had modified the hang, and now it was called the gubal.

"This sounds like a project of a pilgrimage," he concluded. "We are not a place like that."

The email was signed by Felix and Sabina.

In my followup, in case I had come off as a stalker, I made clear that I'd also be writing about other music in Switzerland.

He wrote back that their goal was to stay humble. "We do our daily work like monks."

I tried one last angle. Would he at least put me in touch with other hang players?

The maker of the hang didn't respond to that question. He had, essentially, hung up on me.

But Switzerland had more hang players than any other country —I'd seen them in the videos. I'd simply find one myself. Somehow. And if I struck out completely, well, there was other material to be had: the country was crawling with yodelers.

After the clarinetist and drummer in the alley, I went to meet Thomas Burkhalter, a musicologist who runs a worldmusic website called Norient. He had interviewed Felix Rohner in 2001 about his new creation.

"He was very open, but then, he wanted to sell the hang, you know," Thomas said.

Thomas, 41, started Norient in 2002 to showcase experimental music. "I traveled as a journalist—as a print and radio journalist —to places like Istanbul and Cairo," he said, "and I was sometimes a bit annoyed that in Europe people always wanted to hear the cliché side of these places, you know? Like reggae in Jamaica, or if you were in Istanbul, you just want to hear Turkish music."

When we talked about the traditional music of Switzerland— yodeling, accordions, alphorns—Thomas said its popularity had gotten a boost because of the recent rise of the conservative movement.

"In Switzerland we have a big struggle between the left and the right," he said. "You have the conservative side, and that is against Europe, against foreigners, against everything, basically. And then you have the more left side, where we are the part that wants to show another feature of Switzerland—that is modern and open to the world."

The alphorn and the accordion had been co-opted by the conservatives, he said, as if to say, *Why would we ever need anything else?* "So there's the motivation to show, for these musicians, that they are not part of the right wing."

As it happened, I was devoting the next day to getting better rooted in traditional Swiss music in a region few tourists visit. I wasn't likely to find the hang there, but I'd get a good education in the instruments that had helped shape part of the country's musical image for the rest of the world.

The Emmental is a countryside of rolling hills, chalet-style farmhouses, and cows and sheep dotting the plush landscape like snowflakes. East of Bern, it's most famous for its cheese production, which plays a major role in the Swiss economy, but there's another production that goes on here to create some of the country's most recognizable music.

Our first stop was what my driver and interpreter, Christian Billau, called "the Rolls-Royce" of accordion makers: Hansruedi Reist's workshop. Hansruedi made a Schwyzerörgeli, a type of accordion marked by buttons, not keys, and notable for its slender size and elegant craftsmanship.

When we walked into the two-story factory, the air was so thick with the scent of lumber it was like walking into wood itself. Generally, the place would have been teeming with its employees, but many Swiss were on holiday, and there was just Hansruedi, his son, and one other. As Hansruedi, 59, spoke, Christian translated the business's origins:

Hansruedi's father, Rudolf, was an uneducated mechanic out of work in 1966. The family wasn't sure how they could continue putting food on the table, so he had to sell everything he owned —even his beloved accordion. His only idea to earn money was to build an accordion to sell. But how to make it distinctive from all the others in the marketplace?

Rudolf's stroke of genius was to make the treble key arms, which control the air coming in and out, of metal instead of wood. The difference was significant. In humid conditions, the wooden parts made the sound inconsistent. Metal solved that.

That first instrument he sold to a good friend, "and the good friend was a truck driver," Hansruedi said. "When he was making a break at the truck stop somewhere, he [brought out] his instrument and played in the restaurant. And the people came and asked, 'Hey, what kind of instrument is this?' And then he said, 'Ah, it's an instrument my buddy does.'" And that, Hansruedi said, was how "it keeps rolling" today.

In 1994 Hansruedi took over the business from his father, and now Hansruedi's two sons work under him. Rudolf, at 88, still liked to come in each day.

As we toured the shop, where saw blades hung on the wall like family portraits, Hansruedi said the waiting list for a Schwyzerörgeli was at least a year. They produce roughly 140 annually, ranging from $3,000 to $13,000.

Before we left, I fished out my picture of the hang and asked if he had ever seen it. He studied it and shook his head no.

Back in the car, Christian said we were now about to meet the "Rolls-Royce of alphorn makers." (Was this just a Swiss way of seeing things? Was there also a Rolls-Royce of the country's vegetable peelers? Fondue pots?)

The alphorn is a key sound of traditional Swiss music, but you might know it more for the way it looks: usually about 10 feet long, its silhouette conjures indoor plumbing pipes. One plays the alphorn like a bugle: no keys or buttons. All the variations of sound come from the musician, whose notes push down through the instrument like downhill skiers.

Bachmann's Alphornmacherei sits in a valley as green as a Scottish golf course. Inside, Walter Bachmann greeted us in the dimly lit workshop as his father, also named Hansruedi, sanded an instrument on the far end. And just as with Hansruedi Reist, Walter, 42, had a story to tell about the company's origin.

His grandfather Ernst Schuepbach was 13 when he wanted to play the alphorn, but his family was too poor to buy one, so he set out to make his own, which he completed in 1925. He, too, sold his creation to a friend—for 2 francs. When he made his next sale, it went for 50.

Originally, Walter said, "the idea of this alphorn was this communication instrument because you can hear it [from] 10 kilometers, so . . . you can communicate with different tones—about the weather, different things. Warnings."

"The melody explained the mood," he continued. "They played it, and the people on the opposite hill could imagine what the needs were."

Unlike the accordion, though, the alphorn didn't have an easy time finding acceptance, because it was a poor farmer's instrument, Walter said. Farmers came into the city during winter to play for spare coins.

The alphorn's prospects would eventually find a sweeter note, but carrying the instrument could make you wish you played the flute. During World War II, Walter said, the "main transportation was the bike." Fortunately, the alphorn was usually made up of two pieces that could be screwed together instead of a whole cut of wood. That didn't make the instrument any lighter, but it might have cut down on cyclists clotheslining one another.

The alphorn got an unlikely boost by way of Pepe Lienhard, a Swiss bandleader who appeared on TV in 1977 performing the hit "Swiss Lady." The song not only featured the alphorn, it was about the alphorn! (*But when we're playin' our music, it's like a dream coming true / My little Swiss lady—she's a little bit crazy / But when we're playin' our music, I'd like to be an alphorn too.*)

Suddenly, an alphorn boom began, and even furniture makers with no musical background decided to get in on the newfound popularity. They produced alphorns more with machines than with their hands. "They made the quality go down, and the price went down," Walter said.

These days, there are 30 professional alphorn makers in Switzerland, he said, but only 3 others, like Bachmann's, make them all by hand. Their waiting list was even longer than Hansruedi Reist's: two years. (If the country is ever in need of a motto, they might try "Visit Switzerland: The Waiting Capital of the World!")

Walter went trolling through a collection of mouthpieces and fitted one onto the grand horn in front of us. He motioned for me to give it a try.

I put my lips to it and had the distinct feeling I was about to summon a dragon. I inhaled a huge breath, then made a long, sad, gurgling note that, had someone been listening over the hills, might have been translated like this: "Hi, Didier, it's David. From the *Post*. So I don't guess you or Yasmina play the hang, by chance? And I'm hearing good things about your cows this year!"

As we were leaving, I took out my hang picture. Bachmann hadn't seen one in person, but he knew a little about Felix Rohner: "He's quite extreme."

Next, Christian, who is the head of an Emmental tourist office, drove us 12 miles to Switzerland's foremost expert on the zither, if not the world's. (I was sorry, though, to learn that his name wasn't also Hansruedi.) On the way, Christian talked about his own hopes for the Emmental, though they weren't musical ones.

It pained him that visitors to Switzerland came to this region in such few numbers—not more than 3 percent, he said. "This is a lovely countryside of Switzerland, undiscovered countryside," he said. He couldn't help but think that people would love the chance to sleep on these beautiful farms, to hike here and see "the real culture of Switzerland and the real Swiss people." Part of the challenge was that there were too few restaurants, too few inns to accommodate visitors. He had good relationships with the people of the Emmental, though. He was sure he could make it work. But, he said, change didn't come easily here.

While the alphorn and the accordion were doing brisk business, fate hadn't proved so kind to the zither, which might date back as far as the 1500s. Generally the zither is a flat, wooden structure with multiple strings you pluck or strum while either holding it on your lap or in front of you.

At the zither museum, I took out my picture of the hang right away to show Lorenz Mühlemann, who spoke English. Lorenz, 54, said he had heard it on the streets of Bern. "Sometimes it's there, and sometimes it's not," he said.

I told him about my quest and trotted out my premise that the hang was one of Switzerland's great musical contributions. His face tightened, as if he'd just suffered a long, hypodermic needle injection. "There are also other great things in Switzerland concerning music," Lorenz said evenly. "For example, the zither." And so began his tour.

Lorenz's museum is made up of two rooms that showcase an astonishing range of zithers from earlier centuries, some with frescolike art on the main body, or sound box, with the number of strings from 4 to 122.

Why isn't the zither better known today? I asked.

He showed the needle face again. "Well, just because," he said.

Running the museum was just one aspect of his labor of love. He gave concerts, wrote books, gave lessons, did repairs, researched and collected old zither sheet music. He got on the radio and TV about the zither. He had also made more than a dozen recordings himself.

And when he played a zither, its euphony cascaded through the room. Lorenz played exquisitely, intensely, and it was easy to think of him as a man simply born about 100 years too late. In another time, he could have been the Eric Clapton of the zither.

Had it been easy to get visitors to the museum? I asked.

"In Switzerland, nothing is easy," Lorenz said, and released a tight smile.

Considering the zither's long life, its struggle for attention has been relatively recent. "Before World War II," he said, "it was absolutely cool to play this for the young people, and after World War II, it was absolutely uncool." As jazz took off, the trumpet and saxophone became more popular, then, as rock-and-roll emerged, the electric guitar made the zither feel like . . . the zither.

Lorenz picked up one from the 20th century and coaxed out a rather sad melody, but it seemed to fill him up again to strum it. When he was done, the echo of notes drifted through the room like mist. He sat very still.

"Nobody plays it anymore," he said. "It's absolutely forgotten."

In Bern I was staying at the Hotel Innere Enge, also known as the Jazz Hotel. I had taken it as a positive sign that I was booked into the Ahmad Jamal room because Jamal, who was a major influence on Miles Davis and used to play at Washington's Blues Alley every New Year's Eve, is my favorite pianist.

Downstairs, Marian's Jazzroom, which the hotel boasts as being one of the top jazz clubs in the world, was closed that evening, but peering through the window, you see a hologram of Dizzy Gillespie. On the way to the second floor is a wide-eyed bust of Louis Armstrong. And on the third floor is a set of vibes Lionel Hampton used while touring Europe.

One of the chief advantages of staying at the delightful Innere Enge, it turned out, was its proximity to PANArt.

Even though Felix had been clear he didn't want to meet with me, I decided that a single drop-in couldn't hurt. I bargained with myself that I would go just this once, and whatever happened, that would be it. But by the time I got there, after all the stops in the Emmental, the lights were off. I pushed my nose to the glass and peered in.

What I could see, about four feet away, was a shelf of 16 gubals. The new design resembled Saturn. For several minutes I stood there and studied this wine rack of extraordinary music.

It was raining, which seemed appropriate enough. They were right there, yet I felt as if I were still 4,000 miles away.

If I had had an alphorn, the message I would have sent would have been shorter this time. And in the key of D.

"Damn."

On my third day, I walked over to a music store called Musik Müller to talk to Tom Gunzburger, 42, the head of the drums and percussion section. Tom had had his own experience with Felix Rohner. In the beginning, Felix had let him sell the hang in the store.

"And then suddenly [Felix] says, 'Stop.' He doesn't want to have to do something with shops. He just wants to sell by himself. That was it."

Over time, Musik Müller began to sell the knockoffs that slipped into the marketplace. (PANArt was late and, ultimately, unsuccessful in trying to patent its design.) There was the German-made caisa that Musik Müller displayed in the front window. One day, Felix happened to be walking by. "He saw that, and he came in and was very angry," Tom said. "And said, 'Well, with this instrument you destroy your shop.'"

"What the hell?" Tom said now, at the memory of that encounter. Sometime after, there was a repeat performance when the store started carrying another knockoff, produced in France, called the Spacedrum. "This is not a good copy," Tom said Felix told him. "They all make shit."

There was, of course, a waiting list for the Spacedrum, too. For me, the Spacedrum was like encountering a Marilyn Monroe impersonator. A little stirring at first, sure, but to feel anything more is to give yourself permission to feel dishonest. And I hadn't come all this way for a substitute.

I fished out my map of Bern and went looking for a spot where someone said they'd seen a hang player recently. It happened to be in front of the Einstein House, where Albert Einstein lived from 1903 to 1905, when he was developing his special theory of relativity. Inside, you see the parlor room where the great thinker might have scribbled notes on the spacetime continuum.

When I came out, there was no hang player around, but a dulcimer player had set up. He was playing something familiar, but it took me a minute to place it: "Smoke on the Water," by Deep Purple, with its simple, Neanderthalish guitar riff. On dulcimer, though, it sounded as if Deep Purple had been turned into a phalanx of fairies.

I walked across the street to the Bern Conservatory, where Markus Plattner, 62, the assistant director and an accomplished guitarist, had agreed to meet me. Markus's office was airy and orderly, with a keyboard and acoustic guitar at easy reach from his desk. Long windows opened to a pleasant breeze.

Years ago, he told me, he and the director were invited to Felix's house to see the hang. "We went there because we were generally interested in maybe having the hang at the school," he said. "I remember, I felt a bit strange. We never got to talk to [Felix]. He didn't actually talk. [Sabina] took care of the conversation."

The conservatory did get a hang, but after a while, Markus said, Felix demanded to have it back without explanation.

At that point, the plinking sounds of round two of "Smoke on the Water" cascaded in. Markus stopped to listen and said, "What we're hearing out there, the dulcimer, that's very popular right now." He said there was a new folk scene in Switzerland, with influences from jazz, pop, and rock. Injected with a modern sensibility. That got him onto the subject, as it had for Thomas at Norient, about the identity of the country. Conservatives, he believed, were saying, "We don't need all that modern stuff. We have our folk music, our yodeling, our Schwyzerörgeli." But, he pointed out, "for artistic musicians, that doesn't cover it all, does it?"

Before we said goodbye, I asked him if he'd play something on the guitar. He cradled it in his arms as if it were a toddler and began to pluck "The Nearness of You." It was soulful and strained with a little melancholy, I thought. Or maybe that was just the mood I had fallen into. It was late afternoon, and I had only one full day left to find the hang.

Journalist Jessica Dacey had interviewed Felix and Sabina for a story on the website SWI (Swissinfo.ch) two months earlier. She agreed to meet, and when we sat down that evening in a wine bar she said she was still surprised she had even gotten the interview.

In her story, she referred to the hang as "a kind of Holy Grail for tens of thousands of people around the world."

In the piece, Felix says: "20,000 letters and everyone is talking about the same thing. They tell us the story of when they first encountered this sound."

"They want to keep it a small production," she said, as a guess as to why they wouldn't talk with me. "They're not interested in making money. For them it's all about the artifice. In fact, they don't even call it an instrument—they call it a sound sculpture."

Jessica, 43, knew plenty about music: her husband is a British recording artist who goes by the name Merz (in one of his videos, set in the woods, he plays with a drum ensemble that keeps the beat by hitting trees and rustling leaves—perhaps to invoke nontraditional forces. Or maybe the budget was just really low). She suggested that the musical experimentation in the country, and also the jazz influence and the very openness in Swiss culture, was a perfect combination for the unique qualities of the hang.

"It's one of those things that kind of transcends culture," she said.

The evening sky was turning pink and violet, and she needed to head off. The streets were quiet, and all the way back to my hotel it occurred to me that my being booked in the Ahmad Jamal room had been all wrong. I was in search of a percussion instrument; I should have asked for the Louie Bellson room. Bellson pioneered the use of two bass drums at once, and Duke Ellington called him "the world's greatest musician." The Louie Bellson room had drumsticks on the wall, a mounted snare drum!

I felt more behind the beat than ever.

A musician who lived in Liestal, a 50-minute train ride north, had expressed an openness to meeting, but the way my luck was going, I figured I'd reach the town and spend the next hours waiting in vain.

On my last day in Switzerland, though, Andreas Gerber, 57, pulled up on his bicycle exactly when we said we'd meet. Andreas, who has the wiry build of someone who has been too busy his whole life to eat, took me up to the loft of a building that also housed a movie theater, and opened the door.

The cavernous room was like Santa's workshop if Santa Claus were a Nigerian percussion master. There were steel drums and a whole wall of African bells. There were shakers and gongs and pouches of decorative mallets posted on wooden beams, berim-baus and a balafon. There was a piano and string instruments, and more hand drums than I could count. And in front of all of that, Andreas had set out two hangs—not unlike the way a date might set the table for a romantic dinner—next to each other on stands, shimmering like blue diamonds.

Here is what followed:

We played the same hang together, and we played the hangs separately. Improvising melodies. He jumped on the piano as I played, and he picked up the guitar and grabbed shakers and the melodica and lorded over the rantang. Sometimes he sang as we played—in English, in German, in no language at all.

For me, playing the hang was like a first kiss, in that it was both wonderful and maybe not exactly what I had imagined. Or maybe it was like driving an exquisite foreign sports car for the first time: I didn't always know where to put my hands. I went too fast. I felt unworthy. (Wait, did I just describe my first kiss again?)

Andreas would have a story for each of his five hangs (here was the one his wife sang most beautifully with; here was the one he loaned to a friend whose friend was dying and wanted to play it while he still could . . .), and he would have me play each one.

He told me of his travels and studying music in Brazil, Korea, Africa, India, Bali, California.

His father had been a preacher, and he was raised in a fundamentalist Christian environment. Church music pervaded the house. But there was no denying Andreas "Satisfaction" when his two older brothers made him aware of the Rolling Stones. "That was a turning point," he said. "It gave me electrifying feeling for my body."

It led him, eventually, into the study of TaKeTiNa, which emphasizes the healthy effects rhythm has on the mind, body, and soul. He has been teaching that and improvisation for decades. But even for a world traveler and musician, the discovery of the hang cast a spell.

"It's the most beautiful sound I ever heard," he said.

Over the years he kept going back to Felix for more. No two hangs are exactly the same, and Andreas kept falling in love with another and expanding the family like a musical polygamist. He wanted to use them in groups, with choirs, whatever musical context interested him. But, he says, Felix became disapproving of this approach, and eventually their relationship became more tense.

"He started more and more saying the hang is not a drum, not a percussion instrument," Andreas said. "'The hang brings you back to yourself. The role of this instrument in the world is to bring people back to their self, their center.' Which is a beautiful thing . . . I respect this vision, but here's my 'but': I find it not OK to say that people who do something else with it mistreat it, are doing wrong."

We kept playing.

Andreas understood that when this story came out, Felix might end their relationship. This would be particularly difficult, he explained, since Felix and Sabina were the only people he knew who could tune a hang.

But, he said, "I'm a free man."

We both knew when we had played our last notes together.

By the time I stepped outside again, I was amazed to realize that, as much as I had loved playing the hang, I no longer harbored the fantasy of owning one. I had something better now: the memories of meeting all these good people over these four days and hearing their stories—and their wonderful playing. And memories wouldn't need tuning.

Maybe Felix was right: maybe I had had the virus. Now I seemed to be cured.

At the station, as the train rounded the bend to take me back to Bern, I reached out to shake Andreas's hand, but he pulled me into an embrace. We broke into laughter—over the fact that I'd come so far for this encounter, that we were two people who took such immense pleasure in the beating of a drum.

The endless roads you could travel to find harmony.

Peak Havana

FROM *Outside*

IN FEBRUARY I was rolling in an old, squeaking taxi through Havana, headed back to my rented digs atop a house in the tiny Chinatown. I got the room in a way many travelers to Cuba will recognize: a friend passed me a phone number, which was never answered. Eventually, days after arriving in Havana and after pursuing the owner halfway across the city in person, I booked the room, which had been available all along. That was how Cuba worked, or didn't work. After 23 years reporting all over the island, I'd grown accustomed to the frustrating mixture of disciplined dictatorship and tropical chaos, the steady state of an island where nothing seemed to change, ever.

But travel is best in the cracks, in the unexpected encounters between appointments, in the crucial subtleties revealed when —according to our expectations and schedules—nothing is happening. So it was that night. My taxi passed by a restaurant, and I looked with exhausted envy at the warm interior, the soft lights, the well-dressed people eating from nice plates. Vibrant, disorganized music spilled out the doors, and a woman was dancing, spinning alone.

We kept moving, and I vowed to come back another day. But then a sudden doubt hit me. The place looked fun now, but would it be tomorrow? At the end of the block, I jumped out of the taxi and walked back.

The restaurant, Siá Kará Café, was unusual for Cuba, even weird: lots of cushions and low seating, eclectic décor, and a large and attentive staff serving food that arrived promptly. What's with that? Even more unusual were the guests. I was used to Europeans and Canadians idling in the bars, but here were actual Cubans, including a pair of uniformed flight attendants for an airline I'd never heard of and a loud family celebrating something over beers and beef skewers. There was a good piano player and then a great one, playing song after song, many of them improvised or unheralded, a fusion of jazz and classical, an almost heedless performance cheered on by the increasingly drunken customers.

Was this really Havana, the grim citadel I'd been obsessing over for two decades? Was this the real Havana at last? A place as good as the legend?

Outside, cooling off, I noted the rest of the block. Dead. Dead and dark in the truly Cuban way. Both sides of the street were a long run of shuttered entrances and windows.

So what? I'd bought countless meals for Cubans in tourist places that they could never afford—or even enter—on their own. But this was the first time in 23 years I'd sat, eaten, danced on an equal footing with Cubans themselves, and it was for one simple reason: they could pay for it.

A nice restaurant, a good song, a cold drink. So what? So long to the old Cuba, that's what.

Americans always say we want to see Cuba *before*. We don't really say before what.

Before it changes into something else? Before Burger King gets there, before Nike and Spotify and global Taylorism turn Cuba into just another place? This is Cuba's dilemma. Isolation and authenticity are its greatest lures, proof that the rebel island isn't just anywhere. But they come at a terrible price. For Cubans, the quaint sleepiness that pops up in our viewfinders is a rusted poverty. And for foreigners, nothing is ever authentic enough.

Even stomach bugs don't plague the modern traveler as much as the nagging suspicion that *this* isn't really *it*. The *it* was always some time ago, in some other place. We fear we are missing Cuba the way it was, or was supposed to be. We don't want to be those people, the ones who arrived too late.

But that's nearly impossible. Today's jet-setter expects, as travel writer and historian Tony Perrottet told me, "to be the only traveler in a remote Amazon village, the first to find a quote-unquote untouched outpost in New Guinea. This is at the heart of the frustration travelers will no doubt feel in Cuba."

In other words, we want to see the island before we ourselves can get there to ruin it.

Bad news: everybody but us is already there. Cuba's 60,000 hotel rooms are booked solid by more than two million tourists each year, mostly Canadians and Europeans who spend their visits at wristband beach resorts that have precisely zero correlation to unspoiled anything. The United States severed diplomatic ties and cut off trade with Cuba back in 1961, and for decades the Treasury Department has blocked Americans from using credit cards in the country. Those who visited Cuba legally had to book educational or cultural tours that were nominally sponsored by universities or nonprofits and supervised by polite functionaries of the Cuban state tourism authority. That meant being shuttled from the Museum of the Revolution to a canned cabaret at the Tropicana, with a stop in the colonial hill town of Trinidad and one afternoon of free time to encounter a Cuba off the books. It wasn't all so bad: in the remote town of Baracoa, I once met a busload of drunk Americans who were here legally "studying Cuban rhythm."

But tens of thousands of U.S. citizens snuck into Havana illegally every year, passing through Cancún or Nassau. (In some years, I tallied four of those visits.) During his first term, Obama zeroed out the funding to pursue such scofflaws, and since December a cascade of travel reforms has seen JetBlue's first flight to Havana — a nonstop from JFK for authorized travelers — and a new plan for ferry service from Key West. Florida-based Carnival Cruise Line, the largest operator on the planet, has won approval from U.S. authorities to begin biweekly landings in Cuba next May, using the *Adonia,* a 710-passenger ship themed around "social impact" voyages. At press time, in early August, Congress was debating lifting the trade embargo entirely. When that happens, up to a million Americans are expected to join the existing crowds.

The abrupt onset of reforms inside Cuba means that for the first time, individual, self-organized travel is becoming less onerous and expensive. A new generation of Americans will soon be able to explore Cuba at their own pace, doing things that should be perfectly routine but aren't, like renting cars, climbing crags, or setting their own itineraries — all difficult or banned under Fidel

Castro. Obama's diplomatic opening gets much of the credit, but Raúl Castro has been making changes ever since he took the reins from his ailing brother nearly a decade ago. Only now, after years of glacial Cuban bureaucracy, have his simple economic reforms —legal self-employment, cheaper Internet access, increased rights to travel abroad, the licensing of hundreds of thousands of private businesses—begun to take effect.

As recently as 2013 I noticed little change in the day-to-day life of Cubans, but this February I was stunned to come back after two years and find the island transformed. I saw this even in small towns like Cárdenas and Sancti Spíritus, but it is most obvious in Havana, where everything seemed to have a new coat of paint, including the old cars. For decades those old Chevys and Buicks were among the few private cars in Cuba, but they are increasingly shoved aside by fleets of Korean Kias and Chinese Geelys that are easier to import for the small new business class. Some 360,000 such enterprises, from repair shops to media companies, have been licensed since 2011, and out of 11 million Cubans, a million were released from mandatory and practically unpaid state employment to earn their own living. The result has been a surge in economic growth and optimism unseen in half a century.

The tourism business was the obvious winner, and Havana in particular is booming, the hotels full and the ancient alleys thronged with foreigners. Airbnb launched last April with 1,000 members —and doubled that number in 40 days. TripAdvisor now reviews 522 restaurants in Havana alone. (About one of my favorites, the hipster bar 304 O'Reilly: "Everything was very good, which is an especially rare thing in Cuba.") The home cafés called *paladares,* little places with just 12 chairs, have been superseded by large private restaurants with scores of employees and ingredients sourced from the first wave of private farms in the countryside. You already have to elbow your way through a crowd to get a mojito where Errol Flynn used to drink. But the changes go much deeper: the population is better fed, better dressed, and (crucially) sure that, with Havana and Washington both changing, their future has finally arrived.

I never fell in love with Cuba, not quite. My first visit, in 1991, was mercenary, a writer's attempt to find a story no one else was seeing. The Cuban Revolution may have started with a giant party, but long before I arrived it became a dead hand on Cuban life, the easygoing, tropical version of a Warsaw Pact summer vacation. That first trip, I slept in a spartan "national" hotel in Havana that cost just $7 a night and came with a radio and an air conditioner labeled in Cyrillic. In 1993, in Cienfuegos, a once-elegant sugar port on the south coast, food was so scarce that I waited in line for an hour and was questioned by two plainclothes cops before I was allowed to eat a small dish of paella. Flavored with iron and diesel, it was unforgettably the worst meal of my life—and yet a privilege in a country that was starving. Back in Havana, I watched two dogs fight to the death for a tiny pile of garbage.

Those were the hunger years, but for two decades I came back, inspired and awed by the ability of Cubans to not just survive but adapt and even thrive. I chronicled the island's weaknesses—that would be the commie dictatorship, the repression of human and political rights, the petty controls over every aspect of life. But I also found and described strengths. I wrote about the stunning oceans and untouched coastlines, benignly neglected for decades by a revolution that could provide no gasoline and whose fishing boats disappeared routinely to Key West. I once lived for a month in Havana on the average Cuban salary, which amounted to dimes a day—an exercise in hunger but also solidarity. Cubans gave me a lesson in survival and an answer to why the best people live in the worst places.

Two books emerged from my obsession—one on Che Guevara, another on Fidel. Cuba's edge was darker than other places, if less sharp. The benefits of free education and health care, as well as a ruthless police state, drowned out all opposition, and Havana in the 1990s was a city of whispering and petty corruption, squalid deals and transparent jockeying for plates of chicken. Everyone lied every day. If you could swim in this queer pool, it was an unforgettable experience.

But was it authentic? No. Foreigners want a Cuba that doesn't change, but Cubans want exactly that: change. "They want their iPhones," says Alfredo Estrada, the Cuban American author of *Havana: Autobiography of a City*. "They've been living in a very unnatural state of isolation, and they want to join the global community," to get "very modern very quickly."

We want them to keep driving those cute old cars. We're nostalgic for a Cuba that shouldn't exist—constrained by our embargo and crippled by dictatorship. Estrada calls the desire to visit an unchanged Cuba patronizing, as if the island is a museum, not a nation entitled to a future.

That future, he says, should include the careful preservation of all that does make Cuba distinct. Some of the first towns built in the Americas are here, including Santiago de Cuba, now the island's second-largest city, a charming Caribbean destination despite losing much of its early architecture in fires and earthquakes. Havana, once the New York City of Latin America, avoided wholesale redevelopment after 1959 in "a fortunate accident," says Estrada. "So let's prolong the accident, because that's what's going to draw people to Havana. Keep the beauty and it will bring a lot of prosperity to the people of Havana."

Foreigners still can't buy real estate, but someday hotel companies and investors will snatch up the properties now moldering in historic parts of Cuba, and choice Old Havana houses may be worth millions in ten years. The Cuban government has mostly protected ordinary residents from displacement, but that will probably change. "A lot of those people are going to get screwed," Estrada says with a sigh, before adding, "Hopefully not."

But Havana, along with Cuba as a whole, is deservedly ripe for improvements. Much of Old Havana has been without running water for decades. The famous Malecón seafront promenade is in desperate condition, even abandoned in parts. "You are going to have all the usual tourist crap," Estrada acknowledged, "but with that will come economic development, growth, restaurants, vendors. And it's not just the physical hotels—it's the industry, the people, the systems."

"Go," Estrada tells people. "Go as soon as possible. Who knows what will happen in five or ten years, what kind of transition will occur? Go now."

Simple advice. We should go to Havana, not before it changes but so that it does change. So that it can change. The most authentic Cuba is the one still to come.

My own Cuban fantasy isn't the *daiquiri mulata*, made with crème de cacao, or an old Nash Rambler rumbling slowly through the rugged streets. There was always a time before we got there, but the past is easy in Cuba. What I want is the next chapter.

Once, a few years ago, I set off across Old Havana with Estrada's history of the city in hand, reading as I walked, crossing from the founding stones at the Plaza de Armas to the *extramural,* literally the outside-the-walls development of the modern metropolis. This old colonial city, the largest remaining in the hemisphere, was belted with defensive walls in the late 17th century, some of which are still visible among the bars of Monserrate Street. Havana continued growing outward, an encyclopedia of architecture, often on the same block, with turn-of-the-century baroque and Catalan art nouveau, Mudéjar movie palaces from the early 20th century, and an ambitious blast of 1950s modernism, like the insanely atmospheric Riviera Hotel, a casino built by gangster Meyer Lansky far from the prying eyes of the FBI. This built history is the single most unshakable thing about Cuba, but the revolution added almost no gestures of its own to the city—the empty Plaza of the Revolution, the never-finished National Art School, and a few monuments to Che. The power elite preferred a modest setting like El Aljibe, a restaurant thatched like a peasant hut that still serves the best black beans and orange-marinated chicken in Cuba.

The pickled authenticity of Old Havana and a few magnets like Trinidad, a UNESCO World Heritage town to the southeast, will change quickly under the assault of decentralized tourism. But most of Cuba needs change. Continue just a mile or two from the gentrified zone along Obispo Street and you'll find plenty of untouched, neglected authenticity, like El Cerro, where wrecked 19th-century mansions decorated with laundry spill down a long road, people living as if they have no holes in their roofs. Tourism has had little effect on such places. You can drink a thimble of sweet coffee from a street vendor and see no other foreigners, no matter how long you wait. Sometimes raw El Cerro feels more authentic than polished Old Havana.

Still, it can be hard to tell the real from the fake. Santeria, the Afro-Cuban religion, is packaged nightly for tourists in Nikon-friendly events. A Cuban devotee assured me that this was faux Santeria, not the true thing. Yet the chaotic, sweat-soaked home ceremonies I'd attended over the years were much the same: crowded initiation rites and birth celebrations that weren't complete without rum, demonic possessions, and gifts of cash. What about the Riviera, for that matter? It was confiscated by the Castro government in 1959, but Lansky would be proud: it's still a notorious hotel full of prostitutes, just like he always wanted.

Every walk around Havana unspools 500 complex years. In 15 minutes you pass from the stones laid by conquistadors to *la esquina caliente,* the "hot corner," where men argue baseball all day. A few blocks and half a millennium later you're in El Floridita, where they serve the Hemingway daiquiri, a double made with grapefruit juice and (gasp!) no sugar at all.

Hemingway spent decades on the island, and called himself a *sato,* a run-of-the-mill Cuban. But I don't know what he was thinking. Why would you want Cuba without the sweet stuff?

JEFFREY TAYLER

Fyodor's Guide

FROM *The Atlantic*

TENS OF THOUSANDS of dragooned serfs perished while draining the swamps to lay the foundations of St. Petersburg, and residents like to remind visitors that their city, enchanting though it
may be, "rests on bones." Its charnel mansion has fed the imagination of some of Russia's greatest writers, most notably Fyodor
Dostoyevsky, whose works are lodged deep in mine: *Crime and
Punishment* and *Notes from Underground* are two masterpieces of the
many in Russian literature that inspired me to become a writer.
I recently traveled to St. Petersburg to reconnect with him and
his environs, hoping to rediscover something of the passion that
drove me to move to Moscow 21 years ago—a passion dimmed by
the return of the authoritarian state, with its soul-numbing gloom.
An unlikely mission, I know, to seek uplift from the high priest of
alienation.

I began my tour at the last of Dostoyevsky's many apartments:
in his 28 years in the city, the Moscow-born writer moved some 20
times, ending up in Kuznechny Lane 5/2, a stately fin-de-siècle
building. The flat has been converted into the Dostoyevsky Liter-
ary-Memorial Museum. My spirits rose as I was warmly welcomed
by a coterie of motherly, middle-aged women, who broke the long-
standing tradition that museum employees in Russia must excel in
gruffness to get their jobs.

Despite the grim oil paintings adorning the walls—one depicting the Last Supper (in the dining room, of course) and another,
in the drawing room, showing the biblical Agony in the Garden
—nothing suggests that Dostoyevsky, psychologist of tortured out-

casts, was anything but a conscientious family man, born to the gentry class. His sanctum sanctorum was his study, a modest chamber with green-patterned wallpaper, a parquet floor, and a desk the size of a pool table, covered in green felt.

To the accompaniment of heavy tick-tocks—in the hush, the grandfather clock in the adjacent drawing room sounded loud —I stood perusing an explanatory placard, marveling that Dostoyevsky could have been quite so domestic, even if a night owl. "The least disorder would annoy father," one of his daughters reported. Starting at 11:00 p.m., he wrote in candlelit solitude, tolerating no interruptions. Around dawn he would retire, burrowing into the bed in his study, with his overcoat laid on top of the sheets. He slept until noon. He adored super-strong tea, scalding coffee, Kiev jam, chocolate, and blue raisins, which he shopped for on nearby Nevsky Prospekt, to this day the most glamorous commercial avenue in St. Petersburg. He enjoyed reading his works in public, in his "high but piercing sharp voice."

The kindly docent posted in the sedate drawing room sabotaged my calm, supplementing the homey scene with her own narrative. Emperor Nicholas I, unsettled by the revolutions of 1848 in Europe, began cracking down on subversives not long after Dostoyevsky started attending meetings of the Petrashevsky Circle—intelligentsia who gathered to read the forbidden works of European socialists. My guide spared no details of the special punishment the emperor had in store for Dostoyevsky and his fellow members. Arrested and ultimately thrown into the city's hulking prison, they were first stripped to their underwear in minus-30-degree weather to face a firing squad, sacks over their heads. The drums rolled —and then, instead of gunshots, they heard a messenger galloping up to grant them commuted sentences. Dostoyevsky got four years in prison and exile in Siberia. He also got material for *House of the Dead,* one of the great prison novels of world literature.

Heading out into the wind-whipped streets, I went in search of 104 Griboyedov Canal Embankment, where, on the third floor, in apartment 74 of entryway No. 5, the troubled young antihero of *Crime and Punishment,* Rodion Raskolnikov, splits open the skull of a usurious old pawnbroker with an ax butt—a scene so graphic and disturbing that I suffered nightmares after first reading it three decades ago.

When I had last visited, in September 2000, I had opened the door to the entryway and climbed the stairs, inhaling a reek of mold and urine. Standing before the apartment, I had examined its door (covered by a layer of reddish leatherette, as I remember): here Raskolnikov had hesitated before he knocked, his ax concealed beneath the folds of his ratty coat. I had the feeling that nothing, not the decrepitude, the smells, or the sepulchral light, had changed since Dostoyevsky's day.

This time, after entering the vast courtyard, I found the entryway secured by a code-locked steel door. Frustrated, I looked up: the courtyard's walls, streaked with grime, seemed concave and irregular, as if drawing together toward the top. A feeling of claustrophobia seized me, as it had so many of Dostoyevsky's heroes, trapped in rooms variously described as "closets," "dog holes," "cabins," and "coffins."

I was luckier, and took refuge in the Idiot Restaurant, a hangout of the city's artsy intelligentsia. Soothed by plush blue carpeting, brocaded oaken sofas and easy chairs, spangled chandeliers, and flickering candles, patrons nursed mugs of beer and glasses of French wine, sprawled in a relaxed way unusual in Russia. I tossed back the complimentary shot of vodka and read the menu's salute, in twisted English, to my hero. The probably apocryphal tale of Dostoyevsky's fleeting ownership of the place—he was forced to sell it, the story goes, to pay gambling debts—inspired a tribute that was as close to a pick-me-up as I was going to get:

> Human masses were puddying in mud and dust and misery in city districts roaming public and gambling establishments. He was young, slim, and poor, maybe not handsome, but energetic talented and hot-tempered, a gambler to the bone.

I wasn't young or energetic, but a glass of red Bordeaux helped to rally the gambling spirit that has made me the expatriate I am. Ever more stifling though the Putin era gets—and I'm betting on worse to come—I'm sticking around to watch.

Return of the Mockingbird

FROM *Smithsonian*

THE TWIGGY BRANCHES of the redbuds were in bloom, the shell-like magnolia petals had begun to twist open, the numerous flowering Bradford pear trees—more blossomy than cherries —were a froth of white, and yet this Sunday morning in March was unseasonably chilly in Monroeville, Alabama. A week before, I had arrived there on a country road. In the Deep South, and Alabama especially, all the back roads seem to lead into the bittersweet of the distant past.

Over on Golf Drive, once a white part of town, Nannie Ruth Williams had risen at 6:00 in the dim light of a late winter dawn to prepare lunch—to simmer the turnip greens, cook the yams and sweet potatoes, mix the mac and cheese, bake a dozen biscuits, braise the chicken parts and set them with vegetables in the slow cooker. Lunch was seven hours off, but Nannie Ruth's rule was "No cooking after church." The food had to be ready when she got home from the Sunday service with her husband, Homer Beecher Williams—"H. B." to his friends—and anyone else they invited. I hadn't met her, nor did she yet know that one of the diners that day would be me.

The sixth of 16 children, born on the W. J. Anderson plantation long ago, the daughter of sharecropper Charlie Madison (cotton, peanuts, sugarcane, hogs), Nannie Ruth had a big-family work ethic. She had heard that I was meeting H.B. that morning, but had no idea who I was, or why I was in Monroeville, yet in the southern way, she was prepared to be welcoming to a stranger, with plenty of food, hosting a meal that was a form of peacemaking and fellowship.

Monroeville styles itself "the Literary Capital of Alabama." Though the town had once been segregated, with the usual suspicions and misunderstandings that arise from such forced separation, I found it to be a place of sunny streets and friendly people, and also—helpful to a visiting writer—a repository of long memories. The town boasts that it has produced two celebrated writers, who grew up as neighbors and friends, Truman Capote and Harper Lee. Their homes no longer stand, but other landmarks persist, those of Maycomb, the fictional setting of *To Kill a Mockingbird*. Still one of the novels most frequently taught in American high schools, Lee's creation has sold more than 40 million copies and been translated into 40 languages.

Among the pamphlets and souvenirs sold at the grandly domed Old Courthouse Museum is *Monroeville: The Search for Harper Lee's Maycomb*, an illustrated booklet that includes local history as well as images of the topography and architecture of the town that correspond to certain details in the novel. Harper Lee's work, published when she was 34, is a mélange of personal reminiscence, fictional flourishes, and verifiable events. The book contains two contrasting plots, one a children's story, the tomboy Scout, her older brother, Jem, and their friend Dill, disturbed in their larks and pranks by an obscure housebound neighbor, Boo Radley; and in the more portentous story line, Scout's father's combative involvement in the defense of Tom Robinson, the decent black man, who has been accused of rape.

What I remembered of my long-ago reading of the novel was the gusto of the children and their outdoor world, and the indoor narrative, the courtroom drama of a trumped-up charge of rape, a hideous miscarriage of justice and a racial murder. Rereading the novel recently, I realized I had forgotten how odd the book is, the wobbly construction, the arch language and shifting point of view, how atonal and forced it is at times, a youthful directness and clarity in some of the writing mingled with adult perceptions and arcane language. For example, Scout is in a classroom with a new teacher from North Alabama. "The class murmured apprehensively," Scout tells us, "should she prove to harbor her share of the peculiarities indigenous to that region." This is a tangled way for a six-year-old to perceive a stranger, and this verbosity pervades the book.

I am now inclined to Flannery O'Connor's view of it as "a child's book," but she meant it dismissively, while I tend to think that its appeal to youngsters (like that of *Treasure Island* and *Tom Sawyer*) may be its strength. A young reader easily identifies with the boisterous Scout and sees Atticus as the embodiment of paternal virtue. In spite of the lapses in narration, the book's basic simplicity and moral certainties are perhaps the reason it has endured for more than 50 years as the tale of an injustice in a small southern town. That it appeared, like a revelation, at the very moment the civil rights movement was becoming news for a nation wishing to understand, was also part of its success.

Monroeville had known a similar event, the 1934 trial of a black man, Walter Lett, accused of raping a white woman. The case was shaky, the woman unreliable, no hard evidence; yet Walter Lett was convicted and sentenced to death. Before he was electrocuted, calls for clemency proved successful; but by then Lett had been languishing on death row too long, within earshot of the screams of doomed men down the hall, and he was driven mad. He died in an Alabama hospital in 1937, when Harper Lee was old enough to be aware of it. Atticus Finch, an idealized version of A. C. Lee, Harper's attorney father, defends the wrongly accused Tom Robinson, who is a tidier version of Walter Lett.

Never mind the contradictions and inconsistencies: novels can hallow a place, cast a glow upon it and inspire bookish pilgrims —and there are always visitors, who'd read the book or seen the movie. Following the free guidebook *Walk Monroeville*, they stroll in the downtown historic district, admiring the Old Courthouse, the Old Jail, searching for Maycomb, the locations associated with the novel's mythology, though they search in vain for locations of the movie, which was made in Hollywood. It is a testament to the spell cast by the novel, and perhaps to the popular film, that the monument at the center of town is not to a Monroeville citizen of great heart and noble achievement, nor a local hero or an iconic Confederate soldier, but to a fictional character, Atticus Finch.

These days the talk in town is of Harper Lee, known locally by her first name, Nelle (her grandmother's name, Ellen, spelled backward). Avoiding publicity from the earliest years of her suc-

cess, she is back in the news because of the discovery and disinter-
ment of a novel she'd put aside almost six decades ago, an early
version of the Atticus Finch–Tom Robinson story, told by Scout
grown older and looking down the years. Suggesting the crisis of
a vulnerable and convicted man in the Old Jail on North Mount
Pleasant Avenue, the novel is titled *Go Set a Watchman.*

"It's an old book!" Harper Lee told a mutual friend of ours
who'd seen her while I was in Monroeville. "But if someone wants
to read it, fine!"

Speculation is that the resurrected novel will be sought after
as the basis of a new film. The 1962 adaptation of *To Kill a Mockingbird,* with Gregory Peck's Oscar-winning performance as Atticus Finch, sent many readers to the novel. The American Film
Institute has ranked Atticus as the greatest movie hero of all time
(Indiana Jones is No. 2). Robert Duvall, who at age 30 played the
mysterious neighbor, Boo Radley, in the film, recently said: "I am
looking forward to reading the [new] book. The film was a pivotal
point in my career and we all have been waiting for the second
book."

According to biographer Charles Shields, author of *Mockingbird:
A Portrait of Harper Lee,* Nelle started several books after her success
in 1960: a new novel, and a nonfiction account of a serial murderer. But she'd abandoned them, and apart from a sprinkling of
scribbles, seemingly abandoned writing anything else—no stories,
no substantial articles, no memoir of her years of serious collabo-
ration with Truman Capote on *In Cold Blood.* Out of the limelight,
she had lived well, mainly in New York City, with regular visits
home, liberated by the financial windfall but burdened—mad-
dened, some people said—by the pressure to produce another
book. (Lee, who never married, returned to Alabama permanently
in 2007 after suffering a stroke. Her sister, Alice, an attorney in
Monroeville who long handled Lee's legal affairs, died this past
November at age 103.)

It seems—especially to a graphomaniac like myself—that
Harper Lee was perhaps an accidental novelist: one book and
done. Instead of a career of creation, a refinement of this profession of letters, an author's satisfying dialogue with the world, she
shut up shop in a retreat from the writing life, like a lottery winner
in seclusion. Now 89, living in a care home at the edge of town,

she is in delicate health, with macular degeneration and such a degree of deafness that she can communicate only by reading questions written in large print on note cards.

"What have you been doing?" my friend wrote on a card and held it up.

"What sort of fool question is that?" Nelle shouted from her chair. "I just sit here. I don't do anything!"

She may be reclusive but she is anything but a shrinking violet, and she has plenty of friends. Using a magnifier device, she is a reader, mainly of history, but also of crime novels. Like many people who vanish, wishing for privacy—J. D. Salinger is the best example—she has been stalked, intruded upon, pestered, and sought after. I vowed not to disturb her.

Nannie Ruth Williams knew the famous book, and she was well aware of Monroeville's other celebrated author. Her grandfather had sharecropped on the Faulk family land, and it so happened that Lillie Mae Faulk had married Archulus Julius Persons in 1923 and given birth to Truman Streckfus Persons a little over a year later. After Lillie Mae married a man named Capote, her son changed his name to Truman Capote. Capote had been known in town for his big-city airs. "A smart-ass," a man who'd grown up with him told me. "No one liked him." Truman was bullied for being small and peevish, and his defender was Nelle Lee, his next-door neighbor. "Nelle protected him," that man said. "When kids would hop on Capote, Nelle would get 'em off. She popped out a lot of boys' teeth."

Capote, as a child, lives on as the character Dill in the novel. His portrayal is a sort of homage to his oddness and intelligence, as well as their youthful friendship. "Dill was a curiosity. He wore blue linen shorts that buttoned to his shirt, his hair was snow-white and stuck to his head like duck-fluff; he was a year my senior but I towered over him." And it is Dill who animates the subplot, which is the mystery of Boo Radley.

Every year a highly praised and lively dramatization of the novel is put on by the town's Mockingbird Players, with dramatic courtroom action in the Old Courthouse. But Nannie Ruth smiled when she was asked whether she'd ever seen it. "You won't find more than four or five black people in the audience," a local man told me later. "They've lived it. They've been there. They don't want to be taken there again. They want to deal with the real thing that's going on now."

H. B. Williams sighed when any mention of the book came up. He was born in a tenant farming family on the Blanchard Slaughter plantation where "Blanchie," a wealthy but childless white landowner, would babysit for the infant H. B. while his parents worked in the fields, picking and chopping cotton. This would have been at about the time of the Walter Lett trial, and the fictional crime of *Mockingbird*—mid-'30s, when the Great Depression gripped "the tired old town" of the novel, and the Ku Klux Klan was active, and the red clay of the main streets had yet to be paved over.

After the book was published and became a bestseller, H. B., then a school principal, was offered the job of assistant principal, and when he refused, pointing out that it was a demotion, he was fired. He spent years fighting for his reinstatement. His grievance was not a sequence of dramatic events like the novel, it was just the unfairness of the southern grind. The pettifogging dragged on for 10 years, but H. B. was eventually triumphant. Yet it was an injustice that no one wanted to hear about, unsensational, unrecorded, not at all cinematic.

In its way, H. B.'s exhausting search for justice resembles that of the public-interest attorney Bryan Stevenson in his quest to exonerate Walter McMillian, another citizen of Monroeville. This was also a local story, but a recent one. One Saturday morning in 1986, Ronda Morrison, a white 18-year-old clerk at Jackson Cleaners, was found shot to death at the back of the store. This was in the center of town, near the Old Courthouse made famous 26 years earlier in the novel about racial injustice. In this real case, a black man, Walter McMillian, who owned a local land-clearing business, was arrested, though he'd been able to prove he was nowhere near Jackson Cleaners that day. The trial, moved to mostly white Baldwin County, lasted a day and a half. McMillian was found guilty and sentenced to death.

It emerged that McMillian had been set up; the men who testified against him had been pressured by the police, and later recanted. Bryan Stevenson—the founder of the Equal Justice Initiative in Montgomery, Alabama, who today is renowned for successfully arguing before the Supreme Court in 2012 that lifetime sentences for juveniles convicted of homicide constituted cruel and unusual punishment—had taken an interest in the case.

He appealed the conviction, as he relates in his prizewinning 2014 account, *Just Mercy*. After McMillian had been on death row for five years, his conviction was overturned; he was released in 1993. The wheels of justice grind slowly, with paper shuffling and appeals. Little drama, much persistence. In the town with a memorial to Atticus Finch, not Bryan Stevenson.

And that's the odd thing about a great deal of a certain sort of Deep South fiction—its grotesquerie and gothic, its high color and fantastication, the emphasis on freakishness. Look no further than Faulkner or Erskine Caldwell, but there's plenty in Harper Lee too, in *Mockingbird*, the Boo Radley factor, the Misses Tutti and Frutti, and the racist Mrs. Dubose, who is a morphine addict: "Her face was the color of a dirty pillowcase and the corners of her mouth glistened with wet which inched like a glacier down the deep grooves enclosing her chin." This sort of prose acts as a kind of indirection, dramatizing weirdness as a way of distracting the reader from day-to-day indignities.

Backward-looking, few southern writers concern themselves with the new realities, the decayed downtown, the Piggly Wiggly and the pawnshops, the elephantine Walmart, reachable from the bypass road, where the fast-food joints have put most of the local eateries out of business (though AJ's Family Restaurant and the Court House Café in Monroeville remain lively). Monroeville people I met were proud of having overcome hard times. Men of a certain age recalled World War II: Charles Salter, who was 90, served in the 78th Infantry, fighting in Germany, and just as his division reached the west bank of the Rhine he was hit by shrapnel in the leg and foot. Seventy years later he still needed regular operations. "The Depression was hard," he said. "It lasted here till long after the war." H. B. Williams was drafted to fight in Korea. "And when I returned to town, having fought for my country, I found I couldn't vote."

Some reminiscences were of a lost world, like those of the local columnist George Thomas Jones, who was 92 and remembered when all the roads of the town were red clay, and how as a drugstore soda jerk he was sassed by Truman Capote, who said, "I sure would like to have something good, but you ain't got it . . . a Broadway Flip." Young George faced him down, saying, "Boy, I'll flip you off that stool!" Charles Johnson, a popular barber in town, worked his scissors on my head and told me, "I'm from the child-abuse era—hah! If I was bad my daddy would tell me to go out and cut a switch from a bridal wreath bush and he'd whip my legs with it. Or a keen switch, more narrah. It done me good!"

Mr. Johnson told me about the settlement near the areas known as Franklin and Wainwright, called Scratch Ankle, famous for in-breeding. The poor blacks lived in Clausell and on Marengo Street, the rich whites in Canterbury, and the squatters up at Lime-stone were to be avoided. But I visited Limestone just the same; the place was thick with idlers and drunks and barefoot children, and a big toothless man named LaVert stuck his finger in my face and said, "You best go away, mister—this is a bad neighborhood." There is a haunted substratum of darkness in southern life, and though it pulses through many interactions, it takes a long while to perceive it, and even longer to understand.

The other ignored aspect of life: the Deep South still goes to church, and dresses up to do so. There are good-sized churches in Monroeville, most of them full on Sundays, and they are sources of inspiration, goodwill, guidance, friendship, comfort, outreach, and snacks. Nannie Ruth and H. B. were Mount Nebo Baptists, but today they'd be attending the Hopewell CME Church because the usual pianist had to be elsewhere, and Nannie Ruth would play the piano. The pastor, the Reverend Eddie Marzett, had indi-cated what hymns to plan for. It was "Women's Day." The theme of the service was "Women of God in These Changing Times," with appropriate Bible readings and two women preachers, Rever-end Marzett taking a back pew in his stylish white suit and tinted glasses.

Monroeville is like many towns of its size in Alabama—indeed the Deep South: a town square of decaying elegance, most of the downtown shops and businesses closed or faltering, the main in-dustries shut down. I was to discover that *To Kill a Mockingbird* is a minor aspect of Monroeville, a place of hospitable and hard-working people, but a dying town, with a population of 6,300 (and declining), undercut by NAFTA, overlooked by Washington, dumped by manufacturers like Vanity Fair Mills (employing at its peak 2,500 people, many of them women) and Georgia Pacific, which shut down its plywood plant when demand for lumber declined. The usual Deep South challenges in education and housing apply here, and almost a third of Monroe County (29 percent) lives in poverty.

"I was a traveling bra and panty salesman," Sam Williams told me. "You don't see many of those nowadays." He had worked for Vanity Fair for 28 years, and was now a potter, hand-firing cups and saucers of his own design. But he had lucked out in another way: oil had been found near his land—one of Alabama's surprises—and his family gets a regular small check, divided five ways among the siblings, from oil wells on the property. His parting shot to me was an earnest plea: "This is a wonderful town. Talk nice about Monroeville."

Willie Hill had worked for Vanity Fair for 34 years and was now unemployed. "They shut down here, looking for cheap labor in Mexico." He laughed at the notion that the economy would improve because of the *Mockingbird* pilgrims. "No money in that, no sir. We need industry, we need real jobs."

"I've lived here all my life—eighty-one years," a man pumping gas next to me said out of the blue, "and I've never known it so bad. If the paper mill closes, we'll be in real trouble." (Georgia-Pacific still operates three mills in or near Monroeville.) Willie Hill's nephew Derek was laid off in 2008 after eight years fabricating Georgia-Pacific plywood. He made regular visits to Monroeville's picturesque and well-stocked library (once the La Salle Hotel: Gregory Peck had slept there in 1962 when he visited to get a feel for the town), looking for jobs on the library's computers and updating his résumé. He was helped by the able librarian, Bunny Hines Nobles, whose family had once owned the land where the hotel stands.

Selma is an easy two-hour drive up a country road from Monroeville. I had longed to see it because I wanted to put a face to the name of the town that had become a battle cry. It was a surprise to me—not a pleasant one, more of a shock, and a sadness. The Edmund Pettus Bridge I recognized from newspaper photos and the footage of Bloody Sunday—protesters being beaten, mounted policemen trampling marchers. That was the headline and the history. What I was not prepared for was the sorry condition of Selma, the shut-down businesses and empty once-elegant apartment houses near the bridge, the whole town visibly on the wane and, apart from its mall, in desperate shape, seemingly out of work. This decrepitude was not a headline.

Just a week before, on the 50th anniversary of the march, President Obama, the First Lady, a number of celebrities, civil rights leaders, unsung heroes of Selma, and crowders of the limelight had observed the anniversary. They invoked the events of Bloody Sunday, the rigors of the march to Montgomery, and the victory, the passage of the Voting Rights Act of 1965.

But all that was mostly commemorative fanfare, political theater and sentimental rage. The reality, which was also an insult, was that these days in this city, which had been on the frontline of the voting-rights movement, voting turnout among the 18-to-25 age group was discouragingly low, with the figures even more dismal in local elections. I learned this at the Interpretive Center outside town, where the docents who told me this shook their heads at the sorry fact. After all the bloodshed and sacrifice, voter turnout was lagging, and Selma itself was enduring an economy in crisis. This went unremarked by the president and the civil rights stalwarts and the celebrities, most of whom took the next plane out of this sad and supine town.

Driving out of Selma on narrow Highway 41, which was lined by tall trees and deep woods, I got a taste of the visitable past. You don't need to be a literary pilgrim; this illuminating experience of country roads is reason enough to drive through the Deep South, especially here, where the red-clay lanes—brightened and brick-hued from the morning rain—branch from the highway into the pines; crossing Mush Creek and Cedar Creek, the tiny flyspeck settlements of wooden shotgun shacks and old house trailers and the white-planked churches; past the roadside clusters of foot-high anthills, the gray witch-hair lichens trailing from the bony limbs of dead trees, a mostly straight-ahead road of flat fields and boggy pinewoods and flowering shrubs, and just ahead a pair of crows hopping over a lump of crimson road-kill hash.

I passed through Camden, a ruinous town of empty shops and obvious poverty, just a flicker of beauty in some of the derelict houses, an abandoned filling station, the whitewashed clapboards and a tiny cupola of old Antioch Baptist Church (Martin Luther King Jr. had spoken here in April 1965, inspiring a protest march that day and the next), the imposing Camden Public Library, its façade of fat white columns; and then the villages of Beatrice—

Bee-ah-triss—and Tunnel Springs. After all this time-warp decay, Monroeville looked smart and promising, with its many churches and picturesque courthouse and fine old houses. Its certain distinction and self-awareness and its pride were the result of its isolation. Nearly 100 miles from any city, Monroeville had always been in the middle of nowhere—no one arrived by accident. As southerners said, You had to be going there to get there.

Hopewell CME Church—in a festive Women's Day mood—was adjacent to the traditionally black part of town, Clausell. The church's sanctuary had served as a secret meeting place in the 1950s for the local civil rights movement, many of the meetings presided over by the pastor, R. V. McIntosh, and a firebrand named Ezra Cunningham, who had taken part in the Selma march. All this information came from H. B. Williams, who had brought me to a Hopewell pew.

After the hymns (Nannie Ruth Williams on the piano, a young man on drums), the announcements, the two offerings, the readings from Proverbs 31 ("Who can find a virtuous woman, for her price is far above rubies"), and prayers, Minister Mary Johnson gripped the lectern and shouted: "Women of God in These Changing Times, is our theme today, praise the Lord," and the congregation called out "Tell it, sister!" and "Praise his name!"

Minister Mary was funny and teasing in her sermon, and her message was simple: Be hopeful in hard times. "Don't look in the mirror and think, 'Lord Jesus, what they gonna think 'bout my wig?' Say 'I'm coming as I am!' Don't matter 'bout your dress—magnify the Lord!" She raised her arms and in her final peroration said, "Hopelessness is a bad place to be. The Lord gonna fee-all you with hope. You might not have money—never mind. You need the Holy Spirit!"

Afterward, the hospitable gesture, my invitation to lunch at the Williams house, a comfortable bungalow on Golf Drive, near the gates to Whitey Lee Park, which was off-limits to blacks until the 1980s, and the once-segregated golf course. We were joined at the table by Arthur Penn, an insurance man and vice president of the local NAACP branch, and his son Arthur Penn Jr.

I raised the subject of *Mockingbird,* which made Nannie Ruth shrug. Arthur senior said, "It's a distraction. It's like saying, 'This is all we have. Forget the rest.' It's like a four-hundred-pound comedian on stage telling fat jokes. The audience is paying more attention to the jokes than to what they see."

In Monroeville, the dramas were intense but small-scale and persistent. The year the book came out all the schools were segregated and they remained so for the next five years. And once the schools were integrated in 1965, the white private school Monroe Academy was established not long after. Race relations had been generally good, and apart from the freedom riders from the North (whom Nelle Lee disparaged at the time as agitators), there were no major racial incidents, only the threat of them.

"Most whites thought, 'You're good in your place. Stay there and you're a good nigger,'" H. B. said. "Of course it was an inferior situation, a double standard all over."

And eating slowly he was provoked to a reminiscence, recalling how in December 1959 the Monroeville Christmas parade was canceled, because the Klan had warned that if the band from the black high school marched with whites, there would be blood. To be fair, all the whites I spoke to in Monroeville condemned this lamentable episode. Later, in 1965, the Klan congregated on Drewry Road, wearing sheets and hoods, 40 or 50 of them, and they marched down Drewry to the Old Courthouse. "Right past my house," H. B. said. "My children stood on the porch and called out to them." This painful memory was another reason he had no interest in the novel, then in its fifth year of bestsellerdom.

"This was a white area. Maids could walk the streets, but if the residents saw a black man they'd call the sheriff, and then take you to jail," Arthur Penn said.

And what a sheriff. Up to the late 1950s it was Sheriff Charlie Sizemore, noted for his bad temper. How bad? "He'd slap you upside the head, cuss you out, beat you."

One example: A prominent black pastor, N. H. Smith, was talking to another black man, Scott Nettles, on the corner of Claiborne and Mount Pleasant, the center of Monroeville and steps from the stately courthouse, just chatting. "Sizemore comes up and slaps the cigarette out of Nettles's mouth and cusses him out, and why? To please the white folks, to build a reputation."

That happened in 1948, in this town of long memories.

H. B. and Arthur gave me other examples, all exercises in degradation, but here is a harmonious postscript to it all. In the early

'60s, Sizemore—a Creek Indian, great-grandson to William Weath-
erford, Chief Red Eagle—became crippled and had a conversion.
As an act of atonement, Sizemore went down to Clausell, to the
main house of worship, Bethel Baptist Church, and begged the
black congregation for forgiveness.

Out of curiosity, and against the advice of several whites I met
in town, I visited Clausell, the traditionally black section of town.
When Nelle Lee was a child, the woman who bathed and fed her
was Hattie Belle Clausell, the so-called mammy in the Lee house-
hold, who walked from this settlement several miles every day to
the house on South Alabama Avenue in the white part of town
(the Lee house is now gone, replaced by Mel's Dairy Dream and a
defunct swimming pool–supply store). Clausell was named for that
black family.

I stopped at Franky D's Barber and Style Shop on Clausell
Road, because barbers know everything. There I was told that I
could find Irma, Nelle's former housekeeper, up the road, "in the
projects."

The projects was a cul-de-sac of brick bungalows, low-cost housing, but Irma was not in any of them.

"They call this the hood," Brittany Bonner told me—she was on
her porch, watching the rain come down. "People warn you about
this place, but it's not so bad. Sometimes we hear guns—people
shooting in the woods. You see that cross down the road? That's
for the man they call James T—James Tunstall. He was shot and
killed a few years ago right there, maybe drug-related."

A white man in Monroeville told me that Clausell was so dangerous that the police never went there alone, but always in twos.
Yet Brittany, 22, mother of two small girls, said that violence was
not the problem. She repeated the town's lament: "We have no
work, there are no jobs."

Brittany's great-aunt Jacqueline Packer thought I might find
Irma out at Pineview Heights, down Clausell Road, but all I found
were a scattering of houses, some bungalows and many dogtrot
houses, and rotting cars, and a sign on a closed roadside café,
SOUTHERN FAVORITES — NECKBONES AND RICE, TURKEY NECKS
AND RICE, and then the pavement ended and the road was red
clay, velvety in the rain, leading into the pinewoods.

Back in town I saw a billboard with a stern message: NOTHING

IN THIS COUNTRY IS FREE. IF YOU'RE GETTING SOMETHING WITHOUT PAYING FOR IT, THANK A TAXPAYER. Toward the end of my stay in Monroeville, I met the Reverend Thomas Lane Butts, former pastor of the First United Methodist Church, where Nelle Lee and her sister, Alice, had been members of his congregation, and his dear friends.

"This town is no different from any other," he told me. He was 85, and had traveled throughout the South, and knew what he was talking about. Born 10 miles east in what he called "a little two-mule community" of Bermuda (Ber-moo-dah in the local pronunciation), his father had been a tenant farmer—corn, cotton, vegetables. "We had no land, we had nothing. We didn't have electricity until I was in the twelfth grade, in the fall of 1947. I studied by oil lamp."

The work paid off. After theology studies at Emory and Northwestern, and parishes in Mobile and Fort Walton Beach, Florida, and civil rights struggles, he became pastor of this Methodist church.

"We took in racism with our mother's milk," he said. But he'd been a civil rights campaigner from early on, even before 1960 when in Talladega he met Martin Luther King Jr. "He was the first black person I'd met who was not a field hand," he said. "The embodiment of erudition, authority, and humility."

Reverend Butts had a volume of Freud in his lap the day I met him, searching for a quotation in *Civilization and Its Discontents*.

I told him the essay was one of my own favorites, for Freud's expression about human pettiness and discrimination, "the narcissism of minor differences"—the subtext of the old segregated South, and of human life in general.

His finger on the page, Reverend Butts murmured some sentences: "'The element of truth behind all this . . . men are not gentle creatures who want to be loved . . . can defend themselves . . . a powerful share of aggressiveness . . .' Ah here it is. '*Homo homini lupus* . . . Man is a wolf to man.'"

That was the reality of history, as true in proud Monroeville as in the wider world. And that led us to talk about the town, the book, the way things are. He valued his friendship with H. B. Williams: the black teacher, the white clergyman, both in their 80s, both of them civil rights stalwarts. He had been close to the Lee family, had spent vacations in New York City with Nelle, and still saw her. An affectionately signed copy of the novel rested on the side table, not far from his volume of Freud.

"Here we are," he intoned, raising his hands, "tugged between two cultures, one gone and never to return, the other being born. Many things here have been lost. *To Kill a Mockingbird* keeps us from complete oblivion."

WILLIAM T. VOLLMANN

Invisible and Insidious

FROM *Harper's Magazine*

FOR THE PAST three years my dosimeter had sat silently on a
narrow shelf just inside the door of a house in Tokyo, upticking its
final digit every 24 hours by one or two, the increase never failing
—for radiation is the ruthless companion of time. Wherever we
are, radiation finds and damages us, at best imperceptibly. During those three years, my American neighbors had lost sight of
the accident at Fukushima. In March 2011 a tsunami had killed
hundreds, or thousands; yes, they remembered that. Several also
recollected the earthquake that caused it, but as for the hydrogen
explosion and containment breach at Nuclear Plant No. 1, that
must have been fixed by now—for its effluents no longer shone
forth from our national news. Meanwhile, my dosimeter increased
its figure, one or two digits per day, more or less as it would have
in San Francisco—well, a trifle more, actually. And in Tokyo, as in
San Francisco, people went about their business, except on Friday
nights, when the stretch between the Kasumigaseki and Kokkai-
Gijidō-mae subway stations—half a dozen blocks of sidewalk,
which commenced at an antinuclear tent that had already been
on this spot for more than 900 days and ended at the prime minister's lair—became a dim and feeble carnival of pamphleteers and
Fukushima refugees peddling handicrafts.

One Friday evening the refugees' half of the sidewalk was demarcated by police barriers, and a line of officers slouched at ease
in the street, some with yellow bullhorns hanging from their necks.
At the very end of the street, where the National Diet glowed white
and strange behind other buildings, a policeman set up a micro-

phone, then deployed a small video camera in the direction of the muscular young people in DRUMS AGAINST FASCISTS jackets who now, at 6:30 sharp, began chanting: "We don't need nuclear energy! Stop nuclear power plants! Stop them, stop them, stop them! No restart! No restart!" The police assumed a stiffer stance; the drumming and chanting were almost uncomfortably loud. Commuters hurried past along the open space between the police and the protesters, staring straight ahead, covering their ears. Finally, a fellow in a shabby sweater appeared, and murmured along with the chants as he rounded the corner. He was the only one who seemed to sympathize; few others reacted at all.

But now the drummers were banging away as if for their very lives, swaying like dancers, raising clenched fists, looking endlessly determined. I was astounded to see that listless scattering of the half-seen become a close-packed, disciplined crowd. There must have been 300 or more. They chanted and raised their hand-lettered placards. It was the last night of February 2014. Perhaps after another three years of Fridays they will still be congregating to express their dissent, which after what happened at Plant No. 1 must be considered pure sanity itself. All the same, they were hurried past, overlooked, and left to chant in darkness while my dosimeter accrued another digit. Another uptick, another gray hair —so what? With radiation, as with time, from moment to moment there may indeed be nothing to worry about.

I was happy to see that dosimeter again. By the time I returned to Japan my interpreter had recalibrated it from millirems to millisieverts, the latter her country's more customary unit of poisonousness. Why not? The thing was hers now; I had given it to her because she had to live here and I didn't. It was the best I could do for her. To be sure, I had come to deplore its inability to detect anything but gamma rays, since plutonium emits alpha particles, and strontium emits beta particles (which present a danger if strontium is inhaled or swallowed); by July of 2013 these and certain other radioactive substances had been detected in a monitoring well at Plant No. 1. (The concentration of cesium was a hundred times greater than the legal maximum. But why be a pessimist? That well was a good six meters away from the ocean.) At least the dosimeter could keep itself occupied measuring gamma-ray emitters such as cesium-134 and cesium-137, which in that same joyful July kept making news. One Wednesday the *Japan Times* reported that the isotopes were "both about 90 times the levels found Friday."

Meanwhile, the JDC Corporation, a construction company, discharged 340 tons of radioactive water into the Iizaka River—but not to worry: it happened, said the *Japan Times,* "during government-sponsored decontamination work." (Well, we all make mistakes. You see, the company had not been aware that water from the river would be used for agricultural purposes.) Ten days later, said the same newspaper, the Tokyo Electric Power Company, or TEPCO, which is the nuclear utility that operates the damaged plant, "now admits radioactive water entering the sea at Fukushima No. 1 . . . fueling fears that marine life is being poisoned." The dangerous hydrogen isotope tritium had already been detected in the ocean back in June, and the amount was climbing. But TEPCO would fix things, no doubt.

In August 2013 the Japanese Nuclear Regulation Authority, which thus far had treated the leak as a level 1 "anomaly," recategorized it at level 3, a "serious accident." Meanwhile, the *Japan Times* was calling the situation "alarming" and speaking of trillions of becquerels of radioactivity, which is to say, "about 100 times more than what TEPCO had been allowing to enter the sea each year before the crisis." A year later TEPCO estimated that tritium emitting 20 to 40 trillion becquerels of radiation per liter may have flowed into the Pacific Ocean since May 2011. To prevent No. 1 from exploding again, and maybe melting down, TEPCO cooled the reactor with water and more water, which then went into holding tanks, which, like all human aspirations, eventually leaked.

By September 2013 South Korea had banned the importation of fish from eight Japanese prefectures. And in February 2014, when I began my second visit to the hot zone, the cesium concentration in one sampling well was more than twice as high as the record set the summer before. A day after that was reported, the cesium figure had again more than doubled. As for strontium levels, TEPCO confessed that it had somehow underreported those; they were five and a half times worse than had been previously stated. Three hundred tons of radioactive water were now entering the ocean every day. (A spokesperson for TEPCO says that the situation has since improved: compared with the period before August 2013, levels of strontium-90 have been reduced by about one-third, and levels of cesium-137 by one-tenth.)

Meanwhile, there were still 150,000 nuclear refugees. Many remained on the hook for the mortgages on their abandoned homes.

Another hilarious little anecdote: many poor souls had toiled for TEPCO in the hideous environs of No. 1, and some had been exposed to a dose of more than 100 millisieverts of radiation. A maximum of *one* millisievert per year for ordinary citizens is the general standard prescribed by the International Commission on Radiological Protection. According to *The First Responder's Guide to Radiation Incidents,* first responders should content themselves with 50 millisieverts per incident, for although radiation sickness manifests itself at 20 times that dose, cancer might well show up after lower exposures. But the tale had a happy ending: the workers would be allowed to undergo annual ultrasonic thyroid examinations free of charge.

TEPCO projected the total cost of the disaster at 978 billion yen, or 8.4 billion U.S. dollars.

Nevertheless, as the Japanese government kept advising in the aftermath of the disaster, there was "no immediate danger." And important plans were being drawn up to save the world. The idea was to build an electric-powered "wall of ice" around Plant No. 1 by inserting over 1,700 pipes 98 feet underground for nearly a mile. Coolant flowing through them at −22 degrees Fahrenheit would then freeze the groundwater in the surrounding soil. Many doubted, however, that it would be possible to maintain the wall in a place where summer temperatures can top 100 degrees. In June 2013, only weeks after construction began, the company met new troubles freezing contaminated water for disposal. "We have yet to form the ice stopper," it admitted, "because we can't make the temperature low enough to freeze water." In July TEPCO announced that it was adding more pipes. The project would cost only 32 billion yen, and with any luck there wouldn't be another tsunami in the area until the radioactivity subsided.

How long might that be? Take tritium, which has a half-life of 12.3 years. Only after 10 half-lives will radiation levels fall to what some realists consider an approximation of precontamination. If the reactors somehow stopped polluting the ocean tomorrow, it would still be well over a century before their tritium became harmless. And tritium is one of the shorter-lived poisons in question.

To be sure, dilution works miracles. And on that bright side, Yamazaki Hisataka, a founder of an NGO called No Nukes Plaza, told me that "the radiation has traveled through the Pacific. As a result, it has reached the waters off of the American west coast. Unless we stop it now, it's going to get worse and worse." When I asked whether the ice wall was practical, he laughed. "No," he said. "Concrete or some permanent barrier would be better." Did I mention that Japan's reactor-studded islands are entering one of their cyclical periods of earthquake activity? This is why TEPCO's wall of ice resembled the fairy tale of Sleeping Beauty, in which it is possible to wall off time with something permeable only to the brave.

When it comes to Japan, arithmetic is now one of my favorite distractions. One sievert is the equivalent of a thousand chest x-rays. A millisievert, the recommended maximum annual dose, is, of course, a thousandth of a sievert; a microsievert a millionth. American first responders are recommended not to exceed 250 millisieverts when saving human lives, but we know surprisingly little about the perils of extended subacute radiation exposure. The so-called linear hypothesis would have it that the multiple of any given dose is the multiple of the danger. For instance: radiation sickness may begin to appear after a dose of one sievert, but the situation described by this statistic is a rapidly delivered dose, such as a nearby H-bomb detonation or a brief foray to the reactor at No. 1. Fifty millisieverts a year delivered over 20 years, which works out to the same total dose of one sievert, may or may not cause perceptible harm; no one seems sure.

Reactor No. 1 exploded at 3:36 on the afternoon of March 12, 2011, when its exposed fuel rods reacted with the air's hydrogen. The authorities quickly drew two rings centered on No. 1. The 40-kilometer radius demarcated the voluntary-evacuation zone. The 20-kilometer radius marked the restricted, or forbidden, zone. As the work of decontamination advanced and wind patterns became better known, the circles were replaced by areas of irregular shape. Once I decided to base my explorations near the 40-kilometer mark, the most convenient place looked like a midsize city called Iwaki. Here the radiation had achieved its maximum at four o'clock on the morning of March 15, 2011: 23.72 microsieverts per hour, or about 600 times Tokyo's average normal background exposure. Iwaki's municipal authorities distributed iodine tablets to residents under 40 years old and to pregnant women. For the others, as always, there was "no immediate danger." During my stay in Iwaki, three years later, the dosimeter almost invariably registered its daily microsievert, which is to say, about 0.042 microsieverts each hour. Reader, what might this mean to you? Later that year, when I could afford to buy a scintillation meter, I measured the following good old American values:

> 0.12 µSv/hr: Average San Francisco reading, June 13, 2014
> 0.18 µSv/hr: Volume II of 1880 census, Boone-Madison Public Library, West Virginia, June 21, 2014
> 0.30 µSv/hr: Marble countertop in my room at the Embassy Suites, Charleston, West Virginia, June 22, 2014
> 0.48 µSv/hr: Ten Commandments granite tablet in front of courthouse, Pineville, West Virginia, June 23, 2014
> 2.46 µSv/hr: Airborne, 36,000 feet, 30 minutes out of Washington Dulles, June 30, 2014

After disembarking from the train in Iwaki one chilly afternoon, I asked the girl at the tourist-information office which local restaurants she would recommend. She replied that the town had always been proud of its seafood, but that because of the nuclear accident the fish now had to be imported.

On one of the maps she gave me, I saw that the international port was a few kilometers south. Several beaches lay east, and Route 6 followed the shoreline north toward the reactors. That was the road I would take for my trips to Tomioka, a town partly within the forbidden zone.

In Iwaki, the hotels were nearly always full. One of them smelled of cigarette smoke and was only for decontamination workers. I asked the receptionist at another why she was so busy. She laughed and said, "TEPCO!" Decontamination was a booming business, all right.

In the Iwaki port, which I had expected to find deserted, a dozen sailors in blue coveralls and white hardhats were unwinding a fishing net, planning to travel two hours southward, where the fish were still considered safe; the smaller boats rocked empty on the water. A patrol-boat captain told me that fishing for personal consumption was not restricted, and that fish were tested for radiation once a week. In the meantime, the fishermen, along with so many others in the city, were surviving on what he called "guaranteed money from TEPCO."

I motored up the coast in a taxi. It was a lovely morning, and the pastel sea was very still. The tsunami-destroyed homes had been deconstructed into foundations, concrete squares upgrown with grass. What I remembered from my visit in 2011 was the black stinking filthiness of everything that the tidal wave had reached. Surely Iwaki's affected coastline must have been similarly slimed, but these pits looked merely mellow—historic, like archaeological sites. Soon the taxi reached a gleaming skeleton of half-built apartments for people who had lost their homes in the disaster; later I would see many of the temporary barracks-like buildings, all of them still and raw, where nuclear refugees were housed.

Eventually I arrived at the Northern Iwaki Rubbish Disposal Center, whose monument is its own big smokestack. That is how I first came to see the disgusting black bags of Fukushima: down a 45-degree slope, behind a large wall with a radiation-caution sign, a close-packed crowd of those bags stood five deep and I don't know how many wide. I strode slowly toward the edge of the grass, where the slope began. That was close enough, I thought. The dosimeter did not turn over a new digit.

"This is debris they burned in Iwaki, not fallout," my taxi driver told me. "They don't know where to put it." Several times during our excursion he said that the bags we saw contained ash from the decontamination of Iwaki. In this he was mistaken; the city did not burn radioactive matter. But in saying that they did not know where to put the debris, he uttered a truth. By the time I departed Fukushima I hardly noticed the bags unless many happened to be together. The closer to No. 1 one drew, the more there were.

In spite of the reminders that No. 1 was not far away, Iwaki strove to present itself as safe, and maybe it was, given the innocuous dosimeter readings. Contrary claims were considered to be "harmful rumors." "Even after one week from the earthquake," according to an official city report, "harmful rumors on the nuclear problems kept blocking the distribution of goods to Iwaki." In other words, during that first week some fuel and grocery trucks refrained from making deliveries to the city for fear of contamination. The same document told me that "harmful rumors due to the accidents at nuclear power stations degraded the status of Iwaki local products tremendously. To regain its reputation, Iwaki City has participated in more than fifty events held in Tokyo metropolitan area." Thanks to such efforts, Iwaki had nearly defeated the harmful rumors. Most people's fears seemed to have been repressed, interred behind a wall of ice as effective as TEPCO's. Consider my first taxi driver, who was round-faced and patient, and smiled often, wrinkling up his cheeks. Although his hair was still black, he had entered middle age. I asked what he thought when he heard the radiation warnings after the tsunami.

"Even in Iwaki most people tried to flee, but I didn't mind. I have an elderly person at home, so I couldn't leave, anyhow!" When I asked if anyone was to blame for what happened, he told me that it was "just bad luck." In general, he explained, he felt cheerful and hopeful because the taxi business was now thriving thanks to the nuclear power situation. "Those who work for TEPCO use taxis. If I were a fisherman I would be suffering a lot, but that's not the case for me!"

My driver the next day had almost as merry an outlook. He was a bald and active old man who wore a paper mask over his mouth, as do many Japanese when they have colds or wish to protect themselves from germs. I asked him to describe the disaster, and he very practically replied: "In the beginning we were busy. Now that the bus services have recovered, it's quieter for taxis." On occasion he had entered the prohibited area with Red Cross passengers.

When I asked about the radiation, he replied: "Since it's not close to here, it has no reality. If someone around here got cancer, I might feel something, but it's invisible, so I don't feel anything." A third driver, asked the same question, said: "There's nothing to do but trust them."

I kept asking people in Iwaki how safe they felt; most of their replies were calm and bland. But it did strike me as funny that no doctor I asked would agree to meet me. And it did disconcert me to read in the newspaper that the Fukushima Prefecture Dental Association would now, with family consent, examine the extracted teeth of children aged 5 to 15, first checking for cesium-137 and then, if that was found, for strontium-90. Of course, a test is not a result. Maybe there would be no cesium in anybody's teeth.

One young man, a recent graduate of the local university, told me that when it came to eating local food, he didn't "think twice" about it.

"When you go to a sushi restaurant, do you wonder where the fish came from?" I asked.

"I eat what is in front of me," he replied.

Then there was Kuwahara Akiyo, a weary-looking woman with blue eye shadow and tiny sparkly earrings. She was a part-time employee of the Tomioka Life Recovery Support Center. She told me that she was only allowed to return to her home in Tomioka once a month. Of Tomioka, which I would visit several times, she told me: "There are animals: mice and rats. Also, the pigs interbred with wild boar. The authorities are trying to kill them because they damage the houses, and poop inside and bite the pillars. They don't know humans, so they are fearless. Sometimes you can see them on the street. And there are so many rats! Wherever we go there, they give us some chemicals to kill the rats."

I asked Kuwahara what she thought about when she envisioned radiation.

"Invisible," she said, smiling, "and that is the cause of the anxiety. You don't feel any pain or itching; it just comes into your body."

"Natural radiation also exists," she explained, "and if it is natural, it must be all right. I think it's safe to live in Iwaki. There are nuclear plants all over the world. You can't flee anywhere."

"What is your feeling about nuclear power?" I asked.

"My husband's work is related to nuclear plants. Until the accident we were told that it was totally safe. Nuclear plants we cannot live without." Then she said: "This was a manmade thing, but we made something so evil, so fearful, so dangerous."

Hamamatsu Kōichi, an Iwaki farmer with cropped gray hair, told me that on the urban farm he ran with his wife, an area of 600 tsubo, about half an acre, they raised cucumbers, eggplants, broccoli, lettuce, napa cabbage for kimchi, and green onions, whose fresh smell and enticing jade color far excelled anything I had ever seen in an American supermarket. He wore elastic wrist gaiters over the sleeves of his striped shirt, and his eyebrows rose and curved like caterpillars. His industrious wife carefully trimmed and cleaned green onions during the interview, smiling and sometimes even sweetly laughing at my corny radiation jokes. Local produce was still allowed, the couple told me, provided it tested well at the agricultural union. They did not eat the fish. For the first year after the accident, farmers from affected areas were not allowed to sell anything; in the second year, the radiation levels in their vegetables were lower, but they had to lower their prices too: people were afraid to buy the produce. Now the radioactivity had declined. Later, at the train station, I bought a kilogram of Iwaki tomatoes and sent them off to No Nukes Plaza in Tokyo for analysis. They were fine.

I asked Mr. Hamamatsu how he felt about the radiation.

"The TV news said it went even to Shizuoka and damaged their tea," he told me, "so for sure this place must be contaminated. But we have no place to go."

"In ten years will you be able to go right up to Plant No. 1 if you wish?"

Folding his hands across his apron, he said, "There may be some spots where you can never return."

West of Tomioka, at what was formerly the edge of the forbidden zone, lies Kawauchi Village. I had been there shortly after the accident, when houseplants had just begun to wilt in front of the silent homes. In 2013 the *Japan Times* reported that in Kawauchi the central government's radiation targets had not been met: even after decontamination, almost half of the 1,061 houses in the "emergency evacuation advisory zone" were still receiving atmospheric radiation doses over one millisievert per year. Suspicious villagers had performed their own gamma-ray surveys. As the newspaper said: "Since the [environmental] ministry hasn't explicitly promised to do such work again, municipalities are increasingly concerned about the future of the decontamination process."

A snowed-over tatami store, snow smooth and high across a little bridge over the river, snow heaped on a cemetery's dark steles—such was the town now. It was almost romantic. It was also almost deserted, except for workers in the streets. I did, however, find the Kawauchi Village Residence to Promote Young People's Settlement. There was a path shoveled through the snow to the unlocked foyer, though no one was in.

Walking farther east on that street, which had been the dividing line between the restricted and voluntary-evacuation zones, I came to a house. Inside, a very small old woman was peering at me through a window. When I rang the bell, she came to the door and pretended to be deaf. Soon a middle-aged man with kind eyes, wearing a dark down jacket, came up behind her. He eventually invited me in.

"That's my mother," he said of the woman I'd seen through the window. "My parents live here. They came back in November 2012." He told me that about half the village was inhabited now, but most of the villagers who had returned only stayed four days a week; on the other days they returned to their temporary housing, in Koriyama or elsewhere. Only about 20 percent lived in Kawauchi full-time.

"So your mother feels safe?" I asked.

"Because she is elderly, it's no use worrying about radiation. Of course she feels lonely; that's why I am visiting her. The children will never come anymore. The grandchildren won't come. That is the result of some fear information."

It turned out that he used to work for TEPCO. "I was not directly involved in the nuclear power plant," he told me. "My work had to do with the buying and leasing of land for construction. Basically, my personal opinion is that given that original 1960s design, it was risky to choose this location at all. The major problem with the emergency-power generator was that it was installed at sea level, not in the correct place. All the contract workers were saying so, including me." (TEPCO says that their belief at the time was that this was the safest design.) As emerald-green tea was served by the old mother in her green kerchief and baggy quilted clothes, her son continued, "It's good to gradually reduce the use of nuclear energy, but now it's like our blood, our life. All the nuclear plants are currently stopped. You cannot maintain this situation forever." He spoke of radioactive mushrooms, honey, and wild boar.

When I asked what Kawauchi would look like in the future, he laughed. "Probably it will eventually die out. The families with young children won't live here." His family had been in Kawauchi for close to 100 years. In that small tatami room, with the old lady half-tucked under a blanket, I watched the clouds and dripping snow through the window and thought what a pleasant home it was. I asked the old lady what she most liked about this place. She smiled. Her teeth were a lovely white. She exclaimed: "The air is clean!" Perhaps it was, for during my hour and a half in Kawauchi my dosimeter did not accrue any more digits.

Kida Shōichi, at the time a decontamination specialist in Iwaki's Nuclear Hazard Countermeasures Division, told me that he considered his city not to be badly off, thanks to the winds; as he explained when we spoke in his office, from the TEPCO plant "the northwest direction is high in radiation, so Iwaki is low." On his laptop, he showed me Iwaki's 475 monitoring posts. Then he zoomed in: "Here is the city office where we are right now. And here is the monitoring post. It's 11:05 a.m., and we're receiving 0.121 microsieverts per hour." Clicking on Tomioka he said: "The highest is about 3 microsieverts per hour, so that's only 24.8 times more than here." He cut himself off: "No, here's a place that measures 4. And here's a 5, so that's 41 times higher . . ." He next zoomed in on a monitoring site in Futaba Town, which was still in the prohibited zone: 13.61 microsieverts per hour. If those levels kept up, that unlucky part of Futaba would be 112 times more dangerous than Iwaki.

I asked when he thought Plant No. 1 might be safe; he estimated that it might be 500 years. The next day, he telephoned me with a correction: in only 300 years, barring further accidents, the radiation will have decayed to a thousandth of its original strength!

When I got home, I asked Edwin Lyman, from the Union of Concerned Scientists, what he thought about 300 years as an estimate. "Well, there's radioactive decay, plus transfer to soil; it will go deeper and deeper and get into the water and so forth." He thought that natural decontamination would take hundreds of years at least.

In Japan, the basic guideline for decontamination was to reduce radiation in an area to less than one millisievert per year. Thirty percent of the reduction in cesium isotopes around Iwaki had already happened naturally, and Kida gave me some multicolored information sheets to prove it. In November 2011 almost every part of the area had been yellow, meaning "decontamination required." By December 2012 the yellow had melted into a crescent along the north and east, along with a few patches in the south.

Wasn't this good news? Iwaki was becoming safe much more

quickly than I would have expected. But I wondered what was happening to that cesium. Did it sink deeper into the earth, as Lyman told me? Did it leach into storm drains and rivers? I had read that it sometimes got concentrated in roots. No doubt the radioactivity of the ground must vary just as the ground itself did, and presumably every square meter of Iwaki would need to be measured. (I did not yet have my scintillation meter, but on my next trip, that toy proved that small areas could vary insanely. In Tomioka, one spot might be 2 microsieverts an hour, and another might be 7 or 12. Deeper into the red zone, of course, the numbers were much higher.) At any rate, the Iwaki municipal report explained that topsoil in schoolyards was being removed if it emitted more than 0.3 microsieverts per hour—which works out to 2.63 millisieverts per year.

During my visit, Kida promised me an excursion with a scintillation counter, and so the next day his deputy, Kanari Takahiro, came to collect me. This young man might have been a little cynical, since he referred to nuclear-mitigation efforts as "casual countermeasures." I liked him for that.

In Iwaki, "we have never felt the imminent desperate situation," he said. "In fact, my parents returned home in only two weeks. I myself couldn't flee since I am a civil servant."

"Around here, do people tell any jokes about radiation?" I asked.

"The radiation level is not high enough to create any jokes."

"Are you sad not to eat the local fish?"

"I don't care. Whatever fish, anywhere it comes from . . ."

The scintillation counter (which is to say an Aloka TCS-172B gamma-survey meter) cost about 100,000 yen. As the technical name implied, it measured only gamma waves, like my dosimeter. Kanari said that its operation was "not difficult." The decontamination procedure he described was this: measure radiation; scrape up surface soil and cut tree branches as needed; place the dirt and wood in a bag.

In Iwaki we met a manager and a construction boss. They wore hardhats, work jackets with white belts, and baggy pants tucked into calf-length rubber boots. When I asked whether it was a union job, they curtly replied that it was not. I told them they were he-

260 WILLIAM T. VOLLMANN

roes. Reducing radioactivity by half, as they were doing, was better than nothing, and anyhow they were endangering themselves. The work was all paid for by the central government, they told me.

They said the decontamination workers in Iwaki were exposed to about 4.5 microsieverts a day, which works out to 1.64 millisieverts a year, while the poor souls who were trying to ice away No. 1 were getting up to 40 millisieverts a year. The manager and the boss had to think about their own dose; though they both wore dosimeters, they never checked them. "The radiation level is so low here that we are not worried," one said.

I traveled with them to Hisanohama, about 16 kilometers north of the Iwaki city center, where a traditional Japanese-style house was being decontaminated. I asked Kanari to test things. In the yard, a bag of waste that a worker was filling emitted 0.3 microsieverts per hour. Another bag registered 0.26.

"What happens to these bags?" I asked.

"We remove them and put them in temporary storage for three years," the manager answered.

"Temporary storage" turned out to mean, for instance, those fields all around Iwaki with the black bags.

"Then what?" I asked.

He smiled, laughed, shrugged. Then he explained: "Unlike the United States, where there are rules, here we make up the rules."

I had Kanari test a potted houseplant: 0.14 microsieverts; the construction boss's boot: 0.11; a dirt berm behind the house: 0.33; a rain channel in the sloping concrete driveway: a surprisingly low 0.16; the drainpipe: 0.49. That last reading was not so good; it meant 4.29 millisieverts per year.

I pointed to the pipe and asked him: "How can you decontaminate it?"

"Structurally speaking, unless you break it, it's rather difficult. We must see what the property owner says." The two decontamination men agreed that cesium generally went about five centimeters into the ground. We measured two black bags side by side: 0.35 and 0.38 microsieverts. Across the highway was a field of vegetables. I asked Kanari to read the crops for me, but he said: "The scintillation meter measures only the air, not the thing." All the same, he did as I requested: 0.13 microsieverts away from the ground, 0.18 close to the ground, near a napa cabbage.

We drove to a nearby town called Ohisa. There were some heavy blackish-green tarps decorated by a DO NOT ENTER sign. The air read 0.17 about two meters from the sign. This was about four times more radioactive than downtown Iwaki. There was a forest, but Kanari was reluctant to measure it, since the municipality's only concern was to decontaminate places where people actually lived. I finally coaxed him into a snowy bamboo grove behind a field at the edge of a mountain. We all listened to the sounds of that lovely bamboo, which resembled birdsongs or windy hollow gurglings. The forest read 0.43 microsieverts per hour, nearly four times the goal of 1 millisievert per year. (Kida of course had said that 0.5 microsieverts per hour would be acceptable to him, so he might not have minded this place.) If all went perfectly from here on out, it would take at least 60 years to get the radiation from cesium-137 in the forest to the target level. But the government would do nothing about this, since, as Kanari told me sadly, the forest is "endless." Besides, he said, "This is not the place where people often go."

As we came closer to the restricted zone, we began to see black bags; it was disgusting how they went on and on. "Temporary storage," Kanari remarked. "Once the intermediate disposal site is ready, they'll move there."

"Where will that be?" I asked.

"Well, we hope there will be such a place, but none of us wants it near us," he replied.

We cruised up Highway 6 and came to Tomioka. I had to give Kanari directions. From his expression, it seemed he might have been having second thoughts. At the border of the exclusion zone was a checkpoint where the police stood watch over a double lane of traffic cones. When I asked him to pull over near an abandoned pachinko parlor, he kept the engine running. Was he anxious, or did he simply wish to get back to work?

Right by the pachinko parlor his scintillation counter read 4.2 microsieverts per hour—about 10 times the level of that mildly dangerous drainpipe in Hisanohama. At a nearby house with yellow DANGER tape around it, the base of a drainpipe registered 22.1 microsieverts per hour. The daily dose would be 530.4 microsieverts; the yearly dose, 193.6 millisieverts. A little perilous, I'd say. The grassy field was a cool 7.5 microsieverts per hour—65.7 millisieverts per year—while the main highway on which the decontamination trucks kept raising dust was only 3.72 per hour, which still comes to 32 times the recommended annual dose. After 15 minutes, my dosimeter had gained its own microsievert, which it normally did only once a day, and Kanari wanted to get out of there. So we sped back, to the place where we eat whatever is put in front of us.

For me, Tomioka, whose pre-accident population had been between 10,000 and 16,000, resembled the Iraqi city of Kirkuk, in that each time I returned to it I felt less safe, because each time I knew more and saw more.

There was plentiful vehicle traffic, to be sure — TEPCO workers, mostly, who queued up at the police checkpoint where the exclusion zone began, or dug with shovels, paused, then dragged picks and rakes across gravel, decontaminating. But the rest was quiet enough. I often tasted metal in my mouth there; I don't know why. The first time I visited, days before my excursion with Kanari, I walked past closed garages, a shuttered sliding door, forsaken shells of buildings. On one trip, I entered a garment store where some of the forms lay cast down. The rest were still standing, eerie silhouettes of headless, legless, armless women; a vacuum cleaner had fallen over on its side. All around were dead weeds, tall and half-frozen, outspreading lace-tipped finger stalks, projecting complex and lovely shadows on the white walls of silent houses whose curtains were neatly drawn. Grass rose up on the sides of the buildings, and golden weeds bent before crumpled blinds. Behind a fence, metal banged on metal. The banging went on and on like a telegraph.

In the city center, the streetlights glowed even in the middle of the day, probably to deter theft, of which there was, apparently, a great deal. Over the whole of Tomioka rang an amplified recorded voice, evidently a young woman's, but distorted and metallic. She reminded the workers not to spread radioactivity; they should dispose of their protective gear at the screening place on their way home. She said, "If you incinerate something or use incense, be careful not to start a fire," and she warned the former inhabitants, crackling, "For temporary-housing people, make sure to kill the breaker before you leave, and lock the door to prevent thieves."

The forbidden zone's current boundary was marked by large, narrow signboards, which said, as rendered in my interpreter's rather beautiful English:

TRANSPORTATION IS NOW BEING RESTRICTED.
AHEAD OF HERE IS A "DIFFICULT TO RETURN ZONE."
SO ROAD CLOSED.

The signs were flanked by traffic cones, with knee-high metal rail-
ings behind, which were low enough that a scofflaw such as I might
step over them to enter the forbidden zone. That is what I did, I
confess, but only for a moment or two on that occasion.

On that first visit I thought that Tomioka appeared only a little
shabby—not really, as my interpreter opined, abandoned; weeds
could have done much worse in three years. But after an hour I
checked the dosimeter and saw that it had already registered another microsievert. Within a single hour I had received three times
as much radiation as I had in the previous 24 hours. The dosage
in Tomioka, in other words, was potentially 72 times greater than
in Iwaki.

I cannot tell you all that I wish to about the quiet horror of the
place, much less of its sadness, but I ask you to imagine yourself
looking at a certain weed-grown wooden residence with unswept
snow on the front porch as the interpreter points and says: "This
must have been a very nice house. The owner must have been very
proud."

"I'm not worried about any thieves," Endo Kazuhiro said as we
drove to his old house, "since my home is not gorgeous." This
former resident of Tomioka was now the head of a residents' association in an Iwaki suburb. Both of his parents had been born
in Iwaki. About his house, he said: "I wish the thieves would clean
it up! I was born there. I'm the fourth generation—more than a
hundred years, almost two hundred."

"When did you last visit?"

"I was there last year, in summer. I only went to visit my ancestors' tombs."

In his childhood, he said, the kids played kick the can and hide-
and-seek. "We waded in the river. There were wild boars and foxes
—also raccoons, although we didn't see them so often. Now most
of the humans are gone, so the animals might be more rampant."

"You don't think they die from radiation?"

"I don't think so."

"So they're stronger in that way than humans?"

He laughed. "I don't know. There are some abandoned pets . . ."

"Based on your experience in the field, is decontamination effective?"

"Not at all! It's the most wasteful, useless activity."

"Who's making the money?"

"General contractors from Tokyo City and this prefecture."

"What do you think about nuclear power nowadays?"

"At this stage, I'm against it, because the response to the accident has been so poor. If the government cares to restart any of these nuclear plants, they'd better do a much better job."

Endo took me to his house. "But it's overgrown now," he warned, "not really presentable." Over the snow-covered road, the brassy female voice roared about protective gear. He showed me his garden, saying, "The bamboo grew! It's a forest! Three years ago there wasn't any." Within the dankness of his former home, rat droppings speckled shoes, boots, a fan, a vacuum cleaner, shelves, and chairs. Everything had been tipped and tilted by the earthquake into a waist-high jumble. He did not invite me in, and anyhow I saw no point in further trawling through that melancholy disorder, so I took a photograph or two, and then he closed the door.

"When we were told to evacuate, everyone thought we could come back in a few days, so we didn't take so many things. Residents are allowed to visit for six hours, and only during the daytime." The Endos had taken their bank book and family portraits. His wife had been back only once. As he put it, "she prefers not to see this."

Endo was now 62. The accident had occurred when he was 60. "I wanted to be a subsistence rice farmer in my retirement," he said. "Right here by the road, this was my field, three hundred tsubo. Elsewhere I had two other rice fields; one of them was near a pond. Well, that was my dream. The house is contaminated with radioactivity. Once the location for the waste site has been established, we will demolish the house. Owners are compensated in proportion to tsunami and earthquake damage. My house is less than half collapsed, so I must take care of the demolition myself. It would have been better if it had collapsed."

There he stood with his cap tilted upward on his forehead, staring at the wisteria whose creepers aimed at him, bullwhips frozen mid-crack. I wondered whether he felt any impulse to fight them.

The amplified woman's voice roared and echoed. He looked at his house. "Soon the wisteria will crush it," he said, almost smiling.

One Sunday afternoon in Iwaki, an orator in dark clothes stood, raising his voice, fanning and chopping the air, leaning on the podium, waving, circling, nodding. About 300 people listened to him in the auditorium of the sixth floor of a department-store tower (which also contained the Iwaki city library). There were far more men than women. Few wore suits, for this event had been organized by a national railway union. There was loud applause, and a few listeners raised cameras over their heads to record each speech. One man clambered up a small painter's ladder for a better angle.

A farmer from near Koriyama was speaking. "There is no place for Fukushima people to throw their anger against," he said. "We feel the administration has abandoned us. In my dairy farm I cannot feed my cows with my own grass. It is forbidden. The grass, the hay, and the compost are contaminated with cesium. They are just sitting there. Finally the city of Iwaki claimed to clean them but just moved them from one place to another. The cows are having more difficult births."

A lady in black said, "In the temporary housing where I used to live, in Namie, in two years, out of twenty residents, three died." Another woman added, "Those who make the decisions are not affected by radiation because they live in Tokyo."

After the speeches, the protesters went out to the street for a parade. There were whistles, drums, chants, banners of pink and yellow and blue and crimson. Some of the marchers were almost ecstatic as they banged their drums or raised their clenched fists; others shyly or listlessly touched their hands together.

A banner said: STOP ALL NUCLEAR POWER PLANTS. A banner said: 3–11 ANTINUCLEAR FUKUSHIMA ACTION. There was a musical chant about poison rain and children being guinea pigs. I saw hardly any spectators. In a travel agency, a young couple turned and frowned over their shoulders and through the glass. A restaurant proprietor stood unsmiling in his doorway. Three pretty women peered out of a second-story window. Two little girls were walking by; the younger wished to join the protest but the elder was against it.

A man was shouting: "You guys did it, you large corporations and TEPCO! Why should we have to suffer? Solidarity, everyone! Work together!" The sentiment was underscored by furious drumming. The marchers went to an unmarked TEPCO building and delivered demands to a man waiting on the sidewalk. He bowed slightly when he received their document. I felt a little sorry for him. Behind the glass doors, two other men in suits stood watching.

My visit to Tomioka with Endo was the least radioactive of the eight trips I have taken to that place; during our two hours there, the dosimeter registered only one additional microsievert. Over the course of our conversation, he remarked that what he missed most about Tomioka was the shrine at the mountain. I asked whether we could stop by, and he kindly drove me there. The characters on the gate read HAYAMA SHRINE. Here, the young men of the town had climbed bearing torches during the festival to pray for a good harvest; if you saw the flames at the top of the mountain from your house, the harvest would be fruitful. The festival took place every August 15. Endo had carried the torch every year from age 16 to 40.

At the shrine, one of the two stone guardian dogs had fallen; not far from his cracked corpse rose the wide stone steps, across which a heavy branch had lately collapsed. Together, we climbed up and looked at the forested hill above the shrine, the place of dead leaves and lovely tall pines. We turned and looked down from the torus at the landscape. Then, finally, we descended to the car and drove away, across that plain of black bags and brown grass, with crows flying up everywhere.

THOMAS CHATTERTON WILLIAMS

In Another Country

FROM *Smithsonian Journeys*

MY FATHER, A bookish black man old enough to be my grandfather, grew up in Texas while it was still a segregated state. As soon as he could, he got himself far enough away from there to cover the walls of his study with photographs of his travels to destinations as exotic as Poland and Mali. As far back as I can remember, he was insistent that the one place in the world truly worth going was Paris. Being a child, I accepted the assertion at face value —mostly because of the way his eyes lit up when he spoke of this city that was nothing but two syllables for me—I assumed he must have lived there once or been very close to someone who had. But it turned out this wasn't the case. Later, when I was older, and when he was finished teaching for the day, he would often throw on a loose gray Université de Paris Sorbonne sweatshirt with dark blue lettering, a gift from his dearest student, who had studied abroad there. From my father, then, I grew up with the sense that the capital of France was less a physical place than an invigorating idea that stood for many things, not least of which were wonder, sophistication, and even freedom. "Son, you have to go to Paris," he used to tell me, out of nowhere, a smile rising at the thought of it, and I would roll my eyes because I had aspirations of my own then, which seldom ventured beyond our small New Jersey town. "You'll see," he'd say, and chuckle.

And he was right. My wife, a second-generation Parisian from Montparnasse, and I moved from Brooklyn to a gently sloping neighborhood in the 9th arrondissement, just below the neon glare of Pigalle, in 2011. It was my second time living in France, and by then I was fully aware of the pull this city had exercised throughout the years, not just on my father but also on the hearts and minds of so many black Americans. One of the first things I noticed in our apartment was that, from the east-facing living room, if I threw open the windows and stared out over the Place Gustave Toudouze, I could see 3 Rue Clauzel, where Chez Haynes, a soul food institution and until recently the oldest American restaurant in Paris, served New Orleans shrimp gumbo, fatback, and collard greens to six decades of luminous visitors, black expats, and curious locals. It fills me with pangs of nostalgia to imagine that not so long ago, if I'd squinted hard enough, I would have spotted Louis Armstrong, Count Basie, or even a young James Baldwin—perhaps with the manuscript for *Another Country* under his arm—slipping through Haynes's odd log cabin exterior to fortify themselves with familiar chatter and the larded taste of home.

In many ways, the trajectory of Chez Haynes, which finally shuttered in 2009, mirrors the best-known narrative of the black expat tradition in Paris. It begins in World War II, when Leroy "Roughhouse" Haynes, a strapping Morehouse man and ex-football player, like so many African Americans initially stationed in Germany, made his way to the City of Lights once fighting had concluded. Here he found the freedom to love whomever he wanted, and married a Frenchwoman named Gabrielle Lecarbonnier. In 1949 the two opened Gabby and Haynes on the Rue Manuel. Though later he would tell journalists that "chitterlings and soul food" were a tough sell for the French, the restaurant immediately thrived on the business of fellow black GIs banging around the bars and clubs of Montmartre and Pigalle—early adopters whose presence lured the writers, jazzmen, and hangers-on. After splitting with Gabrielle, the thrice-wed Haynes spent another stint in Germany before returning to Paris and opening his eponymous solo venture, just across the Rue des Martyrs, at the site of a former brothel. The centrality of this new establishment to the era's black demimonde can be summed up in a single, vivid image: an original Beauford Delaney portrait of James Baldwin that Haynes hung casually above the kitchen doorway.

By the time Leroy Haynes died in 1986, the legendary postwar black culture his restaurant had for decades come to epitomize and concentrate—like the relevance of jazz music itself in black life—had largely dissipated. Most of the GIs had long since gone home, where civil rights legislation had been in place for nearly a generation. And it was no longer clear to what extent even artists still looked to Europe in the manner of the author of *Native Son,* Richard Wright, who famously told interviewers in 1946 that he'd "felt more freedom in one square block of Paris than there is in the entire United States of America." Though Haynes's Portuguese widow, Maria dos Santos, kept the restaurant running—for some 23 more years by infusing the menu with Brazilian spice—it functioned more like a mausoleum than like any vital part of the contemporary city. What I remind myself now as I push my daughter's stroller past the hollowed-out shell at 3 Rue Clauzel, offering up a silent *salut* to the ghosts of a previous generation, is that even if I'd arrived here sooner, the magic had long since disappeared.

Or had it? A few years ago, at the home of a young French trader I'd known in New York who'd moved back to Paris and developed the habit of throwing large, polyglot dinners with guests from all over, I met the esteemed black Renaissance man Saul Williams, a poet, singer, and actor of considerable talents. As we got to talking over red wine and Billie Holiday's voice warbling in the background, it occurred to me that Williams—who was at the time living with his daughter in a spacious apartment near the Gare du Nord, recording new music and acting in French cinema —was in fact the genuine article, a modern-day Josephine Baker or Langston Hughes. The thought struck me too that, at least on that evening, I was his witness and therefore a part of some still-extant tradition. It was the first time I had seen my own life in Paris in such terms.

A while after that, Saul moved back to New York, and I continued to toil away on a novel I'd brought with me from Brooklyn— solitary work that doesn't provide much occasion to mingle—but the thought stuck. Was Paris in any meaningful way still a capital of the black American imagination? It's a question I recently set out to try to answer. After all, though there was a singular explosion of blacks here during and after the two world wars, the African American romance with Paris dates back even further. It begins in antebellum Louisiana, where members of the mulatto elite— often wealthy land- and even slave owners who were discriminated against by southern custom—began sending their free, French-speaking sons to France to finish their schooling and live on a socially equal footing. Bizarre as it seems, that pattern continues right up to this day with the semi-expatriation of the superstar rapper Kanye West, who has planted something more than mere international-rich-person roots here, flourished creatively, and made serious headway in the local music and fashion industries. (It is to West's not unrequited love of all things Gallic that we may credit the surreal vision of presidential candidate François Hollande's youth-inspired campaign commercial set to "Niggas in Paris," West and Jay Z's exuberantly ribald anthem.)

Certainly, such a durable, centuries-old tradition must still manifest itself in any number of quotidian ways that I simply hadn't been noticing. In fact, I knew this to be true when several months earlier I had become friendly with Mike Ladd, a 44-year-old hip-hop artist from Boston by way of the Bronx, who turned out also to be my neighbor. Like me, Ladd is of mixed-race heritage but self-defines as black; he's also married to a Parisian, and is often incorrectly perceived in France, his striking blue eyes leading people to mistake him for a Berber. Talking with Mike and then with my friend Joel Dreyfuss, the Haitian American former editor of *The Root* who splits time between New York and an apartment in the 17th arrondissement, I explained that I was searching for today's black scene, whatever that might be. Both men immediately pointed me in the direction of the novelist and playwright Jake Lamar, a Harvard graduate who has been living here since 1992.

Over pints of Leffe at the Hotel Amour, a hive of fashionable social activity just one block uphill from the old Chez Haynes (and also reputedly in the space of a former brothel), Jake, who is bespectacled and disarmingly friendly, explains that he first came to Paris as a young writer on a Lyndhurst Fellowship (a precursor to the MacArthur "Genius" grant) and stayed, like almost everyone you encounter from abroad in this town, for love. He and his wife, Dorli, a Swiss stage actor, have made their adopted home together on the far side of Montmartre. Though his coming to Paris was not explicitly a choice against the United States, as Wright's and Baldwin's had been, "I was happy to get out of America," he concedes. "I was angry about Rodney King and also about the little things: it's a relief to get in an elevator and no one's clutching her purse!"

Is there still a bona fide black community in Paris? I ask him. "The '90s were a moment of community," he explains, "but a lot

of the old generation has passed away." There is no longer, for example, anyone quite like Tannie Stovall, the prosperous physicist
whose "first Friday" dinners for "brothers"—inspired by the spirit
of the Million Man March—became a rite of passage for scores of
African Americans passing through or moving to Paris. But Jake's
generation of black expats—men now mostly in their 50s and 60s,
many of whom first made each other's acquaintance at Stovall's
apartment years ago—continue the tradition as best they can.

A week after meeting him, I tag along with Jake to the group's
next improvised gathering, a dinner held in a large-by-Paris-
standards *rez-de-chaussée* loft on the Rue du Faubourg Saint-Denis.
The host, a native Chicagoan named Norman Powell with an authentic twang, sent out an email invitation that seems to affirm
Jake's assessment: "Hey my brothers . . . Our Friday meetings have
become a thing of the past. Certainly it's not possible for anyone
to host them like Tannie did, but I'm for trying to get together
a couple of times a year." When I arrive, I'm welcomed cordially
and told I've just missed the author and Cal Berkeley professor
Tyler Stovall (no relation to Tannie), as well as Randy Garrett, a
man whose name seems to bring a smile to everyone's face when
it's mentioned. Garrett, I quickly gather, is the jokester-raconteur
of the group. Originally from Seattle, he once, I'm told, owned
and operated a sensational rib joint on the Left Bank, just off the
Rue Mouffetard, and now gets by as a *bricoleur* (handyman) and on
his wits. Still drinking wine in the living room are a young singer
recently arrived in Europe whose name I do not catch, a longtime
expat named Zach Miller from Akron, Ohio, who is married to a
Frenchwoman and runs his own media production company, and
Richard Allen, an elegant Harlemite of nearly 70 with immacu-
lately brushed silver hair. Allen, who confesses that his love affair
with French began as a personal rebellion against the Spanish he'd
heard all his life Uptown, has a small point-and-shoot camera with
him and occasionally snaps pictures of the group. He has been in
Paris since 1972, having, among many other things, worked as a
fashion photographer for Kenzo, Givenchy, and Dior.

Before long we all have relocated into the kitchen, where, even
though it is well past dinnertime, Norm graciously serves us late-
comers generous portions of chili and rice, doused in hot sauce
and sprinkled with Comté instead of cheddar. The conversation
shifts from introductions to the protests that are raging across

America in the wake of Ferguson and Staten Island, and in no time, we are boisterously debating the interminable deluge of allegations ravaging Bill Cosby's legacy. Then, on a tangent, Norm brings up the fact that he recently discovered WorldStarHipHop .com and describes the preposterous website to this room full of expats. "Now the thing is to make a viral video of yourself just acting a fool," he explains. "You just have to shout 'WorldStar!' into the camera." Most of the guys have been out of the States so long, they don't know what he's talking about. I describe an infamous video I recently encountered of Houston teens queuing at a mall for the latest Air Jordan reissue, and suddenly realize that I am crying tears of laughter—laughing in such a way, it occurs to me then, I have not quite experienced in Paris before.

Tannie Stovall is gone, but if there is a centripetal black Parisian today, that distinction must go to Lamar, a modern-day, well-adjusted Chester Himes. Like Himes, Jake is adept in multiple literary forms, from memoir to literary fiction to, most recently, a crime novel entitled *Postérité,* which like Himes's own *policiers,* was published first in French. But unlike Himes—whose stint in France alongside Baldwin and Wright Lamar was recently dramatized for the stage in a trenchant play called *Brothers in Exile*—Lamar speaks the language fluently. "In that regard, I'm more integrated into French life than he was," he clarifies over email. And it's true: Jake is a part of this city's fabric. He knows everyone, it seems. It is at his suggestion that I find myself one Métro stop into the suburb of Bagnolet. I'm here to meet Camille Rich, a former Next agency model and Brown alumna who lives in a handsome, black-painted house with her three children by the African American fashion designer Earl Pickens. I have the feeling that I've been transported inside an adaptation of *The Royal Tenenbaums.* Camille's kids, Cassius, 12, Cain, 17, and Calyn, 21, immediately reveal themselves to be unusually gifted, eccentric, and self-directed. While Calyn lays out a brunch of *tarte aux courgettes,* soup, and scrambled eggs, I learn that Cassius, a self-taught ventriloquist, in addition to being his school's class president and bilingual in French and English, is picking up German and Arabic for fun. Meanwhile, Cain, whose ambition is to be an animator at Pixar, is in his bedroom painting an intricate canvas. He smiles warmly at me, apologizing for being so distracted, and then continues working. Calyn, for her part, along with being a solid cook and a hobbyist computer program-

mer, is a highly skilled and already published illustrator with a wry
and nuanced sense of humor.

After lunch I join Camille by the fireplace and watch Rocksand,
the family's 14-year-old West African tortoise, inch his prehistoric
carapace across the floor. She lights a cigarette and puts on Gil
Scott-Heron's "The Bottle," explaining that Paris has always held a
significant place in the family's mythology. Her father—a Temple
University mathematician—and uncle came as GIs and stayed on
playing jazz and carousing in Pigalle. Camille, tall and beautiful
with glasses and an Afro, grew up in Philadelphia, where alongside
her more standard black roots, she traces her ancestry to the Me-
lungeon Creoles of Appalachia. "I've always been so busy with the
kids," she explains when I ask about the community here, "that I
never really had time for anything else." But to her knowledge,
there are no other fully African American families like hers with
native-born children still living in Paris. It's been an experience of
freedom that she feels her kids could not have had in the United
States. "There's no way a child in today's America can grow without the idea of race as core to their identity," she says, whereas in
Paris it often seems as if they have been spared that straitjacket.

The subtext of this conversation, of course, of which we must
both be aware, is also one of the great ironies of living in France as
a black American: This traditional extension of human dignity to
black expatriates is not the function of some magical fairness and
lack of racism inherent in the French people. Rather, it stems in
large part from the interrelated facts of general French anti-Amer-
icanism, which often plays out as a contrarian reflex to thumb the
nose at crude white-American norms, along with the tendency to
encounter American blacks—as opposed to their African and Caribbean counterparts—first and foremost as *Americans* and not as
blacks. This of course can present its own problems for the psyche
(as the shattering essays of James Baldwin attest), putting the African American in Paris in the odd new position of witnessing—and
escaping—the systemic mistreatment of other lower castes in the
city.

Beyond that, it also never hurts that the black Americans found
in Paris over the years have tended to be creative types, natural
allies of the sophisticated, art-loving French. Jake Lamar put it to
me best: "There are lots of reasons why I decided to stay here,"
he said, "but a big one is the respect the French have for artists in

general and writers in particular. In America, people only really care about rich and famous writers, whereas in France, it doesn't matter if you're a best-selling author or not. The vocation of writing in and of itself is respected." And so it is this default reverence —in turn extended to the GIs and others who hung around, dabbling in jazz or cooking soul food—that has done a lot to insulate American blacks from the harsher sociopolitical realities most immigrant groups must face. But none of this is what I say to Camille and her wonderful kids that evening. What I say to them, before leaving, is the truth: they inspire me to want to have more children and to raise them here in France.

Right before Christmas I meet up with Mike Ladd, the hip-hop artist who lives down the street from me. We're going to see the acclaimed American rap outfit Run the Jewels perform at La RE-cyclerie, a disused train station cum performance space in the predominantly working-class African and Arab outskirts of the 18th arrondissement. Mike is old friends with El-P, the white half of Run the Jewels, and we go backstage to find the duo eating paprika-flavored Pringles and drinking Grey Goose and sodas before the show. I immediately fall into conversation with El-P's partner, Killer Mike, a physically gargantuan man and militantly conscious lyricist from Atlanta who once attended a book reading of mine at the Decatur Public Library (and vigorously debated me from the audience) but who may or may not remember having done this. In any event, we can't avoid talking about Eric Garner, the Staten Island man choked to death on camera by an NYPD officer who has just been cleared of all wrongdoing. "Our lives aren't worth very much in America," Killer Mike remarks at one point, with a sadness in his voice that surprises me.

The performance that night is suffused with a mood of righteous protest. The Parisian crowd swells and seems ready to march and swim all the way to Ferguson, Missouri, by the end of it. Mike Ladd and I linger and are joined at the bar by some other black expats, including Maurice "Sayyid" Greene, a buoyantly good-natured rapper formerly of the group Antipop Consortium. I ask Ladd if he finds Paris to be a black man's haven. "I feel France, and the rest of continental Europe even more so, is behind the curve in understanding diversity," he answers sincerely. "They were very good at celebrating difference in small quantities—a handful of black American expats, a smattering of colonials—but as is widely seen now, France is having a difficult time understanding how to integrate other cultures within their own."

For Sayyid, a six-foot-four-inch, dark-skinned man of 44 who spends 17 and a half hours a week taking intensive French lessons provided by the government, the supposed preferential treatment reserved for American blacks has sometimes proved elusive. "I had just had my little boy," he tells me about the time a group of French cops swarmed and accused him of trying to break into his own car. "He was three days old, and I was in the hospital with my wife. I parked my car and ended up locking the keys inside. I was with my mother-in-law, who's actually white French, and was trying to get them out. Time went by, a white guy from the neighborhood came and helped me, and it started to get dark. The guy left, and I was still out there. A cop rolled up, and suddenly there were six more cops all around on motorcycles. They didn't believe that my mother-in-law was who I said she was. She tried to talk to them. Finally, they accepted my ID and passed on, but my mother-in-law was like, 'Whoa!' Her first reaction had been to just comply, but then her second reaction was like, 'Wait a minute, why is this happening?'"

Is Paris a haven for African Americans, or is it not? Has it truly ever been? "The Paris of our generation is not Paris; it's Mumbai, it's Lagos, it's São Paulo," says Ladd. Which is part of the reason he keeps a recording studio in Saint-Denis, the *banlieue* to the north whose popular diversity, in contrast to central Paris, reminds him why in his New York days he preferred the Bronx to Manhattan. What made Paris so compelling to artists of all types in the early and mid-20th century, he maintains, was the collision of old traditions with what was truly avant-garde thinking. "That electrifying discord happens in other cities now," he stresses. This is something I have also suspected during my travels, though I am no longer so certain it's true. I am not sure that the electrifying discord we have grown up hearing about is gone from Paris or if it only feels this way now because everywhere is increasingly the same. The Internet, cheap flights, the very globalization of American black culture through television, sports, and hip-hop that has Paris-born Africans and Arabs dressing like mall rats from New Jersey—wherever one happens to be, the truth is there are very few secrets left for any of us. When I put the same question to Sayyid, he turns philosophical: "You can only really be in one place at a time," he says. "If I do twenty push-ups in New York or twenty push-ups here, it's the same twenty push-ups."

A week after the *Charlie Hebdo* massacre that decimated this city's false sense of serenity and ethnic coexistence, Jake Lamar has organized a brothers' outing. The acclaimed African American writer and Francophile Ta-Nehisi Coates is giving a talk about "The Case for Reparations," his highly influential *Atlantic* magazine cover story, at the American Library. Richard Allen, the sharp expat with the camera, and I arrive late after a drink at a nearby café. We pull up chairs in the back and find Coates in midlecture to a full, predominantly white house. In the Q&A, an elderly white man asks if in Paris Coates has encountered any racism. Coates hesitates before conceding that, yes, in fact a white woman once approached him shouting, "Quelle horreur, un nègre!" before throwing a dirty napkin at him. No one in the audience, least of all the man who posed the question, seems to know what to say to that, and Coates helpfully chalks up the encounter to this particular lady's evident madness and not to the workings of the entire French society.

(Later over email, I ask him whether he sees himself as part of the black tradition here. He tells me that although he has consciously sought to avoid being lumped with other black writers in Paris, "I'm not really sure why I even feel that way. I love Baldwin. ADORE Baldwin . . . [but] it feels claustrophobic, like there's no room for you to be yourself . . . All of that said, it does strike me as too much to write off the black expatriate experience here as a mere coincidence.")

As Richard and I gather with the other brothers and their wives who are now preparing to leave, Jake invites Coates to have a drink with us, but he politely rain checks. We make our way out of the library and into the damp Rue du Général Camou, eventually crossing back to the Right Bank via the Pont de l'Alma, the Eiffel Tower glowing orange over our heads, the Seine flowing fast beneath our feet. The city feels strangely back to normal, except for the occasional presence of submachine gun–wielding cops and military personnel, and black-and-white JE SUIS CHARLIE placards affixed to the windows of all the cafés. Our group is made up of Jake and Dorli; Joel Dreyfuss and his wife, Veronica, a striking cocoa-complexioned woman with blue eyes, from St. Louis; Randy Garrett, the raconteur-*bricoleur;* the filmmaker Zach Miller; Richard Allen; and a dapper English professor from Columbia named Bob O'Meally. We slide into a large table at a café on the Avenue George V and order a round of drinks. I immediately grasp what makes Randy so much fun when in no time he's bought Dorli and Veronica loose roses from the Bangladeshi man peddling flowers table to table.

Everyone seems in very good spirits, and I feel for a moment as if I am actually in another era. Our drinks arrive. We toast, and I ask Richard if in fact there is still really such a thing as black Paris. "It's off and on," he shrugs, taking a sip of wine. "It all depends on who is here and when." Right now, Bob O'Meally is here, and the table feels fuller for it. He has organized an exhibition of Romare Bearden's paintings and collages at Reid Hall, Columbia University's outpost near Montparnasse. I tell him I'm excited to see it, and maybe because these older men remind me so much of him, my thoughts turn back around to my father.

One of the great enigmas of my childhood was that when he did finally get his chance to come here in the early '90s, after a fortnight of beating the pavement and seeing all that he could, my father returned home as though nothing at all had happened. I waited and waited for him to fill me with stories about this magical city but was met only with silence. In fact, I don't think he ever spoke euphorically about Paris again. I have always suspected it had something to do with the reason that, in the scariest movies, the audience should never be allowed to look directly at the monster. In either circumstance, the reality, however great, can only dissolve before the richness of our own imagination—and before the lore we carry inside us.

Contributors' Notes
Notable Travel Writing of 2015

Contributors' Notes

Michael Chabon is the best-selling and Pulitzer Prize–winning author of *The Mysteries of Pittsburgh, A Model World, Wonder Boys, Werewolves in Their Youth, The Amazing Adventures of Kavalier and Clay, The Final Solution, The Yiddish Policemen's Union, Maps and Legends, Gentlemen of the Road,* and the middle-grade book *Summerland.* He lives in Berkeley, California, with his wife, the novelist Ayelet Waldman, and their children.

Sara Corbett is a contributing writer at *The New York Times Magazine* and coauthor of *A House in the Sky.*

Dave Eggers is the author of ten books, including *The Circle* and *A Hologram for the King,* which was a finalist for the 2012 National Book Award. He is the founder of McSweeney's, an independent publishing company based in San Francisco that produces books, a quarterly journal of new writing (*McSweeney's Quarterly Concern*), and a monthly magazine, *The Believer.* McSweeney's also publishes Voice of Witness, a nonprofit book series that uses oral history to illuminate human rights crises around the world. Eggers is the cofounder of 826 National, a network of eight tutoring centers around the country, and ScholarMatch, a nonprofit organization designed to connect students with resources, schools, and donors to make college possible.

Gretel Ehrlich is the author of 15 books of nonfiction, fiction, and poetry —including *The Solace of Open Spaces, Heart Mountain, This Cold Heaven,* and *Facing the Wave,* which was longlisted for the National Book Award. Her books have won many awards, including the first Henry David Thoreau Prize for nature writing, the PEN Center USA Award for Creative Nonfiction, the American Academy of Arts and Letters Harold D. Vursell

Memorial Award, a Guggenheim Fellowship, three National Geographic Expeditions Council grants for travel in the Arctic, a Whiting Award, and a National Endowment for the Arts grant. Her work has appeared in *Harper's Magazine, The Atlantic, Orion, The New York Times Magazine,* and *The Best Essays of the Century,* among many other publications. Her poetry was featured on the *PBS NewsHour.* She lives with her partner, Neal Conan, on a farm in the highlands of Hawaii and on a ranch in Wyoming.

William Finnegan is the author of *Barbarian Days: A Surfing Life; Cold New World: Growing Up in a Harder Country; A Complicated War: The Harrowing of Mozambique; Dateline Soweto: Travels with Black South African Reporters;* and *Crossing the Line: A Year in the Land of Apartheid.* He has been a staff writer at *The New Yorker* since 1987. He has won numerous journalism awards, including two Overseas Press Club awards since 2009. He lives in New York.

Alice Gregory is a contributing editor at *T: The New York Times Style Magazine* and a columnist for *The New York Times Book Review.* She lives in New York and has contributed to many publications, including *The New Yorker, The New York Review of Books,* and *n+1.*

Pico Iyer is the author of two novels and ten works of nonfiction, covering between them subjects as varied as globalism, the Cuban Revolution, Islamic mysticism, and the 14th Dalai Lama. His most recent books are *The Art of Stillness* (on the virtue of not traveling) and *The Man Within My Head* (on the inner and outer inquiries of Graham Greene). Though based in rural Japan since 1992, he currently serves as a Distinguished Presidential Fellow at Chapman University in Orange, California, and continues to write frequently for *The New York Review of Books, Harper's, Granta,* and many others.

Andrew W. Jones is the author of *Two Seasons in the Bubble: Living and Coaching Basketball in Bulgaria.* In 2014 he won the Norman Mailer Middle and High School Teachers Creative Nonfiction Award for his essay "The Inca Champions League." He currently lives, teaches, and writes in Brasília, Brazil.

Kea Krause has written for *The Believer, The Toast, Vice, Narratively,* and *The Rumpus.* She holds an MFA from Columbia University, where she also taught creative writing. Born and raised in the Pacific Northwest, she now resides in Queens, New York.

Helen Macdonald is an English writer, a naturalist, and an Affiliated Research Scholar at the University of Cambridge Department of History and

Philosophy of Science. She is the author of the best-selling *H Is for Hawk,* which won the 2014 Samuel Johnson Prize and Costa Book Award. She is also the author of the poetry collection *Shaler's Fish.*

Patricia Marx is a staff writer for *The New Yorker* and a former writer for *Saturday Night Live* and *Rugrats.* Her most recent book is *Let's Be Less Stupid: An Attempt to Maintain My Mental Faculties.* She teaches at Columbia University and Stony Brook University. She was the first woman elected to *The Harvard Lampoon* and in 2015 received a Guggenheim Fellowship. Her children's book *Now Everybody Really Hates Me* was the first and only winner of the Friedrich Medal, an award made up by Patty and named after her air conditioner. She can take a baked potato out of the oven with her bare hand.

D. T. Max is a graduate of Harvard University and a staff writer at *The New Yorker.* As a young man he learned Italian during visits to an uncle in Rome who was a writer for Cinecittà. He is the author of the best-selling *Every Love Story Is a Ghost Story: A Life of David Foster Wallace* and *The Family That Couldn't Sleep,* the story of an Italian family with a mysterious insomnia. He is at work on a book about Mark Twain.

Freda Moon is a widely published journalist and the "Frugal Family" columnist for the *New York Times,* where she is a regular contributor to the travel section. She lives with her husband, infant daughter, and rescue dog on a vintage trawler motor yacht in the San Francisco Bay Area.

Mitch Moxley has written for *GQ, The Atlantic, Grantland, Playboy, The Atavist Magazine,* and other publications, and he is an editor at *Roads & Kingdoms,* an online journal of foreign correspondence. He is the author of *Apologies to My Censor: The High and Low Adventures of a Foreigner in China,* about the six years he lived in Beijing.

Justin Nobel writes about science and the environment for magazines and literary journals, and is presently at work on a book of tales about the weather. A book he cowrote with an exonerated death row inmate will be published in November 2016. He lives in New Orleans.

Stephanie Pearson is a contributing editor at *Outside* magazine. After earning her master's degree from Northwestern University's Medill School of Journalism, she served on *Outside's* editorial staff for 12 years and has since logged many hours in the field, reporting stories in wild corners of the world, from Bhutan to Colombia to the Falkland Islands. This is her second story anthologized in the *Best American Travel Writing* series.

Raised in Australia and a denizen of the East Village of Manhattan, **Tony Perrottet** is a contributing writer at *Smithsonian* magazine and a regular at the *New York Times, WSJ Magazine,* and other publications. He is the author of five books combining arcane history and travel, most recently *Napoleon's Privates: 2500 Years of History Unzipped* and *The Sinner's Grand Tour: A Journey Through the Historical Underbelly of Europe.* He is a regular on the History Channel, where he has spoken about everything from the Crusades to the birth of disco. This is his seventh appearance in the *Best American Travel Writing* series.

Steven Rinella is the author of five books and hosts *The MeatEater Podcast* and *MeatEater* television series. He lives in Seattle.

David Rowell is the author of *The Train of Small Mercies,* a novel. His second book, on how and why we make the music we do, will be published in 2018.

Patrick Symmes is the author of two books on the Cuban Revolution and its leaders, *Chasing Che* and *The Boys from Dolores.*

Jeffrey Tayler lives in Moscow. He is a contributing editor at *The Atlantic* who has also written for *National Geographic, Foreign Policy, Condé Nast Traveler, The American Scholar,* and *Harper's Magazine,* among other publications. He is the author of seven books, including *Facing the Congo, River of No Reprieve,* and *Topless Jihadis: Inside Femen, the World's Most Provocative Activist Group.* "Fyodor's Guide" is the sixth work of his chosen for the *Best American Travel Writing* series.

Paul Theroux is the author of many highly acclaimed books. His novels include *The Lower River* and *The Mosquito Coast,* and his renowned travel books include *Ghost Train to the Eastern Star* and *Dark Star Safari.* He lives in Hawaii and Cape Cod. His most recent book is *Deep South: Four Seasons on Back Roads.*

William T. Vollmann has written nine novels, three collections of stories, six works of nonfiction, and a memoir. He has won the PEN Center USA West Award for Fiction, a Whiting Award, and the Strauss Living award from the American Academy of Arts and Letters.

Thomas Chatterton Williams is the author of the 2010 memoir *Losing My Cool.* His writing has appeared in the *New York Times, The New Yorker,* the *Wall Street Journal,* the *Washington Post, Le Monde, New Republic, The Atlantic, n+1, Harper's Magazine,* the *London Review of Books, Virginia Quarterly*

Review, Smithsonian Journeys, The American Scholar, and many other places. He currently lives in Paris, where he is an associate editor at *Purple* and *Holiday* magazines and a regular book critic for the *San Francisco Chronicle.* His next book, a reckoning with how we define race in America, is forthcoming.

Notable Travel Writing of 2015

SELECTED BY JASON WILSON

ATOSSA ARAXIA ABRAHAMIAN
Among Strangers. *Guernica*, December 15.

ELIF BATUMAN
The Big Dig. *The New Yorker*, August 31.
DON BELT
Wild Heart of Sweden. *National Geographic*, October.
BERND BRUNNER
Istanbul Panorama. *Lapham's Quarterly*, Winter.
BRIN-JONATHAN BUTLER
Myths Made Flesh: Last Breaths in a Spanish Bullring. *SB Nation*, August 19.

PABLO CALVI
Secret Reserves. *The Believer*, Fall.
JULIA COOKE
Art in the Time of Politics. *Virginia Quarterly Review*, Fall.

DAVE EGGERS
Understand the Sky. *AFAR*, June/July.

AARON GILBREATH
Three Feet by Six Feet by Three Feet. *The Morning News*, January 27.
WILL GRANT
A Liar Standing Next to a Hole in the Ground. *Outside*, March.
KARL TARO GREENFELD
The Island of No Regrets. *Roads & Kingdoms*, November 10.

PETER HESSLER
  Travels with My Censor. *The New Yorker,* March 9.

LESLIE JAMISON
  The Two Faces of Paradise. *AFAR,* March/April.
MARK JENKINS
  Point of No Return. *National Geographic,* September.

KARL OVE KNAUSGAARD
  My Saga (Part 1 and Part 2). *The New York Times Magazine,* March 1 and March 15.

JHUMPA LAHIRI
  Teach Yourself Italian. *The New Yorker,* December 7.

MITCH MOXLEY
  Superman of Havana. *Roads & Kingdoms,* December 16.

JUSTIN NOBEL
  Walking the Tornado Line. *Oxford American,* Spring.

NORMAN OLLESTAD
  Vertical Snap. *Outside,* May.
LAWRENCE OSBORNE
  The Eagles Have Landed. *Departures,* March/April.

TONY PERROTTET
  Traveler in the Sunset Clouds. *Smithsonian,* April.

EDWARD READICKER-HENDERSON
  Dream Weavers. *AFAR,* October.
ELIZABETH RUSH
  The Saree Express. *Witness,* Spring.

NAT SEGNIT
  Blast from the Past. *Harper's Magazine,* December.
KATE SIBER
  Ghost of a Chance. *Preservation,* Spring.
CHOIRE SICHA
  Summer Fridays. *The New York Times Magazine,* July 19.
THOMAS SWICK
  A Press Trip to Branson. *Roads & Kingdoms,* May 20.

PATRICK SYMMES
> Following in the Inca's Giant Steps. *Smithsonian,* July.

TOM VANDERBILT
> Loudsourcing. *Outside,* April.

LISA WELLS
> All Across the Desert Our Bread Is Blooming! *The Believer,* January/
> February.

EMILY WITT
> The Body Politic. *Harper's Magazine,* January.

THE BEST AMERICAN SERIES®

FIRST, BEST, AND BEST-SELLING

The Best American Comics

The Best American Essays

The Best American Infographics

The Best American Mystery Stories

The Best American Nonrequired Reading

The Best American Science and Nature Writing

The Best American Science Fiction and Fantasy

The Best American Short Stories

The Best American Sports Writing

The Best American Travel Writing

Available in print and e-book wherever books are sold.

Visit our website: *www.hmhco.com/bestamerican*